LOBBYING DISCLOSURE

BACKGROUND AND COMPLIANCE ANALYSIS

GOVERNMENT PROCEDURES AND OPERATIONS

Additional books in this series can be found on Nova's website under the Series tab.

Additional e-books in this series can be found on Nova's website under the e-book tab.

GOVERNMENT PROCEDURES AND OPERATIONS

LOBBYING DISCLOSURE

BACKGROUND AND COMPLIANCE ANALYSIS

KERI MATTHEWS
EDITOR

nova publishers

New York

Copyright © 2014 by Nova Science Publishers, Inc.

For permission to use material from this book please contact us:
Telephone 631-231-7269; Fax 631-231-8175
Web Site: http://www.novapublishers.com

NOTICE TO THE READER

The Publisher has taken reasonable care in the preparation of this book, but makes no expressed or implied warranty of any kind and assumes no responsibility for any errors or omissions. No liability is assumed for incidental or consequential damages in connection with or arising out of information contained in this book. The Publisher shall not be liable for any special, consequential, or exemplary damages resulting, in whole or in part, from the readers' use of, or reliance upon, this material. Any parts of this book based on government reports are so indicated and copyright is claimed for those parts to the extent applicable to compilations of such works.

Independent verification should be sought for any data, advice or recommendations contained in this book. In addition, no responsibility is assumed by the publisher for any injury and/or damage to persons or property arising from any methods, products, instructions, ideas or otherwise contained in this publication.

This publication is designed to provide accurate and authoritative information with regard to the subject matter covered herein. It is sold with the clear understanding that the Publisher is not engaged in rendering legal or any other professional services. If legal or any other expert assistance is required, the services of a competent person should be sought. FROM A DECLARATION OF PARTICIPANTS JOINTLY ADOPTED BY A COMMITTEE OF THE AMERICAN BAR ASSOCIATION AND A COMMITTEE OF PUBLISHERS.

Additional color graphics may be available in the e-book version of this book.

Library of Congress Cataloging-in-Publication Data

ISBN: 978-1-63321-777-5

Published by Nova Science Publishers, Inc. † New York

CONTENTS

PREFACE

The Lobbying Disclosure Act of 1995 (LDA) requires lobbyists to file quarterly lobbying disclosure reports and semiannual reports on certain political contributions. The LDA also requires that GAO annually audit the extent to which lobbyists can demonstrate compliance with disclosure requirements; identify challenges to compliance that lobbyists report; and describe the resources and authorities available to the Office in its role in enforcing LDA compliance and the efforts the Office has made to improve enforcement. This book discusses the 2013 lobbying disclosure; registration and disclosure; and provides a lobbying disclosure act guide.

Chapter 1 – The LDA requires lobbyists to file quarterly lobbying disclosure reports and semiannual reports on certain political contributions. The LDA also requires that GAO annually (1) audit the extent to which lobbyists can demonstrate compliance with disclosure requirements, (2) identify challenges to compliance that lobbyists report, and (3) describe the resources and authorities available to the Office in its role in enforcing LDA compliance and the efforts the Office has made to improve enforcement. This is GAO's seventh report under the mandate.

GAO reviewed a stratified random sample of 104 quarterly disclosure LD-2 reports filed for the third and fourth quarters of 2012 and the first and second quarters of calendar year 2013. GAO also reviewed two random samples totaling 160 LD-203 reports from year-end 2012 and midyear 2013. This methodology allowed GAO to generalize to the population of 65,489 disclosure reports with $5,000 or more in lobbying activity and 31,482 reports of federal political campaign contributions. GAO also met with officials from the Office to obtain updated statuses on the Office's efforts to focus resources on lobbyists who fail to comply.

GAO provided a draft of this report to the Attorney General for review and comment. On behalf of the Attorney General, the Assistant U.S. Attorney for the District of Columbia responded that the Department of Justice had no comments.

Chapter 2 – On September 14, 2007, President George W. Bush signed S. 1, the Honest Leadership and Open Government Act of 2007 (P.L. 110-81), into law. The Honest Leadership and Open Government Act (HLOGA) amended the Lobbying Disclosure Act (LDA) of 1995 (P.L. 104-65, as amended) to provide, among other changes to federal law and House and Senate rules, additional and more frequent disclosure of lobbying contacts and activities. This report focuses on changes made to lobbying registration, termination, and disclosure requirements and provides analysis of the volume of registration, termination, and disclosure reports filed with the Clerk of the House of Representatives and the Secretary of the Senate before and after the HLOGA's passage. This report does not analyze the content of these reports.

Chapter 3 – On September 14, 2007, President George W. Bush signed S. 1, the Honest Leadership and Open Government Act of 2007 (P.L. 110-81), into law. The Honest Leadership and Open Government Act (HLOGA) amended the Lobbying Disclosure Act (LDA) of 1995 (P.L. 104-65, as amended) to provide, among other changes to federal law and House and Senate rules, additional and more frequent disclosures of lobbying contacts and activities. This report explains the role of the Clerk of the House of Representatives and the Secretary of the Senate in implementing lobbying registration and disclosure requirements and summarizes the guidance documents they have jointly issued.

Chapter 4 – Section 6 of the Lobbying Disclosure Act (LDA), 2 U.S.C. § 1605, provides that: The Secretary of the Senate and the Clerk of the House of Representatives shall (1) provide guidance and assistance on the registration and reporting requirements of this Act and develop common standards, rules, and procedures for compliance with this Act; [and] (2) review, and, where necessary, verify and inquire to ensure the accuracy, completeness, and timeliness of registrations and reports.

The LDA does not provide the Secretary or the Clerk with the authority to write substantive regulations or issue definitive opinions on the interpretation of the law. The Secretary and Clerk have, from time to time, jointly issued written guidance on the registration and reporting requirements. This document is both a compilation of previously issued guidance documents and our interpretation of the changes that were made to the LDA as a result of the Honest Leadership and Open Government Act of 2007 (HLOGA).

This compilation supersedes all previous guidance documents. This combined guidance document does not have the force of law, nor does it have any binding effect on the United States Attorney for the District of Columbia or any other part of the Executive Branch. To the extent that the guidance relates to the accuracy, completeness, and timeliness of registrations and reports, it will serve to inform the public as to how the Secretary and Clerk intend to carry out their responsibilities under the LDA.

In: Lobbying Disclosure
Editor: Keri Matthews

ISBN: 978-1-63321-777-5
© 2014 Nova Science Publishers, Inc.

Chapter 1

2013 LOBBYING DISCLOSURE: OBSERVATIONS ON LOBBYISTS' COMPLIANCE WITH DISCLOSURE REQUIREMENTS[*]

United States Government Accountability Office

WHY GAO DID THIS STUDY

The LDA requires lobbyists to file quarterly lobbying disclosure reports and semiannual reports on certain political contributions. The LDA also requires that GAO annually (1) audit the extent to which lobbyists can demonstrate compliance with disclosure requirements, (2) identify challenges to compliance that lobbyists report, and (3) describe the resources and authorities available to the Office in its role in enforcing LDA compliance and the efforts the Office has made to improve enforcement. This is GAO's seventh report under the mandate.

GAO reviewed a stratified random sample of 104 quarterly disclosure LD-2 reports filed for the third and fourth quarters of 2012 and the first and second quarters of calendar year 2013. GAO also reviewed two random samples totaling 160 LD-203 reports from year-end 2012 and midyear 2013. This

---

[*] This is an edited, reformatted and augmented version of the United States Government Accountability Office publication, GAO- 14-485, dated May 2014.

methodology allowed GAO to generalize to the population of 65,489 disclosure reports with $5,000 or more in lobbying activity and 31,482 reports of federal political campaign contributions. GAO also met with officials from the Office to obtain updated statuses on the Office's efforts to focus resources on lobbyists who fail to comply.

GAO provided a draft of this report to the Attorney General for review and comment. On behalf of the Attorney General, the Assistant U.S. Attorney for the District of Columbia responded that the Department of Justice had no comments.

WHAT GAO FOUND

Most lobbyists provided documentation for key elements of their disclosure reports to demonstrate compliance with the Lobbying Disclosure Act of 1995, as amended (LDA). For lobbying disclosure (LD-2) reports and political contribution (LD-203) reports GAO estimated the following:

- Ninety-six percent of newly registered lobbyists filed LD-2 reports as required. Lobbyists are required to file LD-2 reports for the quarter in which they first register.
- Ninety-six percent could provide documentation for income and expenses. However, 33 percent of these LD-2 reports were not properly rounded to the nearest $10,000.
- Ninety-two percent filed year-end 2012 or midyear 2013 LD-203 reports as required.
- Seventeen percent of all LD-2 reports did not properly disclose one or more previously held covered position as required.
- Four percent of all LD-203 reports omitted one or more reportable political contributions that were documented in the Federal Election Commission database.

These findings are generally consistent with GAO's reviews from 2010 through 2012 and can be generalized to the population of disclosure reports.

Most lobbyists in GAO's sample rated the terms associated with LD-2 reporting as "very easy" or "somewhat easy" to understand with regard to meeting reporting requirements. However, some disclosure reports demonstrate compliance difficulties, such as failure to disclose covered positions or misreporting of income or expenses. In addition, lobbyists amended 18 of 104 original disclosure reports in GAO's sample to change previously reported information.

The U.S. Attorney's Office for the District of Columbia (the Office) stated it has sufficient authority and resources to enforce LD-2 and LD-203 compliance with the LDA for lobbying firms and certain individual lobbyists. It has one contract paralegal working full time and six attorneys working part time on LDA enforcement issues. The Office continues its efforts to follow up on referrals for noncompliance with lobbying disclosure requirements by contacting lobbyists by e-mail, telephone, and letter. In March 2014, the Office filed a civil complaint against a lobbyist for failure to comply with LDA reporting requirements.

GAO's first report on lobbying disclosure under the LDA concluded that the lobbying community could benefit from creating an entity to share examples of best practices, provide training, and report annually on opportunities to clarify guidance and minimis sources of potential confusion for the lobbying community. Given the ongoing difficulties with compliance, GAO continues to believe that such an entity could be useful to the lobbying community.

ABBREVIATIONS

Clerk of the House	Clerk of the House of Representatives
FEC	Federal Election Commission
HLOGA	Honest Leadership and Open Government Act of 2007
LDA	Lobbying Disclosure Act of 1995
Office	U.S. Attorney's Office for the District of Columbia

* * *

May 28, 2014

Congressional Committees

Questions regarding the influence of special interests in the formation of government policy have led to a move toward more transparency and accountability with regard to the lobbying community. The Honest Leadership and Open Government Act of 2007 (HLOGA) amended the Lobbying Disclosure Act of 1995 to require lobbyists to file quarterly lobbying disclosure reports and semiannual reports on certain political contributions and increased civil and criminal penalties for failure to comply with lobbying disclosure requirements.[1] The mandate requires us to audit the extent of lobbyists' compliance with the Lobbying Disclosure Act of 1995, as amended (LDA) by reviewing publicly available lobbying registrations and a random sampling of reports filed during each calendar year.[2] Our report shall include any recommendations related to improving lobbyists' compliance with the LDA and information on resources and authorities available to the U.S. Attorney's Office for the District of Columbia (the Office) for effective enforcement of the LDA. This is our seventh mandated review of lobbyists' disclosure reports filed under the LDA.

Consistent with our mandate, our objectives were to: (1) determine the extent to which lobbyists can demonstrate compliance with the requirements for registrations and reports filed under the LDA; (2) identify challenges and potential improvements to compliance by lobbyists, lobbying firms, and registrants, if any; and (3) describe the resources and authorities available to the Office in its role in enforcing LDA compliance and the efforts the Office has made to improve enforcement.

To fulfill our audit requirement in HLOGA, we took the following steps:

- To determine the extent to which lobbyists can demonstrate compliance, we examined a stratified random sample of 102 quarterly lobbying disclosure (LD-2) reports with income and expenses of $5,000 or more filed during the third and fourth quarters of calendar year 2012 and the first and second quarters of calendar year 2013.[3] We selected the randomly sampled reports from the publicly downloadable database maintained by the Clerk of the House of Representatives (Clerk of the House).[4] Appendix II contains a list of lobbyists (registrants and clients) whose LD-2 reports we selected. This methodology allows us to generalize to the population of LD-2 reports. We then contacted each lobbyist or lobbying firm in our sample and asked them to provide written documentation for key elements of their LD-2 reports, including the amount of money received for lobbying activities, the houses of Congress or executive branch agencies lobbied, lobbying issue areas, and lobbyists reported as having worked on the issues.[5] We also reviewed whether lobbyists listed on the LD-2 reports properly disclosed prior covered official positions and whether the lobbyists filed the semiannual report of federal political contributions. Of the lobbyists contacted, all in-scope lobbyists in our sample responded to our requests to meet with us to review documentation.

- To determine whether lobbyists reported their federal political contributions as required by the LDA, we analyzed stratified random samples of year-end 2012 and midyear 2013 semiannual political contributions (LD-203) reports. The samples contain 80 LD-203 reports that list contributions and 80 LD-203 reports that do not. We selected the randomly sampled reports from the publicly downloadable contributions database maintained by the Clerk of the House. See appendix III for a list of lobbyists and lobbying firms randomly selected for our review of LD-203 reports. We then checked the contributions reported in the Federal Election Commission's (FEC) database against those identified in our sample to determine whether all contributions reported in the FEC database also appeared on the LD-203 reports, as required. We contacted lobbyists and asked them to provide documentation to clarify differences we observed. All lobbyists complied with our request to provide documentation. This methodology allows us to generalize to the population of LD-203 reports both with and without contributions.

- To determine whether registrants were meeting the requirement to file an LD-2 report for the quarter in which they registered, we compared new registrations (LD-1) filed in the third and fourth quarters of 2012 and the first and second quarters of 2013 to the corresponding LD-2 reports on file with the Clerk of the House.

- To identify challenges and potential improvements to compliance, we used a structured online survey to obtain views from lobbyists included in our sample of reports. In addition, we considered reporting difficulties that became apparent during our reviews of lobbyists' documentation.

- To describe the resources and authorities available to the Office and its efforts to improve LDA enforcement, we interviewed Office officials and obtained updated information about the capabilities of the Office's systems to track enforcement and compliance trends and referral data that it receives from the Secretary of the Senate and Clerk of the House.

The mandate does not require us to identify lobbyist organizations that failed to register and report in accordance with LDA requirements. The mandate also does not require us to determine whether reported lobbying activity or political contributions represented the full extent of lobbying activities that took place.

We conducted this performance audit from June 2013 to May 2014 in accordance with generally accepted government auditing standards. Those standards require that we plan and perform the audit to obtain sufficient, appropriate evidence to provide a reasonable basis for our findings and conclusions based on our audit objectives. We believe that the evidence obtained provides a reasonable basis for our findings and conclusions based on our audit objectives. For more details on our methodology, see appendix I.

BACKGROUND

The LDA, as amended by HLOGA, requires lobbyists to register with the Secretary of the Senate and the Clerk of the House and file quarterly reports disclosing their lobbying activity. Lobbyists are required to file their registrations and reports electronically with the Secretary of the Senate and the Clerk of the House through a single entry point. Registrations and reports must be publicly available in downloadable, searchable databases from the Secretary of the Senate and the Clerk of the House. No specific statutory requirements exist for lobbyists to generate or maintain documentation in support of the information disclosed in the reports they file. However, guidance issued by the Secretary of the Senate and the Clerk of the House recommends that lobbyists retain copies of their filings and supporting documentation for at least 6 years after they file their reports.

The LDA requires that the Secretary of the Senate and the Clerk of the House provide guidance and assistance on registration and reporting requirements and develop common standards, rules, and procedures for LDA compliance. The Secretary and the Clerk of the House review the guidance semiannually. It was last reviewed December 12, 2013, and revised February 15, 2013. The guidance provides definitions of LDA terms, elaborates on the registration and reporting requirements, includes specific examples of different scenarios, and explains why certain scenarios prompt or do not prompt disclosure under the LDA. The Secretary of the Senate and Clerk of the House told us they continue to consider information we report on lobbying disclosure compliance when they periodically update the guidance. In addition, they told us they send quarterly e-mails to registered lobbyists that address common compliance issues as well as reminders to file reports by the due dates.

The LDA defines a lobbyist as an individual who is employed or retained by a client for compensation, who has made more than one lobbying contact (written or oral communication to a covered executive or legislative branch official made on behalf of a client), and whose lobbying activities represent at least 20 percent of the time that he or she spends on behalf of the client during the quarter.[6] Lobbying firms are persons or entities that have one or more employees who lobby on behalf of a client other than that person or entity.[7]

Lobbying firms are required to register with the Secretary of the Senate and the Clerk of the House for each client if the firms receive or expect to receive more than $3,000 in income or $12,500 in incurred expenses from that client for lobbying activities.[8] Lobbyists are also required to submit a quarterly report, also known as an LD-2 report, for each registration filed. The LD-2s contain information that includes:

- the name of the registrant reporting on his or her quarterly lobbying activities and the name of the client on whose behalf the registrant lobbied;
- the list of individuals who acted as lobbyists on behalf of the client during the reporting period;
- whether any lobbyists served as covered executive branch or legislative branch officials in the previous 20 years;
- codes describing general issue areas and specific lobbying issues;
- houses of Congress and federal agencies lobbied during the reporting period; and
- reported income (or expenses for organizations with in-house lobbyists) related to lobbying activities during the quarter (rounded to the nearest $10,000).

The LDA also requires lobbyists to report certain political contributions semiannually in the LD-203 report. These reports must be filed 30 days after the end of a semiannual period by each lobbying firm registered to lobby and by each individual listed as a lobbyist on a firm's lobbying report. The lobbyists or lobbying firms must:

- list the name of each federal candidate or officeholder, leadership political action committee, or political party committee to which they made contributions equal to or exceeding \$200 in the aggregate during the semiannual period;

- report contributions made to presidential library foundations and presidential inaugural committees;
- report funds contributed to pay the cost of an event to honor or recognize a covered official, funds paid to an entity named for or controlled by a covered official, and contributions to a person or entity in recognition of an official or to pay the costs of a meeting or other event held by or in the name of a covered official; and
- certify that they have read and are familiar with the gift and travel rules of Congress and that they have not provided, requested, or directed a gift or travel to a member, officer, or employee of Congress that would violate those rules.

The Secretary of the Senate, the Clerk of the House, and the Office are responsible for ensuring compliance with the LDA. The Secretary of the Senate and the Clerk of the House notify lobbyists or lobbying firms in writing that they are not complying with reporting requirements in the LDA and subsequently refer those lobbyists who fail to provide an appropriate response to the Office. The Office researches these referrals and sends additional noncompliance notices to the lobbyists or lobbying firms, requesting that they file reports or terminate their registration. If the Office does not receive a response after 60 days, it decides whether to pursue a civil or criminal case against each noncompliant lobbyist. A civil case could lead to penalties up to \$200,000, while a criminal case—usually pursued if a lobbyist's noncompliance is found to be knowing and corrupt—could lead to a maximum of 5 years in prison.

MOST NEWLY REGISTERED LOBBYISTS FILED DISCLOSURE REPORTS AS REQUIRED

Of the 3,034 new registrants we identified for the time periods corresponding to our review, we matched 2,925 reports (96 percent) of registrations filed in the first quarter in which they were first registered. These results are consistent with prior reviews. To determine whether new registrants were meeting the requirement to file, we matched newly filed registrations in the third and fourth quarters of 2012 and the first and second quarters of 2013 from the House Lobbyists Disclosure Database to their corresponding quarterly disclosure reports. We did this using an electronic matching algorithm that allows for misspellings and other minor inconsistencies between the registrations and reports. Figure 1 shows that most newly registered lobbyists filed their disclosure reports as required from 2010 through 2013.

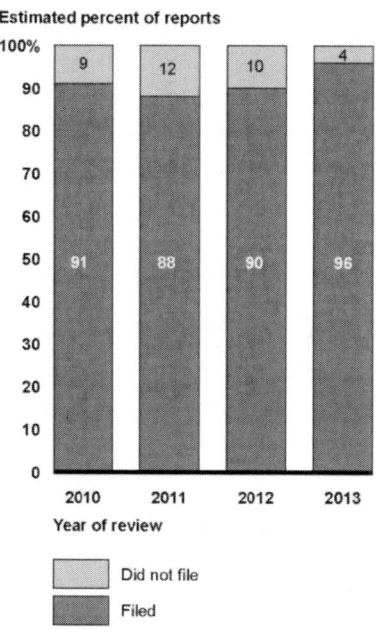

Source: GAO analysis.
Note: Results are based on an analysis of all newly registered lobbyists for the periods corresponding to our reviews.

Figure 1. Comparison of Newly Registered Lobbyists That Filed Disclosure Reports as Required from 2010 through 2013.

For Most LD-2 Reports Lobbyists Provided Documentation for Key Elements, but for Some LD-2 Reports Lobbyists Rounded Their Income or Expenses Incorrectly

For selected elements of lobbyists' LD-2 reports that can be generalized to the population of lobbying reports, unless otherwise noted, our findings were consistent from year to year. We used tests that adjusted for multiple comparisons to assess the statistical significance of changes over time.

Most lobbyists reporting $5,000 or more in income or expenses provided written documentation to varying degrees for the reporting elements in their disclosure reports. For this year's review, lobbyists for an estimated 96 percent of LD-2 reports (98 out of 102) provided written documentation for the income and expenses reported for the third and fourth quarters of 2012 and the first and second quarters of 2013. The most common forms of documentation provided included invoices for income and internal expense reports for expenses. Figure 2 shows that for most LD-2 reports, lobbyists provided documentation for income and expenses for sampled reports from 2010 through 2013.

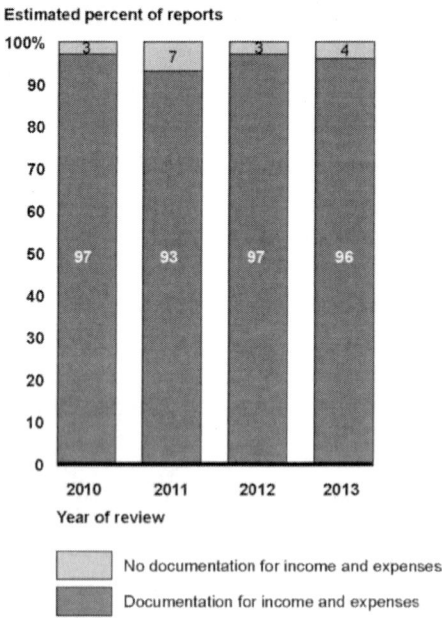

Source: GAO analysis.

Note: Estimates of proportions based on sampled reports, generalizable to the universe of LD-2 reports with lobbying activity. Results have a maximum margin of error of 11 percent. Year-to-year differences are not statistically significant.

Figure 2. Percentage of LD-2 Reports with Documentation for Income and Expenses from 2010 through 2013.

Figure 3 shows that for some LD-2 reports, lobbyists rounded their income or expenses incorrectly. We identified 33 percent of reports as having rounding errors. On 13 percent of those reports, lobbyists reported the exact amount of lobbying income or expenses instead of rounding to the nearest $10,000 as required. Rounding difficulties has been a recurring issue from 2010 through 2013.[9]

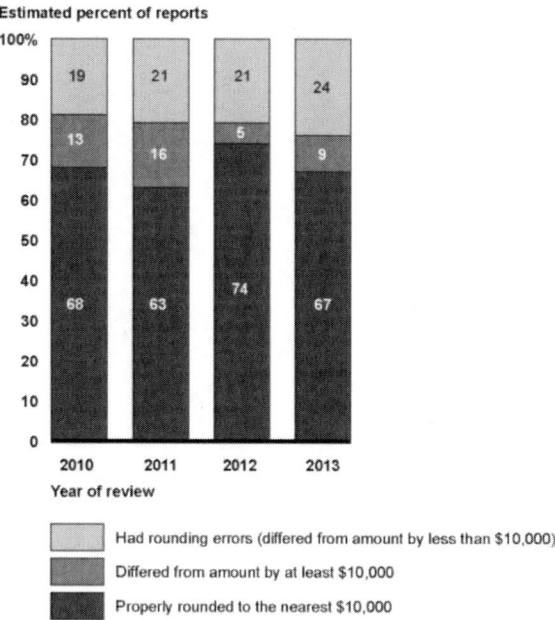

Estimated percent of reports

Had rounding errors (differed from amount by less than $10,000)

Differed from amount by at least $10,000

Properly rounded to the nearest $10,000

Source: GAO analysis.

Note: Estimates of proportions based on sampled reports, generalizable to the universe of LD-2 reports with lobbying activity. Results have a maximum margin of error of 11 percent. With the exception of the decrease in the proportion of reports with a $10,000 or greater discrepancy from 2011 to 2012, results were not statistically significant.

Figure 3. Percentage of LD-2 Reports with Differences in the Amount of Income and Expenses Reported by at Least $10,000 and Rounding Errors from 2010 through 2013.

The LDA requires lobbyists to disclose lobbying contacts made to executive branch agencies on behalf of the client for the reporting period. This year, of the 102 LD-2 reports in our sample, 42 LD-2 reports disclosed lobbying activities at executive branch agencies. Of those, lobbyists provided documentation for all lobbying activities at executive branch agencies for 30 LD-2 reports.[10]

Figures 4 through 7 show that lobbyists for most LD-2 reports were able to provide documentation for selected elements of their LD-2 reports from 2010 through 2013.

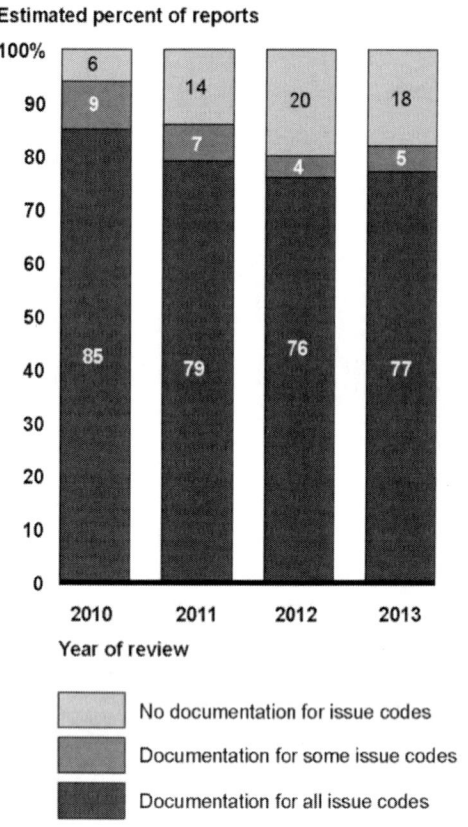

Source: GAO analysis.

Note: Estimates of proportions based on sampled reports, generalizable to the universe of LD-2 reports with lobbying activity. Results have a maximum margin of error of 11 percent. Year-to-year differences are not statistically significant.

Figure 4. Extent to Which Lobbyists Provided Documentation for Issue Codes from 2010 through 2013.

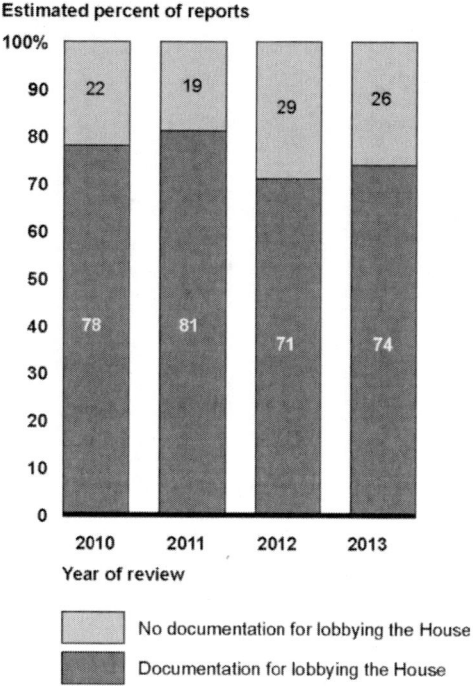

Estimated percent of reports

Source: GAO analysis.

Note: Estimates of proportions based on sampled reports, generalizable to the universe of LD-2 reports with lobbying activity. Results have a maximum margin of error of 11 percent. Year-to-year differences are not statistically significant.

Figure 5. Extent to Which Lobbyists Provided Documentation for Lobbying the House from 2010 through 2013.

For Most LD-2 Reports, Lobbyists Filed LD-203 Reports for All Listed Lobbyists

Lobbyists for an estimated 92 percent of LD-2 reports filed year-end 2012 or midyear 2013 LD-203 reports for all lobbyists and lobbying firms listed on the report as required. Figure 8 shows that lobbyists for most lobbying firms filed contribution reports for lobbyists and lobbying firms as required for LD-2 reports from 2010 through 2013. All individual lobbyists and lobbying firms reporting lobbying activity are required to file LD-203 reports semiannually, even if they have no contributions to report, because they must certify compliance with the gift and travel rules.

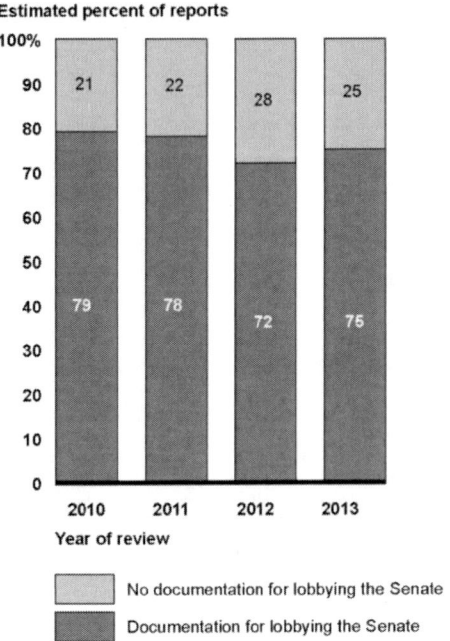

Source: GAO analysis.

Note: Estimates of proportions based on sampled reports, generalizable to the universe of LD-2 reports with lobbying activity. Results have a maximum margin of error of 11 percent. Year-to-year differences are not statistically significant.

Figure 6. Extent to Which Lobbyists Provided Documentation for Lobbying the Senate from 2010 through 2013.

For Some LD-2 Reports, Lobbyists Failed to Disclose Covered Positions

The LDA requires a lobbyist to disclose previously held covered positions when first registering as a lobbyist for a new client. This can be done either on the LD-1 or on the LD-2 quarterly filing when added as a new lobbyist. This year, we estimate that 17 percent of all LD-2 reports did not properly disclose one or more previously held covered positions as required. Figure 9 shows the extent to which lobbyists failed to properly disclose one or more covered positions as required from 2010 through 2013.

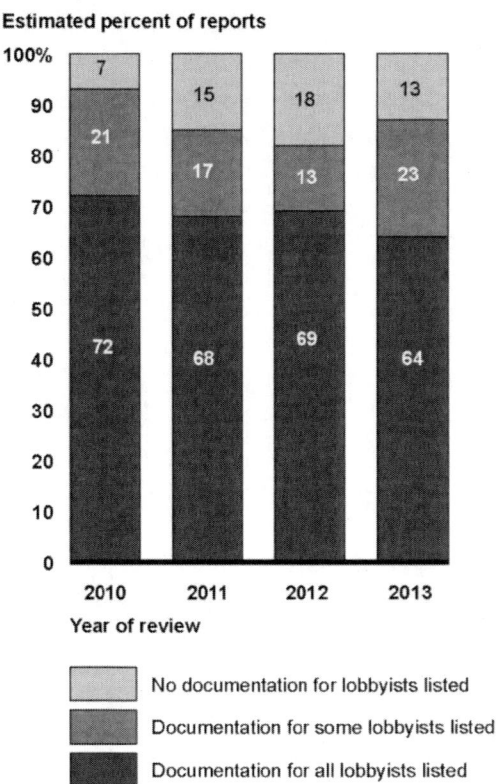

Figure 7. Extent to Which Lobbyists Provided Documentation for Individual Lobbyists Listed from 2010 through 2013.

Source: GAO analysis.

Note: Estimates of proportions based on sampled reports, generalizable to the universe of LD-2 reports with lobbying activity. Results have a maximum margin of error of 11 percent. Year-to-year differences are not statistically significant.

Some Lobbyists Amended Their Disclosure Reports after We Contacted Them

As of April 10, 2014, lobbyists amended 18 of the 104 disclosure reports in our original sample to make changes to previously reported information. One of the 18 reports was amended twice—once after we notified the lobbyists of our review and again after we met with them. An additional 7 of the 18 reports were amended after we notified the lobbyists of our review, but before we met with them. Finally, an additional 10 of the 18 reports were amended after we met with the lobbyists to review their documentation. We cannot be certain how lobbyists not in our sample would have behaved had they not been contacted by us. However, the notable number of amended LD-2 reports in our sample each year following notification of our review suggests that sometimes our contact spurs lobbyists to more closely scrutinize their reports than they would have without our review.

Table 1 lists reasons lobbying firms in our sample amended their LD-1 or LD-2 reports.

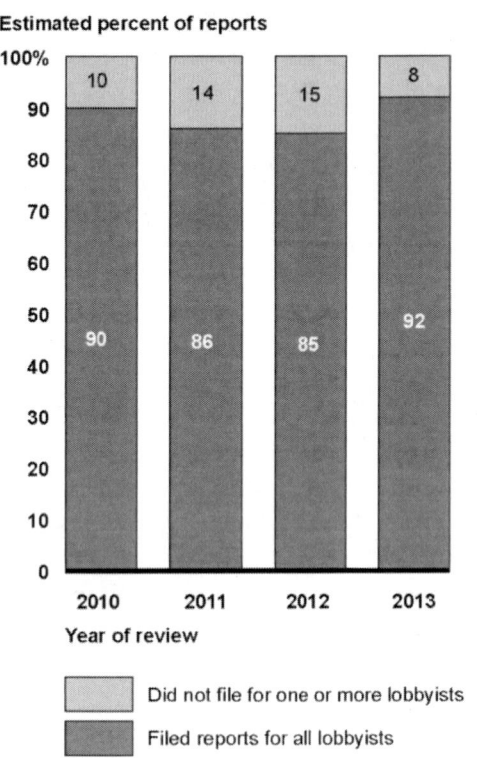

Estimated percent of reports

Year of review

Source: GAO analysis.

Note: Estimates of proportions based on sampled reports, generalizable to the universe of LD-2 reports with lobbying activity. Results have a maximum margin of error of 11 percent. Year-to-year differences are not statistically significant.

Figure 8. Extent to Which Lobbyists on LD-2 Reports Filed Contribution Reports for All Listed Lobbyists and Lobbying Firms from 2010 through 2013.

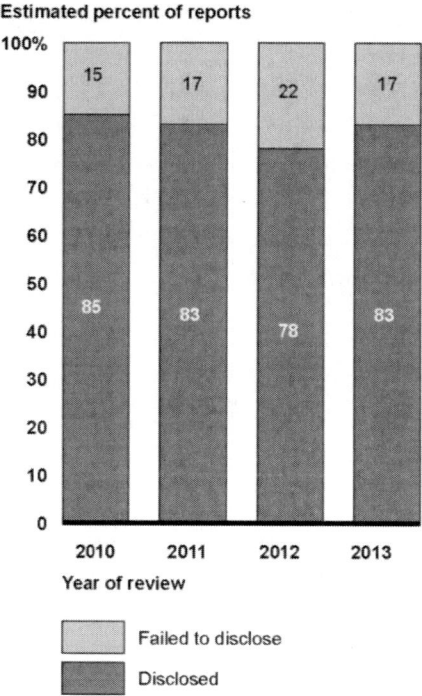

Estimated percent of reports

Year of review

Failed to disclose

Disclosed

Source: GAO analysis.

Note: Estimates of proportions based on sampled reports, generalizable to the universe of LD-2 reports with lobbying activity. Results have a maximum margin of error of 11 percent. Year-to-year differences are not statistically significant. For this element in prior reports, we reported an estimated minimum percentage of reports based on a one-sided, 95 percent confidence interval rather than the estimated proportion as shown here.

Figure 9. Estimated Percent of LD-2 Reports Where Lobbyists Failed to Properly Disclose One or More Covered Positions from 2010 through 2013.

Most LD-203 Contribution Reports Disclosed Political Contributions Listed in the FEC Database

As part of our review, we compared contributions listed on lobbyists' and lobbying firms' LD-203 reports against those political contributions reported in the FEC database to identify whether political contributions were omitted on LD-203 reports in our sample. The sample of LD-203 reports we reviewed originally contained 80 reports with contributions and 80 reports without contributions.[11] We estimate that overall, for 2013, lobbyists failed to disclose one or more reportable contributions on 4 percent of reports.[12] Table 2 illustrates that most lobbyists disclosed FEC reportable contributions on their LD-203 reports as required from 2010 through 2013.

Table 1. Reasons Lobbyists in Our Sample Amended Their Disclosure Reports as of April 2014

Reasons for amending	Number of times reason selected
Update covered position	6
Change reported Income or expenses	5
Change House, Senate, or executive agency lobbying activity	5
Change individuals who acted as a lobbyist	2
Change specific issue areas lobbied	1
Change to no lobbying activity	1
Total	**19**

Source: GAO analysis.

Note: Some firms cited more than one reason for amending. Additionally, one firm amended its disclosure report twice; once after we contacted the firm about the interview and again after the interview. Lobbyists may have amended either their LD-1 or LD-2 reports to change information previously reported on the LD-2 under review.

Table 2. Estimated Percent of LD-203 Reports That Omitted One or More Political Contributions from 2010 through 2013

Year of review	2010	2011	2012	2013
Number of reports with contributions that had one or more omissions	7	12	14	10[a]
Number of reports without contributions that had one or more omissions	1	2	4	0
Estimated percentage of all reports with one or more omissions	4%	9%	9%	4%

Source: GAO analysis.

Note: These results contain contributions that are reportable to the FEC. For this element in prior reports, we reported an estimated minimum percentage of reports based on a one-sided, 95 percent confidence interval rather than the estimated proportion as shown here.

[a] n=80, except where noted with n=79.

Most Lobbying Firms Found It Easy to Comply with Disclosure Requirements and Understood Lobbying Terms

As part of our review, 92 different lobbying firms were included in our 2013 sample.[13] Consistent with prior reviews, most lobbying firms reported that they found it very easy or somewhat easy to comply with reporting requirements. Of the 92 different lobbying firms in our sample, 20 reported that the disclosure requirements were "very easy," 59 reported them "somewhat easy," and 9 reported them "somewhat difficult" or "very difficult" (see figure 10).[14]

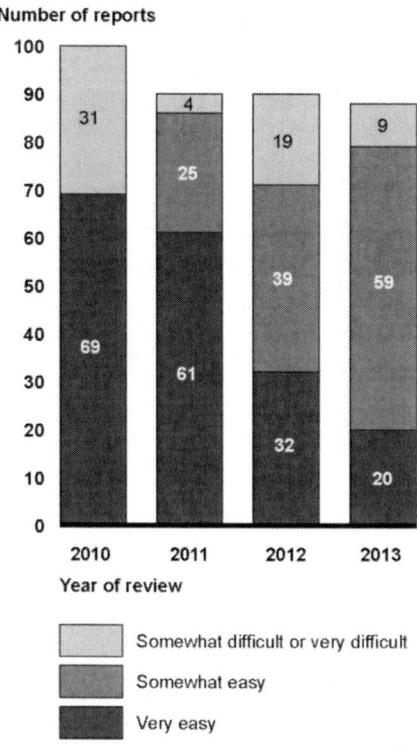

Source: GAO analysis.

Note: In 2011, our scale was easy to meet, somewhat easy to meet, or difficult to meet. In 2010, we asked if it was easy to comply with disclosure requirements. For 2013, 4 of the 92 different lobbying firms did not respond to the question about ease of compliance with reporting requirements.

Figure 10. Ease of Complying with Disclosure Requirements from 2010 through 2013.

Most lobbyists we interviewed rated the terms associated with LD-2 reporting requirements as "very easy" or "somewhat easy" to understand with regard to meeting their reporting requirements. This is consistent with prior reviews. Figures 11 through 15 show how lobbyists reported ease of understanding the terms associated with LD-2 reporting requirements from 2010 through 2013.[15]

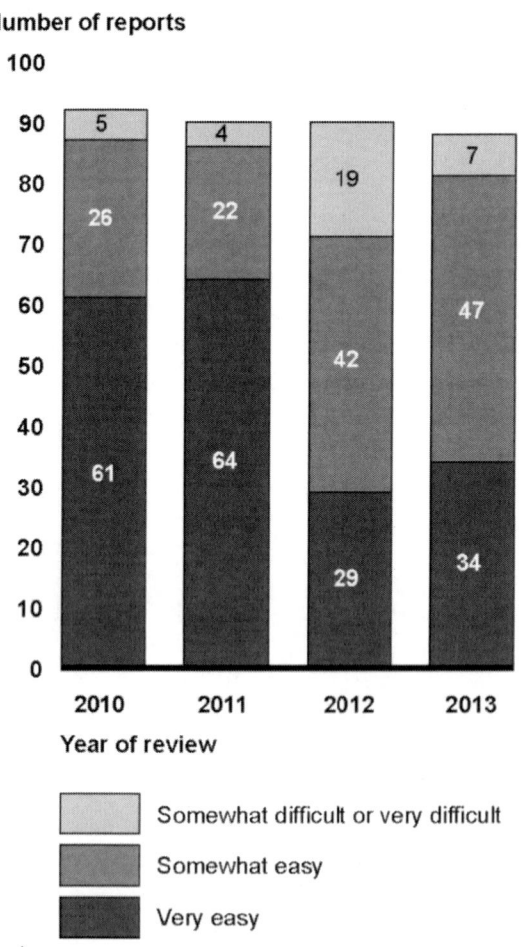

Number of reports

Source: GAO analysis.

Note: In 2011 and 2010, we asked lobbyists to rate the terms associated with LD-2 reporting using the scale clear and understandable, somewhat clear and understandable, or not clear and understandable.

Figure 11. Ease of Understanding Lobbying Definitions from 2010 through 2013.

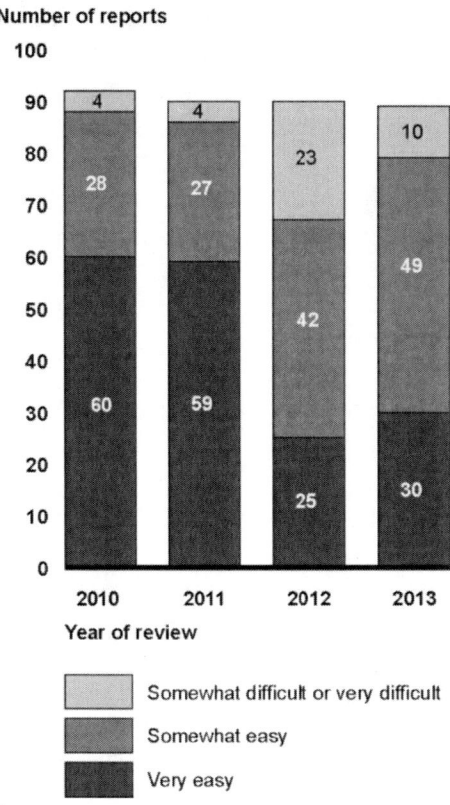

Source: GAO analysis.

Note: In 2011 and 2010, we asked lobbyists to rate the terms associated with LD-2 reporting using the scale, clear and understandable, somewhat clear and understandable, or not clear and understandable.

Figure 12. Ease of Understanding the Term "Lobbying Activities" from 2010 through 2013.

U.S. ATTORNEY'S OFFICE ACTIONS TO ENFORCE LDA

The Office's Authorities, Processes, and Resources to Enforce LDA Compliance

The Office stated it continues to have sufficient personnel resources and authority under the LDA to enforce LD-2 reporting requirements, including imposing civil or criminal penalties for noncompliance of LD-2 reporting.

Noncompliance refers to a lobbyist's or lobbying firm's failure to comply with LDA requirements. According to the Office, it has one contract paralegal specialist assigned full time, as well as five civil attorneys and one criminal attorney assigned part time for LDA compliance work. In addition, the Office stated that it participates in a government-wide program that provides temporary access to attorneys to assist with LDA compliance. The temporarily assigned attorneys work with the contract paralegal specialist to contact referred lobbyists or lobbying firms who do not comply with the LDA.

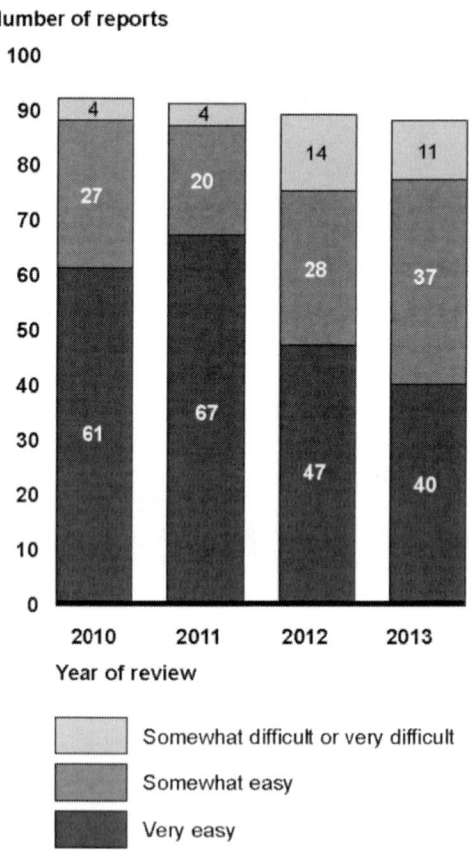

Source: GAO analysis.

Note: In 2011 and 2010, we asked lobbyists to rate the terms associated with LD-2 reporting using the scale, clear and understandable, somewhat clear and understandable, or not clear and understandable.

Figure 13. Ease of Understanding Issue Codes from 2010 through 2013.

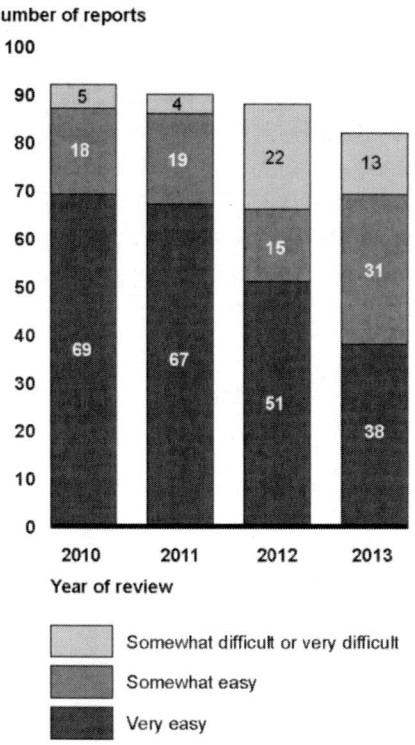

Number of reports

Source: GAO analysis.

Note: In 2011 and 2010, we asked lobbyists to rate the terms associated with LD-2 reporting using the scale, clear and understandable, somewhat clear and understandable, or not clear and understandable.

Figure 14. Ease of Understanding the Term "Covered Positions" from 2010 through 2013.

According to the Office, it has sufficient authority to enforce LD-203 compliance with the LDA for lobbying firms and certain individual lobbyists. However, it has difficulty pursuing hundreds of LD-203 referrals that arise when a lobbying firm does not maintain or a lobbyist does not leave forwarding contact information upon leaving the firm. The LD-203 report does not provide contact information. It only provides the name of the lobbyist and lobbying firm. As a result, the Office does not have contact information to find the referred lobbyist to bring him or her into compliance. Office officials reported that many firms have assisted them by providing contact information for lobbyists, and only a few firms have not been willing to provide contact information for noncompliant lobbyists. Additionally, the Office stated that because the current structure of the LDA requires registered lobbyists to file their LD-203 reports and does not require lobbying firms to ensure that their registered lobbyists have complied with LD-203 filing requirements, the Office has no authority to hold lobbying firms responsible for a registered lobbyist who fails to comply with LD-203 requirements. Accordingly, when the Office does not have contact information to find a lobbyist who left the firm and it cannot hold the lobbying firm responsible for the lobbyist's noncompliance with lobbying disclosure requirements, the Office has no recourse to pursue enforcement action.

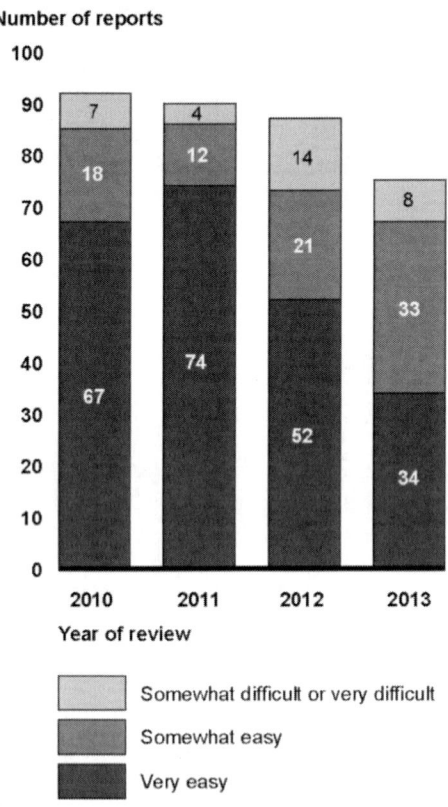

Source: GAO analysis.
Note: In 2011 and 2010, we asked lobbyists to rate the terms associated with LD-2 reporting using the scale, clear and understandable, somewhat clear and understandable, or not clear and understandable.

Figure 15. Ease of Understanding the Term "Terminating Lobbyists" from 2010 through 2013.

In a prior report, we recommended that the Office develop a structured approach for tracking and recording its enforcement actions.[16] The Office developed the LDA database to track the status of referrals and enforcement actions it takes to bring lobbyists and lobbying firms into compliance with the LDA. To enforce compliance, the Office has primarily focused on sending letters to lobbyists who have potentially violated the LDA by not filing disclosure reports as required. The letters request lobbyists to comply with the law by promptly filing the appropriate disclosure reports and inform lobbyists of potential civil and criminal penalties for not complying. In addition to sending letters, a contractor sends e-mails and calls lobbyists to inform them of their need to comply with LDA reporting requirements. Not all referred lobbyists receive noncompliance letters, e-mails, or phone calls because some of the lobbyists have terminated their registrations or filed the required financial disclosure reports before the Office received the referral.

Office officials stated that lobbyists resolve their noncompliance issues by filing the reports or terminating their registration. Resolving referrals can take anywhere from a few days to years depending on the circumstances. During this time, the Office monitors and reviews all outstanding referrals and uses summary reports from the database to track the overall number of referrals that become compliant as a result of receiving an e-mail, phone call, or noncompliance letter. In addition, more referred lobbyists are being contacted by e-mail and phone calls, which has decreased the number of noncompliance letters the Office sends to lobbyists. Officials from the Office stated that the majority of these e-mails and calls result in the registrant becoming compliant without sending a letter. In our last report, the Office told us that its system collects information on contacts made by e-mail and phone calls in the notes section of its database, but the database does not automatically tabulate the number of e-mails and phone calls to lobbyists, as it does for letters sent.[17] In March 2013 as a part of closing discussions with the Office about the findings of our last lobbying disclosure report, as part of its enforcement efforts we urged the Office to develop a mechanism to track e-mails and telephone contacts to individual lobbyists. Since then, the Office has started tracking the number of e-mails and telephone contacts that are associated with its enforcement efforts to bring lobbyists and lobbying firms into compliance. These actions are now included in the number of enforcement actions taken to bring lobbyists and lobbying firms into compliance.

Status of LD-2 Enforcement Efforts from 2009 through 2013 Reporting Periods

As of January 16, 2014, the Office has received 2,722 referrals from both the Secretary of the Senate and the Clerk of the House for failure to comply with LD-2 reporting requirements cumulatively for calendar years 2009 through 2013. Figure 16 shows the number and status of the referrals received and the number of enforcement actions taken by the Office in its effort to bring lobbying firms into compliance. Enforcement actions include the number of letters, e-mails, and calls made by the Office. About 66 percent (1,787 of 2,722) of the total referrals received are now compliant because lobbying firms either filed their reports or terminated their registrations. In addition, some of the referrals were found to be compliant when the Office received the referral, and therefore no action was taken. This may occur when lobbying firms respond to the contact letters from the Secretary of the Senate and Clerk of the House after the Office has received the referrals. About 34 percent (922 of 2,722) of referrals are pending action because the Office was unable to locate the lobbying firm, did not receive a response from the firm, or plans to conduct additional research to determine if it can locate the lobbying firm. According to the Office, resolving referrals can take anywhere from a few days to years depending on the circumstances. Referrals may remain in pending status and may be monitored by the Office until it determines whether to pursue legal action against the registrant or dismiss certain referrals or until the registrant files the disclosure report or terminates his or her registration. The remaining 13 referrals did not require action or were suspended because the lobbyist or client was no longer in business or the lobbyist was deceased. The Office suspends enforcement actions against lobbyists or lobbying firms that are repeatedly referred for not filing disclosure reports but that do not have any current lobbying activity. The suspended lobbying firms are periodically monitored to determine whether they actively lobby in the future. As a part of this monitoring, the Office checks the lobbying disclosure databases maintained by the Secretary of the Senate and the Clerk of the House.

Status of LD-203 Enforcement Actions from 2009 through 2013 Reporting Periods

LD-203 referrals consist of two types: LD-203(R) referrals represent lobbying firms that have failed to file LD-203 reports for the firm, and LD-

203 referrals represent the lobbyists at the lobbying firm who have failed to file their individual LD-203 reports as required. As of January 16, 2014, the Office had received 1,350 LD-203(R) referrals and 3,042 LD-203 referrals from the Secretary of the Senate and Clerk of the House cumulatively for calendar years 2009 through 2013. For LD-203 referrals, the Office sends noncompliance letters for the lobbyists to the registered lobbying firms listed on the LD-203 report because the lobbyist's personal contact information is not listed on the LD-203 report.

Figure 17 shows the status of LD-203(R) referrals received and the number of enforcement actions taken by the Office in its effort to bring lobbying firms into compliance. About 43 percent (581 of 1,350) of the lobbyists who were referred by the Secretary of the Senate and Clerk of the House for noncompliance during the 2009 through 2013 reporting periods are now considered compliant because lobbying firms either have filed their reports or have terminated their registrations. About 57 percent (768 of 1,350) of the referrals are pending action because the Office was unable to locate the lobbyist, did not receive a response from the lobbyist, or plans to conduct additional research to determine if it can locate the lobbying firm.

Figure 18 shows that as of January 16, 2014, the Office had received 3,042 LD-203 referrals from the Secretary and Clerk for lobbyists who failed to comply with LD-203 reporting requirements for calendar years 2009 through 2012. Figure 18 shows the status of the referrals received and the number of enforcement actions taken by the Office in its effort to bring lobbyists into compliance. Figure 18 shows that 55 percent (1,676 of 3,042) of the lobbyists either have come into compliance by filing their reports or are no longer registered as a lobbyist. About 44 percent (1,352 of 3,042) of the referrals are pending action because the Office was unable to locate the lobbyists, did not receive a response from the lobbyists, or plans to conduct additional research to determine if it can locate the lobbyists.

The Office said that many of the pending LD-203 referrals represent lobbyists who no longer lobby for the lobbying firms affiliated with the referrals, even though these lobbying firms may be listed on the lobbyist's LD-203 report. In addition, Office officials stated that they continue to experience challenges with increasing LD-203 compliance because the Office has little leverage to bring certain individual lobbyists into compliance. Many of the LD-203 referrals remain open in an attempt to locate lobbyists who are no longer employed by the lobbying firm and do not leave a forwarding address. As a result, it may take years to resolve the referrals and bring the lobbyists into compliance.

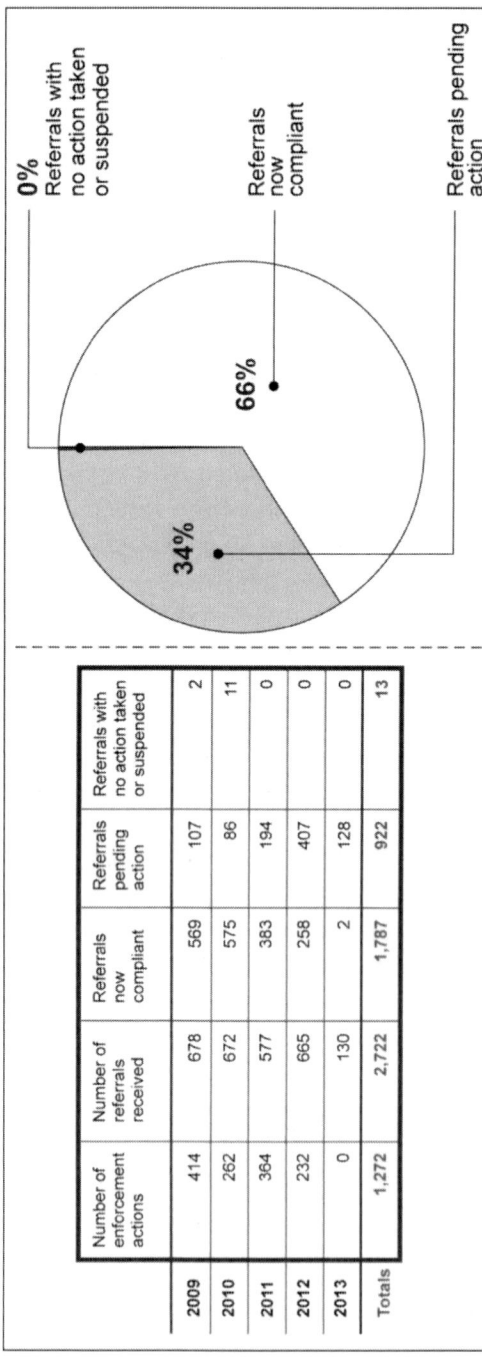

	Number of enforcement actions	Number of referrals received	Referrals now compliant	Referrals pending action	Referrals with no action taken or suspended
2009	414	678	569	107	2
2010	262	672	575	86	11
2011	364	577	383	194	0
2012	232	665	258	407	0
2013	0	130	2	128	0
Totals	1,272	2,722	1,787	922	13

0%
Referrals with no action taken or suspended

Referrals now compliant

66%

34%

Referrals pending action

Source: U.S. Attorney's Office for the District of Columbia.

Figure 16. Status of LDA Enforcement Actions for LD-2 Reporting from 2009 through 2013 (as of January 16, 2014).

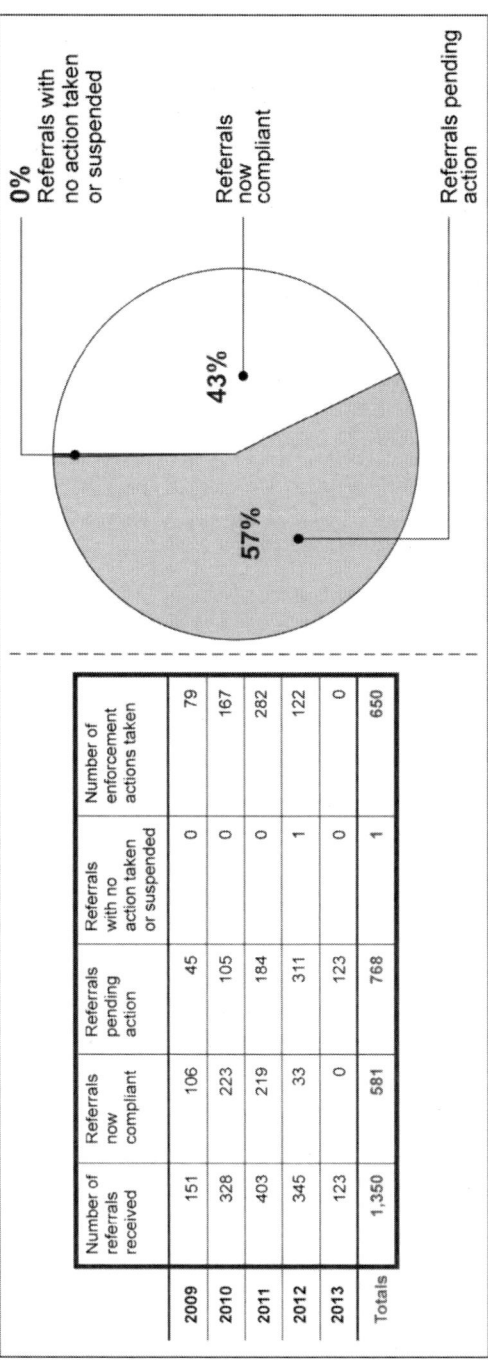

	Number of referrals received	Referrals now compliant	Referrals pending action	Referrals with no action taken or suspended	Number of enforcement actions taken
2009	151	106	45	0	79
2010	328	223	105	0	167
2011	403	219	184	0	282
2012	345	33	311	1	122
2013	123	0	123	0	0
Totals	1,350	581	768	1	650

Source: U.S. Attorney's Office for the District of Columbia.

Figure 17. Status of LDA Enforcement Actions for LD-203(R) Lobbying Firms Only Reporting from 2009 through 2013 (as of January 16, 2014).

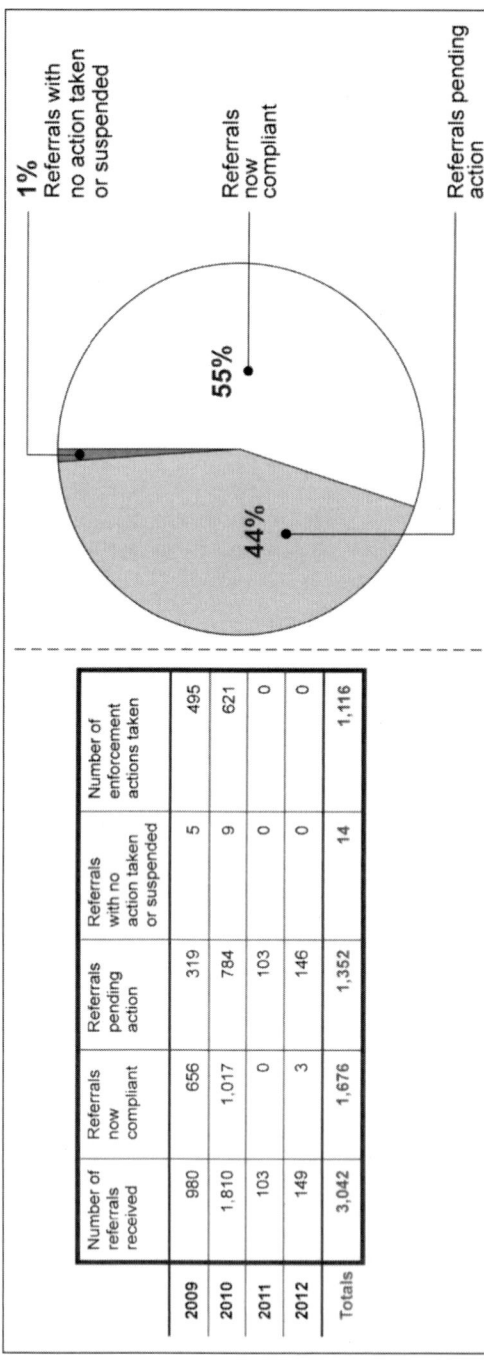

	Number of referrals received	Referrals now compliant	Referrals pending action	Referrals with no action taken or suspended	Number of enforcement actions taken
2009	980	656	319	5	495
2010	1,810	1,017	784	9	621
2011	103	0	103	0	0
2012	149	3	146	0	0
Totals	3,042	1,676	1,352	14	1,116

Source: U.S. Attorney's Office for the District of Columbia.

Figure 18. Status of LDA Enforcement Actions for LD-203 Lobbyists Only for Reporting from 2009 through 2012 (as of January 16, 2014).

Status of Enforcement Settlement Actions

Since the 2012 reporting period, the Office has identified nine registrants on its chronic offenders list for failure to comply with reporting requirements. Of the nine registrants, five filed the outstanding reports or terminated their registration after being contacted by an Assistant U.S. Attorney. The Office reached settlement agreements with two of the registrants for $50,000 and $30,000, respectively, in civil penalties for repeatedly failing to file disclosure reports. In December 2013, the Office filed a default judgment for $200,000 against a registrant for repeated failure to file his LDA reports as required. In March 2014, the Office filed a civil complaint in the U.S. District Court for the District of Columbia for a registrant's failure to comply with LDA reporting requirements.

The Office continues to monitor and review chronic offenders to determine appropriate enforcement actions, which may include considering legal actions or dismissing certain cases.

Concluding Observations

Over the past several years of reporting on lobbying disclosure, we have found that lobbyists reported understanding terms and requirements, but their disclosure filings demonstrated some compliance difficulties. For example, a number of lobbyists had rounding errors in their reports, failed to disclose covered positions, and did not accurately disclose their lobbying activity with the House, the Senate, or executive agencies. As a result, after being contacted by us, lobbyists amended their reports to address these types of compliance difficulties. In our first lobbying disclosure report in September 2008, we concluded that the lobbying community could benefit from creating an organization to

- share examples of best practices of the types of records maintained to support filings;
- use this information gathered over an initial period to formulate minimum standards for recordkeeping;
- provide training for the lobbying community on reporting and disclosure requirements intended to help the community comply with the LDA; and

- report annually to the Secretary of the Senate and the Clerk of the House on opportunities to clarify existing guidance and ways to minimize sources of potential confusion for the lobbying community.

The continuing difficulties that some lobbyists have demonstrated in their disclosure reports, coupled with the sustained public and congressional attention on lobbyists and their interactions with government officials, underscores the importance of accurate and public disclosure of such activities. In that regard, we continue to believe that creating the type of organization we described in our first report could still be beneficial to the lobbying community and the public interest. The activities of such an organization could help enhance the enforcement and compliance with the LDA as amended by HLOGA and improve the accuracy and value of the information reported to Congress.

AGENCY COMMENTS

We provided a draft of this report to the Attorney General for review and comment. The Assistant U.S. Attorney for the District of Columbia responded on behalf of the Attorney General that the Department of Justice had no comments.

Seto J. Bagdoyan
Acting Director, Strategic Issues

APPENDIX I. OBJECTIVES, SCOPE, AND METHODOLOGY

Consistent with the mandate in the Honest Leadership and Open Government Act (HLOGA), our objectives were to

- determine the extent to which lobbyists are able to demonstrate compliance with the Lobbying Disclosure Act of 1995, as amended (LDA) by providing documentation to support information contained on registrations and reports filed under the LDA;
- identify challenges and potential improvements to compliance, if any; and

- describe the resources and authorities available to the U.S. Attorney's Office for the District of Columbia (the Office) and the efforts the Office has made to improve enforcement of the LDA.

To respond to our mandate, we used information in the lobbying disclosure database maintained by the Clerk of the House of Representatives (Clerk of the House). To assess whether these disclosure data were sufficiently reliable for the purposes of this report, we reviewed relevant documentation and spoke to officials responsible for maintaining the data. Although registrations and reports are filed through a single web portal, each chamber subsequently receives copies of the data and follows different data cleaning, processing, and editing procedures before storing the data in either individual files (in the House) or databases (in the Senate). Currently, there is no means of reconciling discrepancies between the two databases caused by the differences in data processing. For example, Senate staff told us during previous reviews that they set aside a greater proportion of registration and report submissions than the House for manual review before entering the information into the database. As a result, the Senate database would be slightly less current than the House database on any given day pending review and clearance. House staff told us during previous reviews that they rely heavily on automated processing. They added that while they manually review reports that do not perfectly match information on file for a given registrant or client, they will approve and upload such reports as originally filed by each lobbyist, even if the reports contain errors or discrepancies (such as a variant on how a name is spelled). Nevertheless, we do not have reasons to believe that the content of the Senate and House systems would vary substantially. For this review, we determined that House disclosure data were sufficiently reliable for identifying a sample of quarterly disclosure (LD-2) reports and for assessing whether newly filed registrants also filed required reports. We used the House database for sampling LD-2 reports from the third and fourth quarters of 2012 and the first and second quarters of 2013, as well as for sampling year-end 2012 and midyear 2013 political contributions (LD-203) reports and finally for matching quarterly registrations with filed reports. We did not evaluate the Offices of the Secretary of the Senate or the Clerk of the House, both of which have key roles in the lobbying disclosure process. However, we did consult with officials from each office and they provided us with general background information at our request.

To assess the extent to which lobbyists could provide evidence of their compliance with reporting requirements, we examined a stratified random sample of 104 LD-2 reports from the third and fourth quarters of 2012 and the first and second quarters of 2013. We excluded reports with no lobbying activity or with income less than $5,000 from our sampling frame.[18] We drew our sample from 65,489 activity reports filed for the third and fourth quarters of 2012 and the first and second quarters of 2013 available in the public House database, as of our final download date for each quarter. One LD-2 report was removed from the sample because we could not contact the firm and it appears the firm has gone out of business. We treated this report as a nonrespondent for the purposes of analysis and adjusted our sampling weights accordingly for analysis. Another LD-2 report was excluded because the lobbyist amended the LD-2 to reflect no lobbying activity after being notified of the review. This report was treated as out of scope.

Our sample of LD-2 reports was not designed to detect differences over time. However, we conducted tests of significance for changes from 2010 to 2013 for the generalizable elements of our review and found that there were generally no statistically significant differences over time. With the exception of one yearly decrease in the estimated proportion of reports with income or expense discrepancies of $10,000 or more, we found no statistically significant differences after using a Bonferroni adjustment to account for multiple comparisons.[19] While the results provide some confidence that apparent fluctuations in our results across years are likely attributable to sampling error, the inability to detect significant differences may also be related to the nature of our sample, which was relatively small and was designed only for cross-sectional analysis.

Our sample is based on a stratified random selection and is only one of a large number of samples that we may have drawn. Because each sample could have provided different estimates, we express our confidence in the precision of our particular sample's results as a 95 percent confidence interval. This interval would contain the actual population value for 95 percent of the samples that we could have drawn. The percentage estimates for 2013 have a 95 percent confidence interval of within plus-or-minus 10.1 percentage points or less of the estimate itself, unless otherwise noted. For 2010 through 2012, the percentage estimates have a 95 percent confidence interval with a maximum of 11 percentage points.

We contacted the lobbyists and lobbying firms in our sample using a structured web-based survey and asked them to confirm key elements of the LD-2 and provide documentation for key elements in their reports, including

- the amount of income reported for lobbying activities,
- the amount of expenses reported on lobbying activities,
- the names of those lobbyists listed in the report,
- the houses of Congress and federal agencies that they lobbied, and
- the issue codes listed to describe their lobbying activity.

After reviewing the survey results for completeness, we conducted interviews with the lobbyists and lobbying firms to review documentation they reported as having on their online survey for selected elements of their LD-2 reports.

Prior to each interview, we conducted an open source search to identify lobbyists on each report who may have held a covered official position. We reviewed the lobbyists' previous work histories by searching lobbying firms' websites, LinkedIn, Leadership Directories, Legistorm, and Google. Prior to 2008, lobbyists were only required to disclose covered official positions held within 2 years of registering as a lobbyist for the client. HLOGA amended that time frame to require disclosure of positions held 20 years before the date the lobbyists first lobbied on behalf of the client. Lobbyist are required to disclose previously held covered official positions either on the client registration (LD-1) or on the first LD-2 report when the lobbyist is added as "new." Consequently, those who held covered official positions may have disclosed the information on the LD-1 or a LD-2 report filed prior to the report we examined as part of our random sample.

Therefore, where we found evidence that a lobbyist previously held a covered official position and it was not disclosed on the LD-2 report under review, we then conducted an additional reviewed the publicly available Secretary of the Senate or Clerk of the House database. This was done to determine whether the lobbyist properly disclosed the covered official position on a prior report or LD-1. Finally, if a lobbyist appeared to hold a covered position that was not disclosed, we asked for an explanation at the interview with the lobbying firm to ensure that our research was accurate. In previous reports, we reported the lower bound of a 90- percent confidence interval to provide a minimum estimate of omitted covered positions and omitted contributions with a 95 percent confidence level. We did so to account for the possibility that our searches may have failed to identify all possible omitted covered positions and contributions. As we have developed our methodology over time, we are more confident in the comprehensiveness of our searches for these items. Accordingly, this report presents the estimated percentages for omitted contributions and omitted covered positions rather than the minimum estimates. As a result, percentage estimates for these items will differ slightly from the minimum percentage estimates presented in prior reports.

In addition to examining the content of the LD-2 reports, we confirmed whether year-end 2012 or midyear 2013 LD-203 reports had been filed for each firm and lobbyist listed on the LD-2 reports in our random sample. Although this review represents a random selection of lobbyists and firms, it is not a direct probability sample of firms filing LD-2 reports or lobbyists listed on LD-2 reports. As such, we did not estimate the likelihood that LD-203 reports were appropriately filed for the population of firms or lobbyists listed on LD-2 reports.

To determine if the LDA's requirement for registrants to file a report in the quarter of registration was met for the third and fourth quarters of 2012 and the first and second quarters of 2013, we used data filed with the Clerk of the House to match newly filed registrations with corresponding disclosure reports. Using an electronic matching algorithm that includes strict and loose text matching procedures, we identified matching disclosure reports for 2,925, or 96 percent, of the 3,034 newly filed registrations. We began by standardizing client and registrant names in both the report and registration files (including removing punctuation and standardizing words and abbreviations, such as "company" and "CO"). We then matched reports and registrations using the House identification number (which is linked to a unique registrant-client pair), as well as the names of the registrant and client. For reports we could not match by identification number and standardized name, we also attempted to match reports and registrations by client and registrant name, allowing for variations in the names to accommodate minor misspellings or typos. For these cases, we used professional judgment to determine whether cases with typos were sufficiently similar to consider as matches. We could not readily identify matches in the report database for the remaining registrations using electronic means.

To assess the accuracy of the LD-203 reports, we analyzed stratified random samples of LD-203 reports from the 31,482 total LD-203 reports. The first sample contains 80 of the 10,227 reports with political contributions. The second contains 80 of the 21,255 reports listing no contributions. Each sample contains 40 reports from the year-end 2012 filing period and 40 reports from the midyear 2013 filing period.[20] The samples allow us to generalize estimates in this report to either the population of LD-203 reports with contributions or the reports without contributions to within a 95 percent confidence interval of plus or minus 9.5 percentage points or less. Although our sample of LD-203 reports was not designed to detect differences over time, we conducted tests of significance for changes from 2010 to 2013 and found no statistically significant differences after adjusting for multiple comparisons.[21] While the results provide some confidence that apparent fluctuations in our results across years are likely attributable to sampling error, the inability to detect significant differences may also be related to the nature of our sample, which was relatively small and designed only for cross-sectional analysis. We analyzed the contents of the LD-203 reports and compared them to contribution data found in the publicly available Federal Elections Commission's (FEC) political contribution database. We interviewed FEC staff responsible for administering the database and determined that the data reliability is suitable for confirming whether a FEC-reportable disclosure listed in the FEC database had been reported on an LD-203 report.

We compared the FEC-reportable contributions reporting on the LD-203 reports with information in the FEC database. The verification process required text and pattern matching procedures, and we used professional judgment when assessing whether an individual listed is the same individual filing an LD-203. For contributions reported in the FEC database and not on the LD-203 report, we asked the lobbyists or organizations to explain why the contributions were not listed on the LD-203 report or to provide documentation of those contributions. As with covered positions on LD-2 disclosure reports, we cannot be certain that our review identified all cases of FEC-reportable contributions that were inappropriately omitted from a lobbyist's LD-203 report. We did not estimate the percentage of other non-FEC political contributions that were omitted because they tend to constitute a small minority of all listed contributions and cannot be verified against an external source.

To identify challenges to compliance, we used a web-based survey and obtained the views from 92 different lobbying firms included in our sample on any challenges to compliance. The number of different lobbying firms total 92 and is less than our sample of 102 reports because some lobbying firms had more than 1 LD-2 report included in our sample. We calculated our responses based on the number of different lobbying firms that we contacted rather than the number of interviews. Prior to our calculations, we removed the duplicate lobbying firms based on the most recent date of their responses. For those cases with the same response date, we kept the cases with the smallest assigned case identification number. To obtain their views, we asked them to rate their ease with complying with the LD-2 disclosure requirements using a scale of "very easy," "somewhat easy," "somewhat difficult," or "very difficult." In addition, using the same scale we asked them to rate the ease of understanding the terms associated with LD-2 reporting requirements.

To describe the resources and authorities available to the Office and its efforts to improve its LDA enforcement, we interviewed officials from the Office and obtained updated information on the capabilities of the system they established to track and report compliance trends and referrals, and other practices established to focus resources on enforcement of the LDA. The Office provided us with updated reports from the tracking system on the number and status of referrals and chronically noncompliant lobbyists and lobbying firms.

The mandate does not include identifying lobbyists who failed to register and report in accordance with LDA requirements, or whether for those lobbyists who did register and report, that all lobbying activity or contributions were disclosed.

We conducted this performance audit from June 2013 through May 2014 in accordance with generally accepted government auditing standards. Those standards require that we plan and perform the audit to obtain sufficient, appropriate evidence to provide a reasonable basis for our findings and conclusions based on our audit objectives. We believe that the evidence obtained provides a reasonable basis for our findings and conclusions based on our audit objectives.

APPENDIX II. LIST OF REGISTRANTS AND CLIENTS FOR SAMPLED LOBBYING DISCLOSURE REPORTS

The random sample of lobbying disclosure reports we selected was based on unique combinations of registrant lobbyists and client names (see table 3).

Table 3. Names of Registrants and Clients Selected in Random Sample of Lobbying Disclosure Reports Filed in the Third and Fourth Quarters of 2012 and the First and Second Quarters of 2013

Registrant name	Client
38 North Solutions, LLC	Gamesa Technology Corporation, Inc.
A.O. Smith Corporation	A.O. Smith Corporation
Akin Gump Strauss Hauer & Feld	CT Corporation
American Continental Group	Monsanto Company

Registrant name	Client
American Continental Group	New York State Association for Affordable Housing
Ascension Health	Ascension Health
Atlantic Strategies Group	Scientific Research Corporation
Baker Donelson Bearman Caldwell & Berkowitz	EO2 Concepts
Barnes & Thornburg LLP	Board of Commissioners of Vanderburgh County
Blank Rome Government Relations	Intelsat
Bob Lawrence & Associates, Inc.	Renaissance Associates S.A.
Breaux Lott Leadership Group	St. Tammany Parish
Brownstein Hyatt Farber Schreck, LLP	Genworth Financial, Inc.
Capitol Representatives	The Greenway Foundation
Capitol Strategies, LLC	Lower Santa Cruz River Alliance
Capitol Tax Partners, LLP	International Paper Company
Cassidy & Associates, Inc. (formerly known as Cassidy & Associates)	Lovelace Respiratory Research Institute
Caterpillar Inc.	Caterpillar Inc.
CJ Lake, LLC	CALSTART
Cornerstone Government Affairs, LLC	Custodial Financial
Covington & Burling LLP	Monster Energy Company
DCI Group, LLC	Exxon Mobil
Denny Miller Associates	General Atomics
East End Group, LLC	The Pharmaceutical Research and Manufacturers of America
Edmund Graber	Santa Rosa County FL
Fleet Street Group	Xcel Energy
Friends Committee on National Legislation	Friends Committee on National Legislation
Hannegan Landau Poersch Advocacy, LLC	Quad Partners
Health Policy Source, Inc.	American Society for Anesthesiologists
Hogan Lovells US LLP	National Chicken Council
Hogan Lovells US LLP	GE Oil & Gas
Hyjek & Fix, Inc.	Assured Information Security, Inc.

Table 3. (Continued)

Registrant name	Client
Intellectual Property Owners Association	Intellectual Property Owners Association
Jackson Lewis LLP	Safeway Inc.
James Desmond	Lockheed Martin
Jamison and Sullivan, Inc.	Douglas County, Oregon
John T. O'Rourke	H&R Block Inc.
K &L Gates LLP	Starbucks Coffee Corp
Kadesh & Associates, LLC	Chuckwalla Farm Land, LLC
Karv Communications, Inc.	German Insurance Association
Kia Motors Corporation	Kia Motors Corporation
League of Women Voters of the US	League of Women Voters of the US
Liberty Square Group	Massachusetts Biotechnology Council
LTD Group, LLC	JP Morgan Chase & Co
Manatt, Phelps & Phillips, LLP	Outdoor Advertising Association of America, Inc.
Marla Grossman	American Continental Group on Behalf of The Authors Guild, Inc.
McAllister & Quinn LLC	Yardney Technical Products
McBee Strategic Consulting, LLC	Corrections Corporation of America
Miller/Wenhold Capitol Strategies, LLC	Taxicab, Limosuine and Partransit Association
Mintz Levin Cohn Ferris Glovsky and Popeo, P.C.	National Cable & Telecommunications Association
Motorcycle Riders Foundation	Motorcycle Riders Foundation
Mr. Khalil Saliba	OSI Restaurant Partners, Inc.
MWW Group	WebMD Health (formerly known as Medscape, Inc.)
Nathanson+Hauck	Freelancers Union
National Beer Wholesalers Association	National Beer Wholesalers Association
National Council for Community Behavioral Healthcare	National Council for Community Behavioral Healthcare
National Council of Farmer Cooperatives	National Council of Farmer Cooperatives
Nelson, Mullins, Riley & Scarborough	University of Massachusetts at Dartmouth

Registrant name	Client
Nelson, Mullins, Riley & Scarborough, LLP	Myrtle Beach Downtown Redevelopment Corp
Omer F. Brown, II Law Office	Contractors International Group on Nuclear Liability
O'Neill, Athy & Casey, P.C	Cape Cod Healthcare
Palmetto Group	Hewlett-Packard Company
Palmetto Group	Association of Clinical Research Organizations
Pennsylvania Farm Bureau	Pennsylvania Farm Bureau
Podesta Group, Inc.	Monster Energy Company
Podesta Group, Inc.	URS Corporation
PPG Industries, Inc.	PPG Industries, Inc.
PRASAM	DigitalGlobe, Inc.
Quinn Gillespie & Associates	National Association of Realtors
R. B. Murphy & Associates, LLC	Google Inc
Robert Talley	TAPS
Russ Reid Company	Covenant House Florida
Scholastic Inc.	Scholastic Inc.
Sustainable Strategies DC	The Ferguson Group on behalf of the City of Ranson, WV
The Advocacy Group	University of Central Florida
The Brightup Group LLC	Association of Nutrition & Foodservice Professionals (FKA-Dietary Managers Assn)
The Ferguson Group, LLC	Climate Communities
The Majority Group, LLC	Numbers USA
The Nickles Group, LLC	American Society of Anesthesiologists
The Nickles Group, LLC	Exxon Mobil Corporation
The Normandy Group, LLC	American Systems Corporation
THE OB-C Group, LLC	Eli Lilly
The Smith-Free Group	Ingram Barge Company
The University of Tennessee	The University of Tennessee
Twenty-First Century Group, Inc.	Verizon
U.S. Apple Association	U.S. Apple Association
Union Square Strategic LLP	American Academy of Otolaryngology-Head and Neck Surgery
University of Notre Dame	University of Notre Dame
Van Ness Feldman, LLP	PacifiCorp

Table 3. (Continued)

Registrant name	Client
Van Scoyoc Associates	New York University Langone Medical Center
Van Scoyoc Associates	Morgan State University Foundation
Venable LLP	Association of Food and Dairy Retailers, Wholesalers and Manufacturers
Venn Strategies, LLC	Campaign to End Obesity Action Fund
Water Strategies, LLC	Diamond Plastic Corporation
Westinghouse Electric Company	Westinghouse Electric Company
Williams & Jensen, PLLC.	CME Group
Williams & Jensen, PLLC.	TE Connectivity, Inc.
Williams & Jensen, PLLC.	Takeda Pharmaceuticals America, Inc.
Williams & Jensen, PLLC	AK Steel

Source: Lobbying disclosure database of the Clerk of the House of Representatives for the third and fourth quarters of 2012 and the first and second quarters of 2013.

APPENDIX III. LIST OF SAMPLED LOBBYING CONTRIBUTION REPORTS WITH AND WITHOUT CONTRIBUTIONS LISTED

See table 4 for a list of the lobbyists and lobbying firms from our random sample of lobbying contribution reports with contributions. See table 5 for a list of the lobbyists and lobbying firms from our random sample of lobbying contribution reports without contributions.

Table 4. Lobbyists and Lobbying Firms in Sample of Lobbying Contribution Reports with Contributions Listed, Filed Year-End 2012 and Midyear 2013

Lobbyist or lobbying firm	Reporting period
Aircraft Owners & Pilots Association	Year-end 2012
Airports Council International — North America	Midyear 2013
Alan Elias	Year-end 2012
Amy Andryszak	Year-end 2012

Lobbyist or lobbying firm	Reporting period
Arthur Cameron. Sr	Year-end 2012
Benjamin Palumbo	Year-end 2012
BP America, Inc	Year-end 2012
Brendan Williams	Year-end 2012
Brooks Brunson	Midyear 2013
Camille Donald	Year-end 2012
Capella University	Year-end 2012
Charles Nuckolls	Midyear 2013
Christopher Heinz	Year-end 2012
CompTIA (Computing Technology Industry Association)	Midyear 2013
Conor Yunits	Midyear 2013
Corley Consulting, LLC	Midyear 2013
David Thompson	Midyear 2013
De'ana Dow	Midyear 2013
Discover Financial Services	Midyear 2013
Frank Vitello	Midyear 2013
Frankie Trull	Midyear 2013
Gary Carpentier	Midyear 2013
Glen Overton	Year-end 2012
Gray & Oscar, LLC (Formerly Bob Gray, LLC)	Year-end 2012
Heather Strawn	Year-end 2012
Henry Bonilla	Midyear 2013
Hobbs Straus Dean & Walker, LLP	Midyear 2013
Independent Insurance Agents & Brokers of America	Midyear 2013
J. Steven Judge	Year-end 2012
James Massie	Year-end 2012
James Nichols	Year-end 2012
Jayne Chambers	Midyear 2013
Jennifer Luray	Midyear 2013
John Albertine	Midyear 2013
John Gallagher	Year-end 2012
John Grzebien	Midyear 2013
John Hollay	Year-end 2012
John Sasso	Year-end 2012
Jonathan Niedzielski	Midyear 2013
Josephine Cooper	Year-end 2012
Julie Pawelczyk	Midyear 2013

Table 4. (Continued)

Lobbyist or lobbying firm	Reporting period
Justin Daly	Midyear 2013
Katherine Cullen	Year-end 2012
Kathryn Fulton	Year-end 2012
Keybank	Year-end 2012
Kimberly Dean	Midyear 2013
Lawrence Markley	Midyear 2013
Mark Holman	Year-end 2012
Martin Bayr	Midyear 2013
Mary Kenkel	Year-end 2012
Mary Savary Taylor	Midyear 2013
McKesson Corporation And Its Affiliate U.S. Oncology (Formerly McKesson Corp.)	Midyear 2013
Michael Nilsson	Year-end 2012
Michele Ballantyne	Midyear 2013
Milam Mabry	Midyear 2013
Monica Healy	Year-end 2012
Mr. James Desmond	Midyear 2013
National Cannabis Industry Association	Midyear 2013
National Funeral Directors Assn	Midyear 2013
Peter Begans	Year-end 2012
Quadripoint Strategies LLC	Year-end 2012
Railway Supply Institute, Inc.	Year-end 2012
Robert Neal	Year-end 2012
Robyn Lippert	Midyear 2013
Ryan Thompson	Midyear 2013
Scott Eckart	Year-end 2012
Scott Lively	Year-end 2012
Sean Richardson	Midyear 2013
Society of American Florists	Year-end 2012
Susan Bodine	Year-end 2012
Susan Neely	Year-end 2012
TECO Energy, Inc.	Year-end 2012
Terry Muilenburg	Midyear 2013
Thomas Danjczek	Year-end 2012
Timothy McGivern	Year-end 2012

Lobbyist or lobbying firm	Reporting period
VCA - Vision Council of America; The Vision Council	Year-end 2012
Wayne Smith	Year-end 2012
William Behrens	Midyear 2013
Xerox Corporation	Midyear 2013
Yahoo! Inc	Midyear 2013

Source: Lobbying contributions database of the Clerk of the House of Representatives, year-end 2012 and midyear 2013 reports.

Table 5. Lobbyists and Lobbying Firms in Sample of Lobbying Contribution Reports with No Contributions Listed, Filed Year-End 2012 and Midyear 2013

Lobbyist or lobbying firm	Reporting period
38 North Solutions, LLC	Year-end 2012
Allan Adler	Midyear 2013
Amelia Consulting Group, LLC	Year-end 2012
American Academy of Actuaries	Midyear 2013
American College of Gastroenterology	Year-end 2012
Andrew McNary	Midyear 2013
Anna Roberts	Midyear 2013
Brian Gantman	Year-end 2012
Business Council for Sustainable Energy	Midyear 2013
Caroline Cooper	Midyear 2013
Carrie Johnson	Year-end 2012
Cathy Dewitt	Midyear 2013
Charles O'Brien	Year-end 2012
Chris Townsend	Year-end 2012
Cord Sterling	Year-end 2012
Craig Saperstein	Year-end 2012
Curators of The University of Missouri	Midyear 2013
Daniel Gans	Year-end 2012
Daniel Hartnett	Year-end 2012
David Roberts	Midyear 2013
Diana Felner	Year-end 2012
Edward Wender	Midyear 2013
Eileen Sottile	Midyear 2013
Elizabeth Fiveash	Midyear 2013

Table 5. (Continued)

Lobbyist or lobbying firm	Reporting period
Elizabeth Kucinich	Year-end 2012
Elizabeth Lawson	Midyear 2013
Emily Sass	Year-end 2012
English First, Inc	Year-end 2012
Fresh Produce Association of the Americas	Year-end 2012
Gerald Hughes	Midyear 2013
Haake and Associates	Midyear 2013
Hank Webster	Midyear 2013
Immigration Equality Action Fund	Year-end 2012
James Backlin	Midyear 2013
James P. Keese	Midyear 2013
Jen Kaleta	Year-end 2012
Jennifer Bendall	Midyear 2013
Jennifer Cervantes	Midyear 2013
Jerry Hadenfeldt	Year-end 2012
John Bartimole	Midyear 2013
Julie Halbert Wright	Midyear 2013
Julie Kirchner	Midyear 2013
Kate Petersen	Year-end 2012
Kevin Schmidt	Year-end 2012
Kristina Butts	Year-end 2012
Laurie Bertenthal	Midyear 2013
Leslie Griffin	Midyear 2013
Lisa Lamkins	Year-end 2012
Lorren Walker	Year-end 2012
Louis Sheldon	Year-end 2012
Lufthansa German Airlines	Year-end 2012
Lynn Henselman	Midyear 2013
Mary Rosado	Midyear 2013
Matthew Coffron	Year-end 2012
Meredith Mull	Year-end 2012
Meredith Nethercutt	Midyear 2013
Michael Roman	Midyear 2013
Michael Willis	Year-end 2012

Lobbyist or lobbying firm	Reporting period
Mike Rock	Year-end 2012
Morgan Brown	Midyear 2013
Mr. Charles Monfort	Year-end 2012
Mr. John Troy	Midyear 2013
Mr. Richard Hirn	Year-end 2012
Mr. Russell Wapensky	Year-end 2012
Native American Contractors Association	Year-end 2012
New York State Society Of CPAs	Midyear 2013
Rebecca Benn	Midyear 2013
Rick Freer	Year-end 2012
Ryan Thomas	Midyear 2013
Selig Merber	Midyear 2013
Shannon Kelly	Year-end 2012
Sohini Gupta	Midyear 2013
Stiefel & Jones Consulting, LLC	Year-end 2012
Susan Johnson	Midyear 2013
The Tomhave Group, Inc.	Year-end 2012
The Winter Group	Year-end 2012
Timothy Dietz	Midyear 2013
Todd Davis	Midyear 2013
Trish Jones	Year-end 2012
William Shute	Midyear 2013

Source: Lobbying contributions database of the Clerk of the House of Representatives, year-end 2012 and midyear 2013 reports.

End Notes

[1] Pub. L. No. 110-81, 121 Stat. 735 (Sept. 14, 2007). Pub. L. No. 104-65, 109 Stat. 691 (Dec. 19, 1995) codified at 2 U.S.C. §§ 1601-1614.

[2] 2 U.S.C. § 1614.

[3] We originally selected 104 reports for review. After notification of our review, one lobbyist amended an LD-2 report to no lobbying activity and the case was excluded from the scope of our review. Another lobbying firm appeared to have gone out of business and we treated this case as a nonrespondent for the purposes of our review.

[4] Our sample is only one of a large number of samples that we might have drawn. Because each sample could have provided different estimates, we express our confidence in the precision of our estimate as a 95 percent confidence interval. This interval would contain the actual population value for 95 percent of the samples we could have drawn. Unless otherwise

stated, all percentage estimates have a maximum 95 percent confidence interval of within 11 percentage points or less of the estimate.

[5] Although we contacted each lobbyist or lobbying firm in our sample, we did not always meet with the lobbyists identified as the point of contact or the actual lobbyists. We met with individuals representing lobbyists or lobbying firms. For the purposes of this review, we use the term lobbyists to refer to lobbyists, lobbying firms, and individuals representing the lobbyists that were present during the review.

[6] The LDA defines a covered executive branch official as the President, Vice President, an officer or employee, or any other individual functioning in the capacity of such an officer or employee of the Executive Office of the President; an officer or employee serving in levels I through V of the Executive Schedule; members of the uniformed services whose pay grade is at or above O-7; and any officer or employee serving in a position of a confidential, policy-determining, policy-making or policy-advocating character who is excepted from competitive service as determined by the Office of Personnel Management (commonly called Schedule C employees). The LDA defines a covered legislative branch official as a member of Congress, an elected officer of either house of Congress, or any employee or any other individual functioning in the capacity of an employee of a member, a committee of either house of Congress, the leadership staff of either house of Congress, a joint committee of Congress, or a working group or caucus organized to provide legislative services or other assistance to members. 2 U.S.C. § 1602(3), (4). Lobbying activities include not only direct lobbying contacts but also efforts in support of such contacts, such as preparation and planning activities, research, and other background work that is intended for use in contacts. 2 U.S.C. § 1602(10).

[7] 2 U.S.C. § 1602(9).

[8] Organizations employing in-house lobbyists file only one registration. An organization is exempt from filing if total expenses in connection with lobbying activities are not expected to exceed $12,500. Amounts are adjusted for inflation and published in LDA guidance.

[9] Lobbyists are expected to provide a good faith estimate on the LD-2 report of income and expenses reported rounded to the nearest $10,000. Our estimate of the number of reports with rounding errors includes reports that disclosed the exact amount of income from or expenditures on lobbying activities, but failed to round to the nearest $10,000 as required.

[10] The sample size of LD-2 reports that reported contact with federal agencies is smaller than the 102 LD-2 reports that were included in our sample and used to generate percentage sums for other selected reporting elements. The size is also too small to generate estimated percentages or to make comparisons across the reviews.

[11] We treated one respondent as a nonrespondent because the itemized contributions in the FEC database were not available at the time of our review to determine whether political contributions were omitted on the respondent's LD-203 report.

[12] We did not estimate the percentage of other non-FEC political contributions that were omitted because they tend to constitute a small minority of all listed contributions and cannot be verified against an external data source.

[13] The number of different lobbying firms total 92 and is less than our sample of 102 reports because some lobbying firms had more than one LD-2 report included in our sample. We calculated our responses based on the number of different lobbying firms that we contacted rather than the number of interviews. Prior to our calculations, we removed the duplicate lobbying firms based on the most recent date of their responses. For those cases with the same response date, we kept the cases with the smallest assigned case identification number.

[14] Four of the 92 different lobbying firms did not respond to the question about ease of compliance with reporting requirements. Although the percentage estimates from our sample of LD-2 reports are generalizable to all LD-2 reports, results from the analysis of lobbying firm opinions are not generalizable. Our sample was designed to develop

population estimates of the accuracy of information on LD-2 reports and was not designed to estimate lobbyist opinions.

[15] Some lobbying firms may not have responded to all of the questions about their ease of understanding the terms associated with LD-2 reporting requirements. Therefore, the number of responses may not be consistent with the number of different lobbying firms in figures 11 through 15.

[16] GAO, *Lobbying Disclosure: Observations on Lobbyists' Compliance with New Disclosure Requirements*, GAO-08-1099 (Washington, D.C.: Sept. 30, 2008).

[17] GAO, *2012 Lobbying Disclosure: Observations on Lobbyists' Compliance with Disclosure Requirements,* GAO-13-437 (Washington, D.C.: Apr.1, 2013).

[18] LD-2 activity reports with "no lobbying issue activity" and reports with less than $5,000 in reported income or expenses are filtered out because they do not contain verifiable information on income, expenses, or activity.

[19] We adjusted for three comparisons to account for the three pairwise tests for each item examined.

[20] One midyear 2013 contributions case was not available in the FEC data because FEC had not processed individual contributions. The case was treated as a nonrespondent for the purposes of data analysis, and the weights for mid-year contributions reports was adjusted using an effective sample of 39 rather than 40 cases as originally sampled for 159 reports.

[21] We used a Bonferroni adjustment to adjust for three comparisons to account for the three pairwise tests for each item examined.

In: Lobbying Disclosure
Editor: Keri Matthews

ISBN: 978-1-63321-777-5
© 2014 Nova Science Publishers, Inc.

Chapter 2

LOBBYING REGISTRATION AND DISCLOSURE: BEFORE AND AFTER THE ENACTMENT OF THE HONEST LEADERSHIP AND OPEN GOVERNMENT ACT OF 2007[*]

Jacob R. Straus

SUMMARY

On September 14, 2007, President George W. Bush signed S. 1, the Honest Leadership and Open Government Act of 2007 (P.L. 110-81), into law. The Honest Leadership and Open Government Act (HLOGA) amended the Lobbying Disclosure Act (LDA) of 1995 (P.L. 104-65, as amended) to provide, among other changes to federal law and House and Senate rules, additional and more frequent disclosure of lobbying contacts and activities. This report focuses on changes made to lobbying registration, termination, and disclosure requirements and provides analysis of the volume of registration, termination, and disclosure reports filed with the Clerk of the House of Representatives and the Secretary of the Senate before and after the HLOGA's passage. This report does not analyze the content of these reports.

Under the LDA, as amended by the HLOGA, the Clerk and the Secretary manage the collection of registration, termination, and disclosure reports

---

[*] This is an edited, reformatted and augmented version of a Congressional Research Service publication, No. R40245, dated April 22, 2011.

made by lobbyists and lobbying firms. Prior to the HLOGA, lobbyists and lobbying firms were required to submit semi-annual reports to the Clerk and the Secretary. The HLOGA amendments to the LDA modified reporting requirements to require quarterly filing of disclosure and termination reports. These forms are available for public inspection from the Clerk's and Secretary's websites.

The filing of registration, termination, and disclosure reports under the HLOGA amendments has continued at approximately the same pace as under the LDA. Examining data for filings between 2001 and 2007 under the LDA, and for 2008 through 2010 under the HLOGA amendments, reveals that the number of new registrations has remained mostly consistent under the HLOGA amendments. The termination reports filed by lobbyists and lobbying firms no longer representing a client have also remained constant following the implementation of the HLOGA amendments. Only disclosure reports, now filed quarterly, show a change between 2007 and 2010. Under the HLOGA amendments, the number of disclosure reports filed in the fourth quarter between 2008 and 2010 has decreased from filings between 2001 and 2007.

Since 1946, Congress has approved, on four occasions, legislation to regulate lobbyist contacts with Members of Congress. In each instance, the legislation was designed to require individuals and companies who lobby Members of Congress to register with the House of Representatives and the Senate and disclose receipts and expenditures related to lobbying.

STATUTORY REGISTRATION AND DISCLOSURE PROVISIONS

Initial registration and disclosure provisions, contained in the Legislative Reorganization Act of 1946, required lobbyists to register with Congress and disclose receipts and expenditures. In 1995, the Lobbying Disclosure Act repealed the 1946 act and created a system of detailed reporting and registration thresholds. In 1998, technical amendments to the 1995 law were passed.[1] In 2007, the Honest Leadership and Open Government Act amended disclosure and reporting requirements to require quarterly, instead of semi-annual reporting.

1946 Act

The Federal Regulation of Lobbying Act, for the first time, established requirements for individuals lobbying Congress to register with and report to the House of Representatives and the Senate. Included as part of the Legislative Reorganization Act of 1946,[2] the Lobbying Act did not impose restrictions on lobbying activities. Instead, it merely required individuals who lobby Congress to register with the House and Senate and disclose certain activities.[3] Perhaps most importantly, the Lobbying Act also imposed the requirement that all registration and disclosure statements be made under oath. Fines and possible jail time were established for incorrectly reporting lobbying contacts.[4]

Registration

The Lobbying Act established the first registration thresholds for individuals lobbying Members, committees, and congressional staff. Section 308 of the act required individuals to register if they contacted Congress about legislation. The section also detailed the information required from the lobbyists:

> Any person who shall engage himself for pay or for any consideration for the purpose of attempting to influence the passage or defeat of any legislation by the Congress of the United States shall, before doing anything in furtherance of such object, register with the Clerk of the House of Representative and the Secretary of the Senate and shall give to those offices in writing and under oath, his name and business address, the name and address of the person by whom he is employed, and in whose interest he appears or works, the duration of such employment, how much he is paid and is to receive, by whom he is paid or is to be paid, how much he is to be paid for expenses, and what expenses are to be included.[5]

Disclosure

Following registration with the House and Senate, the lobbyist was responsible for filing quarterly disclosure statements "detailing money received and expended, persons to whom funds were paid and the purposes of the funding, the names of any publications in which he has caused any articles or editorials to be published, and the proposed legislation he sought to influence. In addition, the registrant was bound to report the names and addresses of persons who made contributions to him of $500 or more."[6]

Since the Federal Regulation of Lobbying Act regulated conduct and activities bearing on First Amendment rights, the Supreme Court narrowly interpreted its reach and breadth, and applied the registration provisions only to those whose "principal purpose" was directly lobbying Members of Congress.[7] This narrow interpretation excluded many persons and organizations who spent substantial time and funds on "lobbying," but for whom such lobbying was not necessarily the principal purpose of the organization, person, or entity.

Lobbying Disclosure Act of 1995

The Lobbying Disclosure Act (LDA) of 1995 repealed the Lobbying Act portion of the Legislative Reorganization Act of 1946. LDA also provided specific thresholds and clear definitions of lobbying activities, lobbying contacts, and who is a lobbyist, compared with the 1946 act.[8] In reporting the LDA, the House Judiciary Committee summarized the need for new lobbying provisions:

> The Act is designed to strengthen public confidence in government by replacing the existing patchwork of lobbying disclosure laws with a single, uniform statute which covers the activities of all professional lobbyists. The Act streamlines disclosure requirements to ensure that meaningful information is provided and requires all professional lobbyists to register and file regular, semiannual reports identifying their clients, the issues on which they lobby, and the amount of their compensation. It also creates a more effective and equitable system for administering and enforcing the disclosure requirements.[9]

The LDA not only required that lobbyists attempting to influence Congress register with the Clerk of the House and the Secretary of the Senate, but that they file semi-annual reports on the nature of their lobbying contacts. See the Appendix for a list of definitions applicable to the LDA, as amended by the HLOGA.

Registration

Pursuant to LDA Section 4, lobbyists must register with the Clerk of the House and Secretary of the Senate no more than 45 days after the lobbyist first makes a lobbying contact or is employed to make a lobbying contact if the "total income for matters related to lobbying activities on behalf of a particular client (in the case of a lobbying firm) does not exceed and is not expected to exceed $5,000" or the "total expenses in connection with lobbying activities (in the case of an organization whose employees engage in lobbying activities on its own behalf) do not exceed or are not expected to exceed $20,000."[10]

Section 4 further required that each registration contain the following six items:

1) the registrant's name, address, business telephone number, principal place of business, and a general description of his or her business or activities.

2) the registrant's client's name, address, principal place of business, and a general description of its business or activities.

3) the name, address, and principal place of business of any organization, other than the client, that contributes more than $10,000 toward the registrant's lobbying activities in a semi-annual reporting period, as described in 2 U.S.C. § 1604(a), and has a major role in planning, supervising, or controlling lobbying activities

4) the name, address, principal place of business, amount of any contribution of foreign entities (if any) that hold at least 20% equitable ownership in the client, directly or indirectly plans, supervises, controls, directs, finances, or subsidizes the activities of the client, or is an affiliate of the client and has a direct interest in the outcome of lobbying activities and contributes more than $10,000 to the registrant's lobbying activity.

5) a statement on the general issue areas the registrant expects to engage in lobbying activities on behalf of the client and, if possible, specific issues that have already been addressed or are likely to be addressed.

6) the names of the registrant's employees who have acted or whom will act as a lobbyist on behalf of the client and if that person has been a covered executive or legislative branch official in the past two years (after December 19, 1995).[11]

A registered lobbyist who has multiple clients must file a separate registration form for each client. A registered lobbyist who makes multiple contacts for the same client only needs to register once. A lobbying organization that employs more than one lobbyist must submit a single registration form for each client listing all lobbyists working on behalf of that client.[12]

When a registered lobbyist is no longer employed by a client or lobbying organization or does not anticipate further lobbying contacts for a specific client, the lobbyist can file a registration termination form with the Clerk and the Secretary.[13]

Disclosure

Once a lobbyist or lobbying firm is registered with the Clerk and the Secretary, the LDA required the filing of semi-annual reports within 45 days of the end of a semi-annual reporting period, with a separate report filed for each client of a registered lobbyist.[14] Pursuant to Section 5 of the LDA, the report was required to contain the following information:

- the registrant's name, the client's name, and any changes or updates to the information provided in the initial registration;
- for each general issue area which the registrant lobbied on behalf of the client (1) a list of specific issues, including bill numbers and specific references to executive branch actions (when practicable) which lobbyists employed by the registrant engaged in lobbying activities; (2) a list of the congressional and executive branch contacts; (3) a list of registrant employees who acted as lobbyists on behalf of the client; and (4) a description of interests by foreign entities, if any;
- a good faith estimate by lobbying firms of the total amount of income generated from the client from lobbying activities on behalf of the client; ;
- if a registrant engaged in lobbying activities on its own behalf, an estimate of the total expenses that the registrant and its employees incurred in connection with lobbying activities.[15]

Following the disclosure by registrants, the Clerk and the Secretary are required to provide guidance to lobbyists and the lobbying community on the implementation of reporting requirements. The Clerk and the Secretary are required to

- review, verify and ensure the accuracy, completeness, and timeliness of the registration and disclosure statements;
- make a list of registered lobbyists, lobbying firms, and clients publicly available;

- create a computerized filing system; make all filing available for public inspection;
- retain registration and disclosure statements for a period of at least six years;
- summarize information contained in registrations and reports on a semi-annual basis;
- notify lobbyists or lobbying firms in writing of non-compliance; and
- notify the United States Attorney for the District of Columbia of non-compliance by a lobbyist or a lobbying firm if the registrant has been notified in writing and has failed to provide an appropriate response within 60 days.[16]

Honest Leadership and Open Government Act of 2007

The Honest Leadership and Open Government Act (HLOGA) of 2007 amended the LDA. HLOGA further refined thresholds and definitions of lobbying activities, changed the frequency of reporting for registered lobbyists and lobbying firms, added additional disclosures, created new semi-annual reports on contributions, and added disclosure requirements for coalitions and associations.[17]

Registration

The HLOGA did not specifically amend the LDA's registration requirements. The Clerk and the Secretary, however, were for the first time required to make registration and disclosure forms available, in a searchable and sortable format, on the Internet, for public inspection.[18]

Disclosure

The HLOGA amendments to the LDA made several changes to disclosure requirements. Under the LDA, lobbyists and lobbying firms were required to submit forms disclosing activities on a semi-annual basis (as discussed above under "Disclosure" of the Lobbying Disclosure Act). The HLOGA amendments created quarterly, instead of semi-annual, reporting periods and shortened the deadline for submission from 45 days to 20 days after the filing period ends. The amended text reads as follows:

No later than 20 days after the end of the quarterly period beginning on the first day of January, April, July, and October of each year in which a registrant is registered under section 4 [2 USCS § 1603], or on the first business day after such 20th day if the 20th day is not a business day, each registrant shall file a report with the Secretary of the Senate and the Clerk of the House of Representatives on its lobbying activities during such quarterly period. A separate report shall be filed for each client of the registrant.[19]

The threshold for filing quarterly reports was also lowered, requiring lobbyists and lobbying firms to file reports of work when total income from lobbying exceeded $2,500 (formerly $5,000) and where total expenses used in connection with lobbying exceeded $10,000 (formerly $20,000) for any given quarterly reporting period.[20]

In addition to the amendments concerning quarterly reports of lobbying activity, Congress amended the LDA to create a new semi-annual reporting requirement for campaign and presidential library contributions by lobbyists and lobbying firms. These reports are due within 30 days of the end of a semi-annual reporting period.[21]

These semi-annual contribution reports are to contain the following information:

- the name of the person (including employer) or organization;
- the names of all political committees established or controlled by the person or organization;
- the name of each federal candidate or officeholder, leadership PAC, or political party committee, to whom aggregate contributions equal to or exceeding $200 were made by the person or organization, or a political committee established or controlled by the person or organization, and the date and amount of each such contribution made;
- the date, recipient, and amount of funds contributed or disbursed during the semiannual period by the person or organization or a political committee established or controlled by the person or organization;[22]
- the name of each Presidential library foundation, and each Presidential inaugural committee, to whom contributions equal to or exceeding $200 were made by the person or organization, or a political committee established or controlled by the person or organization, within the semiannual period, and the date and amount of each such contribution within the semiannual period;[23]

- a certification by the person or organization filing the report that the person or organization has read and is familiar with those provisions of the Standing Rules of the Senate and the Rules of the House of Representatives relating to the provision of gifts and travel; and has not provided, requested, or directed a gift, including travel, to a Member of Congress or an officer or employee of either House of Congress with knowledge that receipt of the gift would violate rule XXXV of the Standing Rules of the Senate or rule XXV of the Rules of the House of Representatives.[24]

REGISTRATION, TERMINATION, AND DISCLOSURE ANALYSIS

The Clerk of the House and the Secretary of the Senate have collected registration and disclosure data since the passage of the LDA in 1995. Using these data, it is possible to analyze registration and disclosure trends under the LDA and changes made by the HLOGA amendments. The following sections examine registration and disclosure data filed under the LDA between 2001 and 2007, and between 2008 and 2010 following the passage of the HLOGA amendments.

All data are presented from the Clerk's lobbying disclosure website. The LDA requires the Clerk and the Secretary to use a single, computer based system for lobbyists and lobbying firms to file registration and disclosure forms.[25] The Clerk and the Secretary, however, use different search engines and display the data differently.[26] Data from the Clerk are utilized because they provide distinctions between paper and electronically filed reports. The distinction between report submission methods shows compliance with the LDA requirements for electronic submissions and the rate of online filing prior to the passage of the HLOGA amendments.

Tracking these numbers is important because it enables a comparison of lobbying registration and disclosure before and after the HLOGA amendments. Analyzing the registration, termination, and disclosure data before and after the HLOGA amendments allows a systematic examination of the amendments impact on the lobbying community. If the goal of the HLOGA was to more closely regulate lobbyists by requiring additional disclosure, the data constitute an opportunity to examine the law's impact.

Registration

Since 2001, almost 50,000 individuals and firms have registered, as lobbyists under the LDA. During that time, the number of individuals and firms that registered has varied annually. While no specific pattern has developed, it appears that with the exception of 2001, more new registrations registered in the first session of a Congress (e.g., 2003, 2005, 2007, and 2009) than in the second session (e.g., 2004, 2006, 2008, and 2010).

In addition to registering with the Clerk and the Secretary, lobbyists and lobbying firms are also required to amend registration forms when changes are made to their status, clients, contact information, or other identifying information. Figure 1 shows the total number of new registrants per year and number of registration amendments filed per year before and after the enactment of the HLOGA amendments.

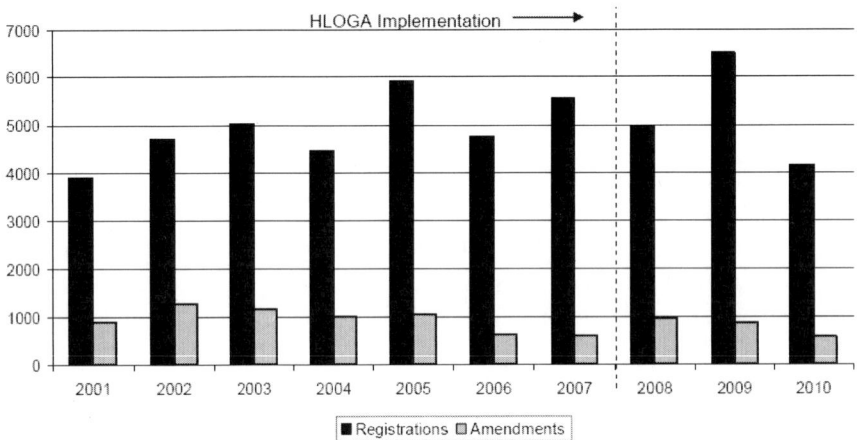

Source: Data compiled from U.S. Congress, Clerk of the House of Representatives, Lobbying Disclosure Search, http://disclosures.house.gov/ld/ldsearch.aspx.

Figure 1. Lobbyist and Lobbying Firm Registrations, 2001-2010; Total Number of New Registrations and Registration Amendments.

Immediately prior to the HLOGA amendments, the number of registrants amending their forms declined from a peak of 1,279 in 2002 to a low of 599 in 2007. Under the HLOGA, the number of registration amendment forms increased to 981 in 2008. The number of registration amendments decreased slightly (884) in 2009 and returned to 2007 levels in 2010 (587). The reason for the variation in registration amendments does not appear to follow a particular pattern. Instead, it appears that the filing of registration amendments might be governed by lobbyists' need to make changes based on hiring and firing of staff and recruitment of new clients.

The HLOGA amendments to LDA, for the first time, required electronic filing to the Clerk and the Secretary. The Clerk and the Secretary, however, have allowed lobbyists and lobbying firms to file registration forms electronically since 2002, when 0.38% of all registrations were filed electronically. Since 2009, 100% of all registrations were filed electronically. Figure 2 shows the number of registrations filed electronically, on paper, and in total since 2001.

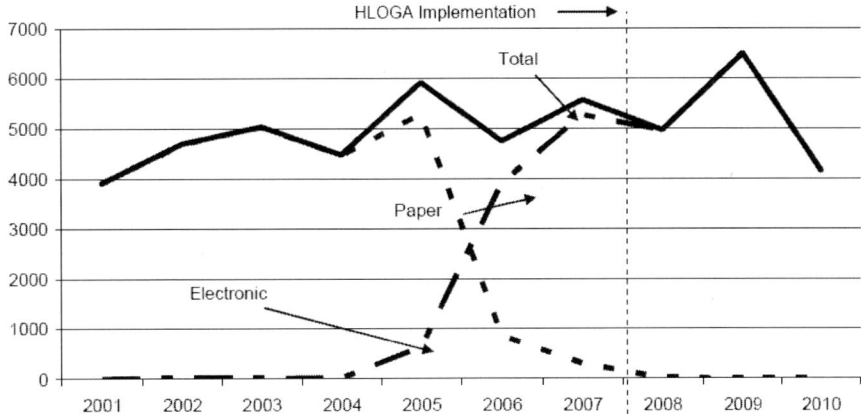

Source: Data compiled from U.S. Congress, Clerk of the House of Representatives, Lobbying Disclosure Search, http://disclosures.house.gov/ld/ldsearch.aspx.

Figure 2. Registration Filing by Method, 2001-2010.

Electronic submission of registration forms began to increase in 2005, when 10.7% of new registrants filed electronically. While filing electronically was not required prior to the HLGOA amendments, the number of registrations filed electronically increased significantly in 2006 and 2007. In 2006, the number of electronic registrations eclipsed paper registrations for the first time (82.2% of all registrations were filed electronically). By 2007, the number of registrations had again increased with 94.7% of lobbyists and lobbying firms filing electronically. Following the enactment of HLOGA, 99.9% of registrations were filed electronically in 2008, and 100% were filed electronically in 2009 and 2010.

Termination

A lobbyist or lobbying firm that has gone out of business or is no longer representing a client is required to file a registration termination report with the Clerk and the Secretary. Under LDA, termination reports were filed on a semi-annual basis. Figure 3 shows the number of registration termination reports filed during the mid-year reporting period (June 30), during the year-end reporting period (December 31), and the total number of terminations for the year (from 2001 to 2010).

Since 2001, the number of terminations has increased every year except for 2007 and 2010 when there was a slight decline in total terminations from the previous year. Overall, between 2001 and 2007 there appeared to be only a slight increase in terminations at year's end, compared with the mid-year reporting period. The difference may have existed because lobbyists and lobbying firms adjust clients and staff more at the end of congressional sessions. The difference could also be tied to the number of registrations. As more lobbyists and lobbying firms register with the Clerk and the Secretary, more termination forms may be submitted.

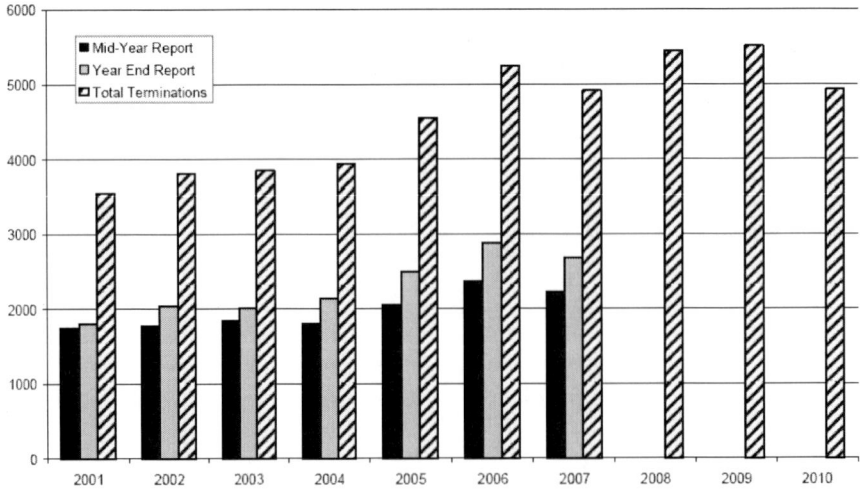

Source: Data compiled from U.S. Congress, Clerk of the House of Representatives, Lobbying Disclosure Search, http://disclosures.house.gov/ld/ldsearch.aspx.

Figure 3. Lobbyist and Lobbying Firms Termination Reports, 2001-2010.

Pursuant to the HLGOA amendments, termination reports were changed from semi-annual reports to quarterly reports. **Figure 4** shows the quarterly termination reports filed between 2008 and 2010.

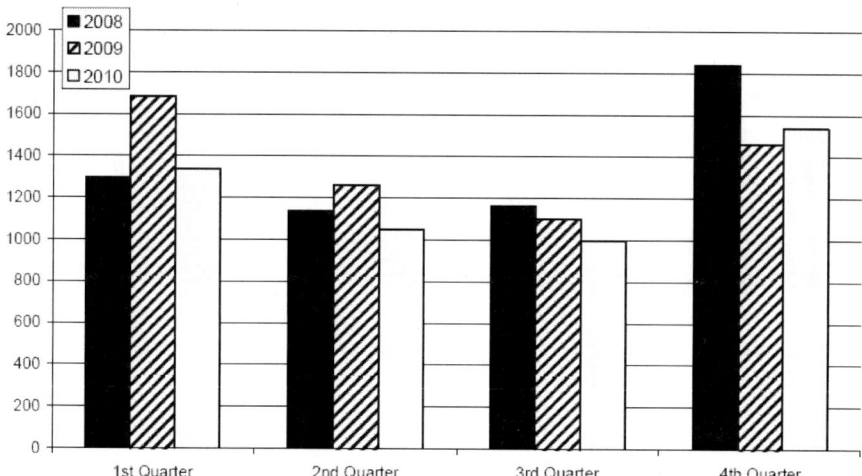

Source: Data compiled from U.S. Congress, Clerk of the House of Representatives, Lobbying Disclosure Search, http://disclosures.house.gov/ld/ldsearch.aspx.

Figure 4. Lobbyist and Lobbying Firm Termination Reports, 2008-2010; Filed Under the LDA, as Amended by the HLOGA.

The trend toward a greater number of year-end terminations evident under the LDA continues under the HLOGA amendments. The number of terminations in the fourth quarter (an average of 1,651) is higher than for any of the previous three quarters. The first quarter (an average of 1,491) has the second-highest number of terminations. The number of registration terminations filed with the Clerk and the Secretary in the second quarter (an average of 1,200) and the third quarter (an average of 1,134) of between 2008 and 2010 were relatively consistent.

The difference in terminations in the fourth quarter of 2008 and the first quarter of 2009 may exist because, as previously stated, lobbyists and lobbying firms change clients and staff more frequently at the beginning and end of a Congress rather than during the sessions. Alternately, the increase in registration terminations could reflect the change in administration from a Republican to a Democratic White House. Since the LDA covers both legislative and executive branch officials, lobbyists and lobbying firms could adjust staffing levels to reflect changes in administration priorities and policy.

Disclosure

Under the LDA, lobbyists and lobbying firms were required to file semi-annual reports disclosing certain information about clients, issues lobbied, government officials lobbied, an estimate of income generated from each client, and an estimate of total expenses incurred in connection with lobbying activities.[27] Since 2001, the number of disclosure reports filed has increased from a low of 12,853 disclosures in 2001 to a high of 19,178 in 2007. Although this could indicate an overall increase in lobbying activity, without additional data for the period under the HLOGA amendments, a definitive conclusion cannot be made. In most years, the number of year-end reports was slightly greater than the number of mid-year reports. This may reflect an increase in lobbying activity towards the end of a congressional session when additional efforts might be needed to ensure the passage of important legislation. Figure 5 shows the number of mid-year and year-end reports filed by lobbyists and lobbying firms between 2001 and 2007.

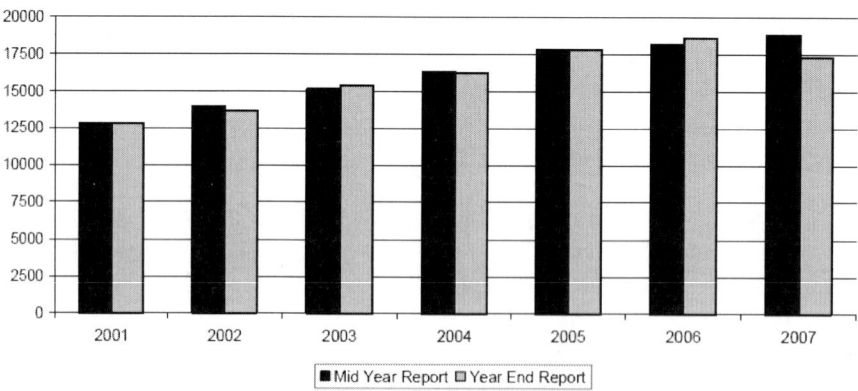

Source: Data compiled from U.S. Congress, Clerk of the House of Representatives, Lobbying Disclosure Search, http://disclosures.house.gov/ld/ldsearch.aspx.

Figure 5. Mid-Year and Year-End Disclosure Reports, 2001-2007.

Pursuant to the HLOGA amendments, disclosure reports were changed beginning in 2008 from semi-annual reports to quarterly reports. For this reason, Figure 5 does not contain a similar accounting of disclosure reports for 2008 and 2009. To reflect the reporting change, Figure 6 shows the volume of quarterly disclosure reports filed between 2008 and 2010.

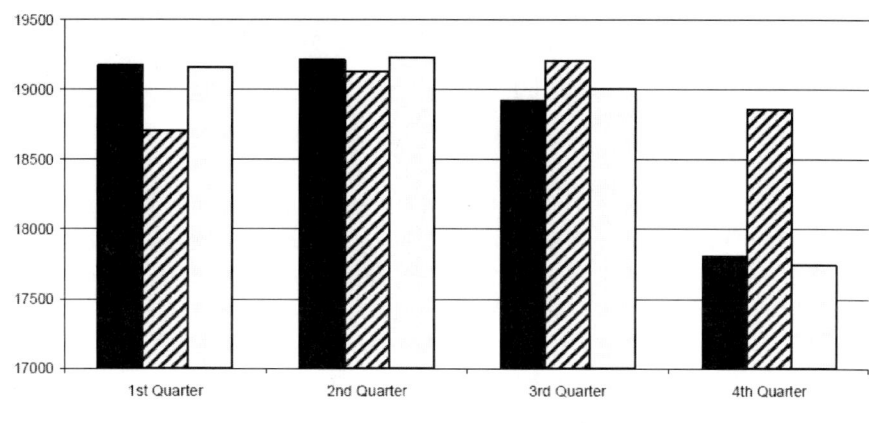

Source: Data compiled from U.S. Congress, Clerk of the House of Representatives, Lobbying Disclosure Search, http://disclosures.house.gov/ld/ldsearch.aspx

Figure 6. Disclosure Reports, 2008-2010.

In 2008, the number of disclosure reports filed from one quarter to the next decreased from 18,615 during the first quarter to 16,372 in the fourth quarter. In 2009, the number of disclosure reports filed each quarter was slightly less than for 2008 for the first and second quarter and higher for the third and fourth quarters. Contrasted with an average of 18,270 mid-year and 17,937 year-end disclosure statements filed between 2005 and 2007 under the LDA, the decline in filings in the fourth quarters of 2008 and 2010 appears to be incongruous with the previous data. Data for 2008 and 2010 represent the end of a Congress. It is possible that the number of disclosures filed in the fourth quarter of 2008 and 2010 was a result of decreased lobbying activity. As a Congress completes its legislative agenda, the need to lobby Members declines.

CONCLUSION

The impact of the HLOGA on the registration, termination, and disclosure of lobbyists and lobbying firms is mixed. In the three years since the HLOGA amendments were implemented, it appears the registration trends that existed between 2001 and 2007 continue under the HLOGA amendments. For termination, overall trends also continue, with an increase in terminations in the fourth quarter of 2008 and the first quarter of 2009. Since the first quarter of 2009, the number of terminations has stabilized and roughly mirrors the 2008 numbers. Overall, while terminations in 2008 and 2009 are greater than anytime between 2001 and 2007, the pattern of increased terminations in congressional election years, followed by a slight decline the following year, continues.

The most significant change in reporting occurred for the filing of disclosure statements. Instead of filing two reports per year on lobbying activity, lobbyists, and lobbying firms are required to report four times per year. Collecting the data in quarters instead of semi-annual periods appears to have uncovered a reporting trend that was otherwise obscured under the semi-annual system. For 2008 and 2010, the data shows an overall decline in disclosure reports for the fourth quarter.

The data suggest that lobbyists and lobbying firms make more contacts and engage in a greater percentage of their lobbying activity in the first three quarters of the year than at the end of a congressional session. The year-end report data from 2001 to 2007, which included both third and fourth quarter activity, may have been motivated by third quarter activity that was previously included in year end reports. It is possible, however, that the 2008 and 2010 upticks in reporting reflect the transition to a new presidential administration coupled with the beginning of a new Congress.

For 2009, the volume of disclosure reports does not easily fit with the volume of reports for 2008 and 2009. Fourth quarter lobbying activity, as shown by the number of disclosure reports continues at a high level. This may reflect the continuation of Congress's legislative agenda from the first to the second session. In the 111th Congress, many issues that were initiated during the first session continued through an after-Thanksgiving session and into the second session. Lobbying for those provisions continued throughout that period.

APPENDIX. LOBBYING REGISTRATION AND DISCLOSURE DEFINITIONS

Pursuant to the Lobbying Disclosure Act, as amended by the Honest Leadership and Open Government Act of 2007 (Chapter 26, Title 2, *United States Code*), the following definitions are applicable to the registration and disclosure process.

Table A-1. Definitions of Terms in the Lobbying Disclosure Act and Honest Leadership and Open Government Act

Term	Definition
Agency	Has the meaning given in 5 U.S.C. § 551 (1).[a]
Client	Any person or entity that employs or retains another person for financial or other compensation to conduct lobbying activities on behalf of that person or entity. A person or entity whose employees act as lobbyists on its own behalf is both a client and an employer of such employees. In the case of a coalition or association that employs or retains other persons to conduct lobbying activities, the client is the coalition or association and not its individual members.
Covered executive branch official	The President; Vice President; any officer or employee, or any other individual functioning in the capacity of such an officer or employee, in the Executive Office of the President; any officer or employee serving in an Executive Schedule position, as designated by statute or Executive order; any member of the uniformed services whose pay grade is at or above O-7 under 37 U.S.C. § 201; and any officer or employee serving in a position of a confidential, policy-determining, policy-making, or policy-advocating character described in section 5 U.S.C. § 7511(b)(2)(B).
Covered legislative branch official	A Member of Congress; an elected officer of either House of Congress; any employee of, or any other individual functioning in the capacity of an employee of—(1) a Member of Congress, (2) a committee of either House of Congress, (3) the leadership staff of the House of Representatives or the Senate, (4) a joint committee of Congress and, (5) a working group or caucus organized to provide legislative services or other assistance to Members of Congress; and any other legislative branch employee serving in a position described under section 109(13) of the Ethics in Government Act of 1978 (5 U.S.C. App.).
Employee	Any individual who is an officer, employee, partner, director, or proprietor of a person or entity, but does not include— independent contractors or volunteers who receive no financial or other compensation for their services.
Foreign entity	A foreign principal as defined by 22 U.S.C. § 611 (b).
Lobbying activities	Lobbying contacts and efforts in support of such contacts, including preparation and planning activities, research and other background work that is intended, at the time it is performed, for use in contacts, and coordination with the lobbying activities of others.

Table A-1. (Continued)

Term	Definition
Lobbying contact	Any oral or written communication (including an electronic communication) to a covered executive branch official or a covered legislative branch official that is made on behalf of a client with regard to—the formulation, modification, or adoption of Federal legislation (including legislative proposals); the formulation, modification, or adoption of a Federal rule, regulation, Executive order, or any other program, policy, or position of the United States Government; the administration or execution of a Federal
	program or policy (including the negotiation, award, or administration of a Federal contract, grant, loan, permit, or license); or the nomination or confirmation of a person for a position subject to confirmation by the Senate. [b]
Lobbying firm	A person or entity that has one or more employees who are lobbyists on behalf of a client other than that person or entity. Also includes a self-employed individual who is a lobbyist.
Lobbyist	Any individual who is employed or retained by a client for financial or other compensation for services that include more than one lobbying contact, other than an individual whose lobbying activities constitute less than 20 percent of the time engaged in the services provided by such individual to that client over a three-month period.
Media organization	A person or entity engaged in disseminating information to the general public through a newspaper, magazine, other publication, radio, television, cable television, or other medium of mass communication.
Member of Congress	A Senator or a Representative in, or Delegate or Resident Commissioner to, the Congress.
Organization	A person or entity other than an individual.
Person or entity	Any individual, corporation, company, foundation, association, labor organization, firm, partnership, society, joint stock company, group of organizations, or State or local government.
Public official	Any elected official, appointed official, or employee of a Federal, State, or local unit of government in the United States; [c] a Government corporation (31 U.S.C. § 9101); an organization of State or local elected or appointed officials (other than officials described in note c); an Indian tribe (25 U.S.C. 450b(e)); a national or State political party or any organizational unit thereof; or a national, regional, or local unit of any foreign government, or a group of governments acting together as an international organization.

Term	Definition
State	Each of the several States, the District of Columbia, and any commonwealth, territory, or possession of the United States.

Source: 2 U.S.C. § 1602.

Notes:

a. Pursuant to 5 U.S.C. § 551 "'agency' means each authority of the Government of the United States, whether or not it is within or subject to review by another agency, but does not include—(A) the Congress; (B) the courts of the United States; (C) the government of the territories or possessions of the United States; (D) the government of the District of Columbia; or except as to the requirements of section 552 of this title— (E) agencies composed of representatives of the parties or of representatives of organizations of the parties to the disputes determined by them; (F) courts martial and military commissions; (G) military authority exercised in the field in time of war or in occupied territory; or (H) functions conferred by sections 1738, 1739,1743, and 1744 of title 12; chapter 2 of title 41; subchapter II of chapter 471 of title 49; or sections 1884, 1891-1902, and former section 1641(b)(2), of title 50, appendix.

b. For a list of exemptions see 2 U.S.C. § 1602 (8)(b).

c. This includes all elected and appointed officials and employees other than those of a college or university; a government-sponsored enterprise (2 USCS § 622 (8); a public utility that provides gas, electricity, water, or communications; a guaranty agency (20 U.S.C. §1085 (j)), including any affiliate of such an agency; or an agency of any State functioning as a student loan secondary market pursuant to 20 U.S.C. § 1085(d)(1)(F).

End Notes

[1] The 1998 technical amendments did not amend the Lobbying and Disclosure Act of 1995's sections on registration and disclosure.

[2] P.L. 79-601, 60 Stat. 839-843, August 2, 1946. Title III of the Legislative Reorganization Act of 1946 is the "Federal Regulation of Lobbying Act."

[3] *Political Activity, Lobbying Laws and Gift Rules Guide*, ed. Trevor Potter and Kirk L. Jowers, 2nd ed., vol. 1 (Little Falls, NJ: Glasser Legal Works, 1999), p. 1-7.

[4] P.L. 79-601, 60 Stat. 843, August 2, 1946. Section 309 requires that statements be made under oath. Section 310 provided for a fine up to $5,000 and jail time of up to twelve months, or both, for individuals convicted of not providing information required under the act. Additionally, a person convicted of a misdemeanor was banned from lobbying for three years following his or her conviction.

[5] P.L. 79-601, 60 Stat. 841, August 2, 1946. Section 308(a) lists the registration requirements for lobbyists.

[6] *Political Activity, Lobbying Laws and Gift Rules Guide*, ed. Trevor Potter and Kirk L. Jowers, 2nd ed., vol. 1 (Little Falls, NJ: Glasser Legal Works, 1999), p. 1-8. See also, P.L. 79-601,

60 Stat. 841-842, August 2, 1946. Section 308(a) contains the full listing of disclosure requirements.

[7] *United States v. Harriss*, 347 U.S. 612 (1954).

[8] P.L. 104-65, 109 Stat. 691, December 19, 1995, as amended by P.L. 105-166, 112 Stat. 38, April 8, 1998.

[9] U.S. Congress, House Committee on the Judiciary, *Lobbying Disclosure Act of 1995*, report to accompany H.R. 2564, 104th Cong., 1st sess., H.Rept. 104-339 (Washington: GPO, 1995), p. 2.

[10] 2 U.S.C. § 1603 (a).

[11] 2 U.S.C. § 1603 (b).

[12] 2 U.S.C. § 1603 (c).

[13] 2 U.S.C. § 1603 (d).

[14] P.L. 104-65, 109 Stat. 697, December 19, 1995.

[15] Ibid.

[16] P.L. 104-65, 109 Stat. 698-699, December 19, 1995. For more information on the role of the Clerk and the Secretary see, CRS Report RL34377, *Honest Leadership and Open Government Act of 2007: The Role of the Clerk of the House and the Secretary of the Senate*, by Jacob R. Straus and U.S. Government Accountability Office, *2010 Lobbying Disclosure: Observations on Lobbyists' Compliance with New Disclosure Requirements*, GAO-11-542, April 2011.

[17] P.L. 110-81, 121 Stat. 735, September 14, 2007.

[18] P.L. 110-81, 121 Stat. 748, September 14, 2007. For more information on the role of the Clerk of the House and the Secretary of the Senate and statutory requirements for the public availability of registration and disclosure documents see CRS Report RL34377, *Honest Leadership and Open Government Act of 2007: The Role of the Clerk of the House and the Secretary of the Senate*, by Jacob R. Straus.

[19] 2 U.S.C. § 1604 (a).

[20] 2 U.S.C. § 1603 (a).

[21] The semi-annual reporting period runs from January 1 to June 30 and July 1 to December 31 each year. The report is due to the Clerk of the House and Secretary of the Senate 30 days later (January 30 and July 30) or on the first business day after the 30th if the 30th falls on a non-business day. (2 U.S.C. § 1604 (d)(1).

[22] Items reported under this provision include funds donated to pay the cost of an event to honor or recognize a covered legislative branch official or covered executive branch official; to an entity that is named for a covered legislative branch official, or to a person or entity in recognition of such official; to an entity established, financed, maintained, or controlled by a covered legislative branch official or covered executive branch official, or to an entity designated by such official; or to pay the costs of a meeting, retreat, conference, or other similar event held by, or in the name of, one or more covered legislative branch officials or covered executive branch officials. For additional information, see CRS Report RL34324, *Campaign Finance: Legislative Developments and Policy Issues in the 110th Congress*, by R. Sam Garrett; and CRS Report R40091, *Campaign Finance: Potential Legislative and Policy Issues for the 111th Congress*, by R. Sam Garrett.

[23] For more information on contributions to Presidential library foundations, see CRS Report R40209, *Fundraising for Presidential Libraries: Recent Legislative and Policy Issues for Congress*, by R. Sam Garrett.

[24] 2 U.S.C. § 1604 (d).

[25] 2 U.S.C. § 1604 (e). "A report required to be filed under this section shall be filed in electronic form, in addition to any other form that the Secretary of the Senate or the Clerk of the House of Representatives may require or allow. The Secretary of the Senate and the Clerk of the House of Representatives shall use the same electronic software for receipt and recording of filings under this Act."

[26] To search for individual filing by lobbyists or lobbying firms, the Clerk of the House maintains a search engine at http://disclosures.house.gov/ld/ldsearch.aspx. The Secretary of the Senate's searchable LDA reports can be found at http://senate.gov/legislative /Public_Disclosure/LDA_reports.htm.

[27] P.L. 104-65, 109 Stat. 697, December 19, 1995.

In: Lobbying Disclosure ISBN: 978-1-63321-777-5
Editor: Keri Matthews © 2014 Nova Science Publishers, Inc.

Chapter 3

LOBBYING REGISTRATION AND DISCLOSURE: THE ROLE OF THE CLERK OF THE HOUSE AND THE SECRETARY OF THE SENATE[*]

Jacob R. Straus

SUMMARY

On September 14, 2007, President George W. Bush signed S. 1, the Honest Leadership and Open Government Act of 2007 (P.L. 110-81), into law. The Honest Leadership and Open Government Act (HLOGA) amended the Lobbying Disclosure Act (LDA) of 1995 (P.L. 104-65, as amended) to provide, among other changes to federal law and House and Senate rules, additional and more frequent disclosures of lobbying contacts and activities. This report explains the role of the Clerk of the House of Representatives and the Secretary of the Senate in implementing lobbying registration and disclosure requirements and summarizes the guidance documents they have jointly issued.

Under the HLOGA and predecessor lobbying laws, the Clerk of the House and the Secretary of the Senate manage the registration, filing, and the collection of documents submitted by the lobbyists and lobbying

[*] This is an edited, reformatted and augmented version of a Congressional Research Service publication RL34377, prepared for Members and Committees of Congress, dated June 20, 2013.

firms. Prior to the HLOGA, lobbyists were required to file paper documents with both the Clerk and the Secretary. These forms are now filed electronically and jointly with the Clerk and the Secretary. In addition, the Clerk and the Secretary are responsible for making documents publicly available and reporting incorrect or false filings to the U.S. Attorney for the District of Columbia.

Beginning in December 2007, the Clerk of the House and the Secretary of the Senate issued joint guidance documents for HLOGA implementation. The guidance document identified eight substantive changes to the 1995 Lobbying Disclosure Act, and discussed how the Clerk and Secretary interpret and implement the HLOGA's provisions. In addition, the guidance document provided direction on successful completion of quarterly registration and disclosure documents, the new semi-annual reporting requirement, and interpretation of the Clerk and Secretary's role in referring non-compliance to the U.S. attorney.

Since its initial issuance, the Clerk of the House and Secretary of the Senate, pursuant to 2 U.S.C. §1605, have conducted periodic reviews of existing guidance and have issued multiple updates. Most recently, the document was updated on February 15, 2013, to update registration threshold requirements as required by the LDA "to reflect changes in the Consumer Price Index ... during the preceding 4-year period." These data are used to determine registration exemptions covered in Section 4 of the guidance.

BACKGROUND

During the past six decades, Congress on four occasions has approved legislation designed to regulate lobbyist contact with Members of Congress. The initial provisions, which were contained in the Legislative Reorganization Act of 1946, required that lobbyists register with the House of Representatives and the Senate and disclose certain receipts and expenditures.[1] In 1995, Congress passed, and the President signed into law, the Lobbying Disclosure Act, which repealed the 1946 act and created a detailed system of reporting thresholds. In 1998, technical amendments to the 1995 law were passed. Finally, in 2007, Congress amended the 1995 act to further enhance disclosure and reporting requirements for lobbyists and lobbying firms.

The Lobbying Disclosure Act (LDA) of 1995 provided specific thresholds and definitions of lobbyists, lobbying activities, and lobbying contacts, compared to the 1946 act.[2] In reporting the LDA, the House Judiciary Committee summarized the need for new lobbying provisions:

The Act is designed to strengthen public confidence in government by replacing the existing patchwork of lobbying disclosure laws with a single, uniform statute which covers the activities of all professional lobbyists. The Act streamlines disclosure requirements to ensure that meaningful information is provided and requires all professional lobbyists to register and file regular, semiannual reports identifying their clients, the issues on which they lobby, and the amount of their compensation. It also creates a more effective and equitable system for administering and enforcing the disclosure requirements.[3]

The technical amendments made to the LDA in 1998 clarified the definition of covered executive branch officials, more clearly defined what constitutes a lobbying contact, and provided that organizations, whose lobbying activities are limited by their Internal Revenue Code (IRC) nonprofit status,[4] could use their tax estimates to report lobbying activities. In reporting the 1998 technical amendments, the Senate Committee on Governmental Affairs explained the need for change:

> Once the LDA was implemented by the Clerk of the House and the Secretary of the Senate, several minor problems with the language of the statute materialized. The offices of the Clerk and the Secretary have sought to interpret the LDA with respect to these problems in accordance with the original intent of the law, but it is necessary and appropriate to conform the language of the law to intent, and that is the motivation behind the introduction of S. 758.[5]

The most recent amendments to the LDA, the Honest Leadership and Open Government Act of 2007 (HLOGA), mandated additional and more frequent disclosures.[6]

Pursuant to the 1946 act, the 1995 LDA, as amended by the 1998 act, and the HLOGA, the Clerk of the House and the Secretary of the Senate have had joint responsibility for implementing systems to register lobbyists. Under the 1946 act, individuals, groups, and organizations involved in lobbying activities were required to keep detailed financial records and to file financial statements with the Clerk. Lobbyists also were required to register before engaging in lobbying activities and file quarterly reports with the Clerk and the Secretary. The Clerk was then required to maintain these records for two years.[7]

The 1995 act, as amended, modified the responsibilities of the Clerk and the Secretary in registering lobbyists and collecting disclosure documents. In addition to collecting registration and disclosure documents from lobbyists the Clerk and the Secretary are required to

1. provide guidance and assistance on the registration and reporting requirements of this Act and develop common standards, rules, and procedures for compliance with this Act;
2. review, and, where necessary, verify and inquire to ensure the accuracy, completeness, and timeliness of registration and reports;
3. develop filing, coding, and cross-indexing systems to carry out the purpose of this Act, including—
    a. a publicly available list of all registered lobbyists, lobbying firms, and their clients; and
    b. computerized systems designed to minimize the burden of filing and maximize public access to materials filed under this Act;
4. make available for public inspection and copying at reasonable times the registrations and reports filed under this Act;
5. retain registrations for a period of at least 6 years after they are terminated and reports for a period of at least 6 years after they are filed;
6. compile and summarize, with respect to each semi-annual period, the information contained in registrations and reports filed with respect to such period in a clear and complete manner;
7. notify any lobbyist or lobbying firm in writing that may be in noncompliance with this Act; and
8. notify the United States Attorney for the District of Columbia that a lobbyist or lobbying firm may be in noncompliance with this Act, if the registrant has been notified in writing and has failed to provide an appropriate response within 60 days after notice was given under paragraph (7).[8]

The 2007 HLOGA further refined the role of the Clerk and the Secretary in collecting and reporting information on lobbyists under the LDA. The Clerk and the Secretary are required to electronically register lobbyists and collect quarterly and semi-annual reports; make registrations and filings available on the Internet; and review each registration and filing for accuracy, notify lobbyists of a misfiling, and refer appropriate cases to the U.S. attorney's office for the District of Columbia.[9] Pursuant to these responsibilities, the Clerk and the Secretary have chosen to use a single electronic filing system, whereby lobbyists and lobbying firms register once and documents are automatically transmitted to both the Clerk and the Secretary.[10]

ROLE OF CLERK OF THE HOUSE AND SECRETARY OF THE SENATE

The Clerk of the House and the Secretary of the Senate are responsible for implementing lobbyist registration and disclosure provisions of the LDA, as amended by the HLOGA, for the House of Representatives and the Senate, respectively. As neither the Clerk nor the Secretary have rule-writing or regulatory authority under the LDA or its amendments, but are directed in law to provide guidance and assistance, they issue a joint guidance document to inform lobbyists and the public of how they intend to carry out their registration and disclosure duties. Under the HLOGA amendments, the first quarterly reports were required by April 21, 2008, and new registrations continued to be required no later than 45 days after the first lobbying contact is made or an individual is employed to make a lobbying contact.[11] All lobbyists and lobbying firms filing registration and disclosure statements are required to file with the Clerk and the Secretary through a joint portal maintained at http://lobbyingdisclosure.house.gov, or http://www.senate.gov/lobby.

Electronic Filing

Prior to the HLOGA amendments, the LDA did not require electronic submission of registration and reporting documents. Under the 1995 act, as amended, the Secretary of the Senate provided lobbyists and lobbying firms the means to file electronically or to use paper forms. The Clerk of the House did not provide a method of electronic filing.[12] The HLOGA amended Section 5 of the LDA to make electronic filing mandatory, except when an individual is amending documents filed under the previous system, or in instances where electronic filing is not possible for an individual with a condition covered by the Americans with Disabilities Act.[13]

Pursuant to Section 5, as amended, the Clerk and Secretary created a single electronic registration system, using the previous Senate system's user ID and password protocols,[14] and have developed a website that provides the necessary software applications to make all filings.[15] The website has features for use on Microsoft Windows and Macintosh operating systems. Detailed instructions on the registration and disclosure process and a summary of filing requirements are available on both the House and Senate lobbying disclosure websites.[16] The Clerk and the Secretary are responsible for maintaining the electronic filing system website and for providing updated information in response to lobbyist questions and congressional amendments.

Civil and Criminal Penalties

2 U.S.C. §1605(a)(7) and (8), as amended by HLOGA Section 210, requires the Clerk and the Secretary to notify lobbyists of noncompliance and to notify the U.S. attorney for the District of Columbia of a lobbyist's or lobbying firm's noncompliance, after giving 60 days' notice.[17]

The Clerk of the House's Legislative Resource Center and the Secretary of the Senate's Office of Public Records have been given responsibility for reviewing each filing to ensure accuracy and for issuing notices to those who have not complied. If a notice is issued to a registrant, the registrant has 60 days to respond, after which the Clerk and the Secretary may forward instances of noncompliance to the U.S. attorney's office for the District of Columbia.[18]

Publicly Available Registration and Disclosure Data

2 U.S.C. §1605(a) (3), (4), and (5), as amended by HLOGA Section 209, instructs the Clerk and the Secretary to make registration and disclosure information publicly available for at least six years.

> (3) develop filing, coding, and cross-indexing systems to carry out the purpose of this Act, including—(A) a publicly available list of all registered lobbyists, lobbying firms, and their clients; and (B) computerized systems designed to minimize the burden of filing and maximize public access to materials filed under this Act; (4) make available for public inspection and copying at reasonable times the registrations and reports filed under this Act; (5) retain registrations for a period of at least 6 years after they are terminated and reports for a period of at least 6 years after they are filed.[19]

To satisfy the requirements of Section 6 of the LDA, as amended by the HLOGA, the Clerk and the Secretary established websites for the public to inspect registration and disclosure documents on the Internet.[20] The Lobbying Disclosure Act Guidance (in Section 10) states that the Clerk and the Secretary will use the Internet to deliver the content of the reports.[21]

LOBBYING DISCLOSURE GUIDANCE DOCUMENT

The HLOGA lobbying provisions were effective as of January 1, 2008. As required by Section 6 of the LDA,[22] the Clerk and the Secretary on December 10, 2007, issued a joint guidance document.[23] The guidance document is updated, as needed, to reflect changes in guidance from the Clerk and the Secretary. *Table 1* lists when the guidance document has been updated since it was first issued. The guidance document is posted on both the Clerk's and Secretary's lobbying websites.[24]

Table 1. Guidance Document Updates

Date	Updates
May 29, 2008	Provided additional guidance on semi-annual reporting requirements under the HLOGA Section 203 (related to political and other contributions and activities).a
July 16, 2008	Clarified the types of disclosures required under the HLOGA Section 203.[a]
January 6, 2009	Revised requirements for special registration circumstances, quarterly reporting of lobbying activities, and semiannual reporting of political and other contributions.
February 3, 2009	Raised registration thresholds to $3,000 in total income from a client for individuals or $11,500 in total income from a client for an organization, in any given quarterly period.[b]
June 9, 2009	Revised requirements for registration, removed provision requiring lobbyists to disclose activities regardless of quarterly activity, clarified the definition of active registrants and lobbyists required to file LD-203 forms, and clarified appropriate registrant termination policies and requirements to file LD-203 forms following termination.[c]
December 23, 2009	Revised language on registration for foreign entities to require reporting of foreign affiliates, added codes to report tariff related lobbying, refined definitions on reporting estimated lobbying expenses, added "in-kind" contributions to required semi-annual campaign contribution disclosures, and incorporated previous notices on lobbyist termination.[d]
June 10, 2010	Modified requirements that lobbyists list previous covered executive or legislative branch positions held within 20 years of first acting as a lobbyist for each client, and updated language to "stress" that lobbyists and registrants must file a semi-annual report for each semi-annual period they remain active.
December 15, 2011[e]	Reorganized definitions to alphabetize section on contribution reports, incorporated previous verbal guidance on "listing of the client name when work is performed on behalf of a third party," and clarified the requirement of reporting on LD-2 forms "when a client is a state and local government."

Table 1. (Continued)

Date	Updates
February 15, 2013	Updated registration thresholds "to reflect changes in the Consumer Price Index ... during the preceding 4-year period," and raised the registration exemption for organizations employing in-house lobbyists "... if total expenses for lobbying activities does not exceed and is not expected to exceed $12,500 during a quarterly period." The income threshold for lobbying firms remains unchanged at $3,000.[f]

Source: U.S. Congress, Clerk of the House of Representatives and Secretary of the Senate, Lobbying Disclosure Guidance, 113th Cong., 1st sess., February 15, 2013, at http://www.senate.gov/legislative/resources/pdf/ S1guidance.pdf, and http://lobbyingdisclosure.house.gov/amended_lda_guide.html.

Notes:

[a] For more information, see 2 U.S.C. §1604.

[b] Changes to the registration thresholds, which are indexed to inflation and adjusted quarterly, were effective as of January 1, 2009. For more information about the registration thresholds see, http://www.senate.gov/ legislative/Public_Disclosure/ new_thresholds.htm

[c] Further clarification of the guidance document on the termination of lobbyists was issued on June 16, 2009. The guidance was amended to permit termination if a registered lobbyist "does not reasonably expect to make further lobbying contacts."

[d] U.S. Congress, Clerk of the House of Representatives and Secretary of the Senate, *Clarification of Recent Notice and Revised Guidance Regarding Conditions for Lobbyist Termination*, 111th Cong., 1st sess., June 16, 2009, http://lobbying disclosure.house.gov/0615_Notice_Lobbyist_Clarification.pdf.

[e] Pursuant to 2 U.S.C. §1605, the Clerk of the House and the Secretary of the Senate reviewed the lobbying disclosure guidance on June 12, 2012. No changes were made at that time.

[f]. Changes were effective January 1, 2013.

The guidance document is divided into 12 sections. The LDA does not provide the Clerk and the Secretary with the authority to write regulations or issue opinions on the law. The guidance document is only meant as an interpretation of the law, and is not enforceable as law.[25] A brief summary of the 12 sections of the guidance document follows:

- *Section 1—Introduction.* Provides background information on the LDA and the responsibilities of the Clerk of the House and the Secretary of the Senate in providing guidance to the lobbying community.

- *Section 2—What's New?* Identifies changes made to the guidance since the last update.
- *Section 3—Definitions.* Repeats terms defined in the LDA. These terms include affiliated organizations, reports of certain contributions, client, covered executive and legislative branch officials, lobbying activities, lobbying contact, lobbying firm, lobbying registration, lobbying report, lobbying, and public official, among others. Section 3 also adds the definition of "actively participates" from Section 207 of HLOGA.
- *Section 4—Lobbying Registration.* Explains the lobbying registration process, including who must register and when registrations are necessary.[26] This section also clarifies the preparations for filing registrations, exceptions to lobbying contacts, the 20% activity threshold,[27] the difference between a lobbying contact and lobbying activity, alternative reporting methods, and the relationship between the 20% activity and monetary thresholds. The monetary thresholds are updated periodically to reflect changes in the Consumer Price Index (CPI). For each area, the guidance document provides examples to illustrate the operation of the section for the lobbying community. In addition, this section provides guidance on when and how to report foreign entity contributions to lobbying activity.[28]
- *Section 5—Special Registration Circumstances.* Outlines conditions that could affect the registration of lobbyists or lobbying firms under the LDA. These special circumstances include lobbying firms retained by contingent fees; registration by entities with subsidiaries or state and local affiliates; the effect of mergers and acquisitions; registration for associations, coalitions, churches, and associations of churches; registration for firms hired by churches or church associations; and the registration of professional associations of elected officials.
- *Section 6—Quarterly Reporting of Lobbying Activities.* Explains when and why quarterly reports are needed, and provides instructions on how to complete lobbying disclosure forms LD-1[29] and LD-2.[30] In addition, Section 6 defines how to report firm income, indicates when it is appropriate to report income or expenses, provides examples on the type of material that should be included in a quarterly report, indicates that organizations that pay dues to other organizations must report the portion of their dues used for lobbying activities,[31] removes previous guidance that registrants who previously filed LD-2 forms could be

required to file again in the future, even if they did not meet reporting thresholds in a given quarter,[32] reminds filers that "all expenses of lobbing activities incurred during a quarterly period are reportable,"[33] provides for a specific reporting code for lobbying on tariff bills,[34] reminds filers that all new lobbyists must list "previous covered executive or legislative branch positions held within twenty (20) years of first acting as a lobbyist for a client,"[35] and reiterates that the "requirement to disclose a foreign interest ... is not contingent upon the entity making a contribution ... to the registrant during that particular reporting period."[36]

- *Section 7—Semiannual Reporting of Certain Contributions.* Discusses when and why semiannual reports are needed, the basics of form LD-203;[37] who is required to file LD-203;[38] the required contents of the semiannual report[39] (regardless of whether they make a reportable contribution),[40] including examples; that third-party preparers should "retain appropriate documentation to demonstrate that they have authorization to make such filing on behalf of all filers (including lobbyist-employees of registrants) using their services,[41] and that in-kind contributions should be reported.[42]

- *Section 8—Termination.* Explains the procedure for the termination, for recording purposes, of a lobbyist from a lobbying firm or of a registrant's relationship with a client, including when removing a registrant is appropriate.[43]

- *Section 9—Relationship of LDA to Other Statutes.* Briefly explains the relationship between LDA and three other statutes. These statutes are the Foreign Agents Registration Act (FARA),44 the Internal Revenue Code (IRC),45 and the False Statements Accountability Act of 1996.[46]

- *Section 10—Public Availability.* States that the LDA requires the Clerk of the House and the Secretary of the Senate "to make all registrations and reports available for public inspection over the Internet as soon as technically practicable after the report is filed."[47]

- *Section 11—Review and Compliance.* States that the Clerk of the House's Legislative Resource Center and the Secretary of the Senate's Office of Public Records "must review, verify, and request corrections in writing to ensure the accuracy, completeness, and timeliness of registrations and reports filed under the Act."[48]

- *Section 12*—Penalties. Restates the civil and criminal penalties for filing incorrect or false information.[49]

SEMI-ANNUAL REPORT OF CERTAIN CONTRIBUTIONS

Pursuant to 2 U.S.C. §1604(e), the Clerk and the Secretary created a contributions reporting system and website that allows lobbying organizations and individual lobbyists to register electronically using their existing ID and password.[50] The website contains a help feature to assist lobbying organizations and lobbyists navigate the new form.[51]

End Notes

[1] P.L. 79-601, 60 Stat. 839-842, August 2, 1946. Title III of the Legislative Reorganization Act of 1946 was the "Federal Regulation of Lobbying Act." It was the first law that required persons who lobbied Congress to register with the House of Representatives and the Senate.

[2] P.L. 104-65, 109 Stat. 691, December 19, 1995, as amended by P.L. 105-166, 112 Stat. 38, April 8, 1998; 2 U.S.C. §1601, et seq.

[3] U.S. Congress, House Committee on the Judiciary, Lobbying Disclosure Act of 1995, report to accompany H.R. 2564, 104th Cong., 1st sess., H.Rept. 104-339 (Washington: GPO, 1995), p. 2.

[4] 26 U.S.C. §501(c)(3). 501(c)(3) organizations are "Corporations, and any community chest, fund, or foundation, organized and operated exclusively for religious, charitable, scientific, testing for public safety, literary, or educational purposes, or to foster national or international amateur sports competition ..., or for the prevention of cruelty to children or animals, no part of the net earnings of which inures to the benefit of any private shareholder or individual, no substantial part of the activities of which is carrying on propaganda, or otherwise attempting, to influence legislation (except as otherwise provided in subsection (h)), and which does not participate in, or intervene in (including the publishing or distributing of statements), any political campaign on behalf of (or in opposition to) any candidate for public office." Lobbying disclosure laws also limit these organizations in their lobbying. See 2 U.S.C. §1603(a)(3), 2 U.S.C. §1604(b)(4), and 2 U.S.C. §1610(a). For further information on tax-exempt organizations, see CRS Report 96- 264, Frequently Asked Questions About Tax-Exempt Organizations, by Erika K. Lunder; and CRS Report RL33377, Tax-Exempt Organizations: Political Activity Restrictions and Disclosure Requirements, by Erika K. Lunder.

[5] U.S. Congress, Senate Committee on Governmental Affairs, Lobbying Disclosure Technical Amendments Act of 1997, report to accompany S. 758, 105th Cong., 1st sess., S.Rept. 105-147 (Washington: GPO, 1997), p. 2.

[6] P.L. 110-81, 121 Stat. 739, September 14, 2007.

[7] P.L. 79-601, 60 Stat. 839-842, August 2, 1946.

[8] 2 U.S.C. §1605(a)(8).

[9] 2 U.S.C. §1606.

[10] U.S. Congress, Clerk of the House of Representatives, "Lobbying Disclosure FAQ," http://lobbyingdisclosure.house.gov/FAQ.html; and U.S. Congress, Secretary of the Senate, "Lobbying Disclosure FAQ," http://www.senate.gov/legislative/Public_Disclosure/ FAQs.htm.

[11] 2 U.S.C. §1603.

[12] U.S. Congress, Secretary of the Senate, Historic Lobbying Disclosure Act Guidance (not valid for post January 1, 2008 filings), http://www.senate.gov/legislative/common/ briefing/lobby_disc_briefing.htm.

[13] P.L. 110-81, §205, 121 Stat. 746, September 14, 2007.

[14] The Secretary of the Senate maintains a website http://soprweb.senate.gov/ for lobbyists and lobbying firms to obtain user IDs and passwords online. When requesting a password, lobbyist information is simultaneously transmitted to both the Clerk of the House and Secretary of the Senate for immediate use.

[15] U.S. Congress, Clerk of the House of Representatives, "Lobbying Disclosure Forms and Software," http://lobbyingdisclosure.house.gov/software.html.

[16] U.S. Congress, Clerk of the House of Representatives, "Lobbying Disclosure, Office of the Clerk," http://lobbyingdisclosure.house.gov, U.S. Congress, Secretary of the Senate, "Public Disclosure," http://www.senate.gov/lobby.

[17] 2 U.S.C. §1605(a)(7). The LDA states that the Clerk of the House and the Secretary of the Senate must "(7) notify any lobbyist or lobbying firm in writing that may be in noncompliance with this Act; and (8) notify the United States Attorney for the District of Columbia that a lobbyist or lobbying firm may be in noncompliance with this Act, if the registrant has been notified in writing and has failed to provide an appropriate response within 60 days after notice was given under paragraph (7)."

[18] For more information on the role of the U.S. Attorney's Office for the District of Columbia prosecution of HLOGA related violations see, U.S. Government Accountability Office, Lobbying Disclosure: Observations on Lobbyists' Compliance with New Disclosure Requirements, GAO-08-1099, September 30, 2008, pp. 15-18.

[19] 2 U.S.C. §1605(a)(3)-(5).

[20] The Secretary of the Senate's searchable LDA reports are accessible through http://senate.gov/legislative/ Public_Disclosure/LDA_reports.htm. The Clerk of the House's searchable reports are accessible through http://ldsearch.house.gov.

[21] U.S. Congress, Clerk of the House of Representatives and Secretary of the Senate, Lobbying Disclosure Guidance, 110th Cong., 2nd sess., July 16, 2008. [Hereinafter, LDA Guidance July 2008.]

[22] Pursuant to Section 6 of the LDA, "The Secretary of the Senate and the Clerk of the House of Representatives shall (1) provide guidance and assistance on the registration and reporting requirements of this Act and develop common standards, rules and procedures for compliance with this Act; [and] (2) review, and, where necessary, verify and inquire to ensure the accuracy, completeness and timeliness of registrations and reports[.]" (2 U.S.C. §1605).

[23] U.S. Congress, Clerk of the House of Representatives, "Statement regarding the issuance of revised guidance concerning the Lobbying Disclosure Act," press release, December 10, 2007, http://clerk.house.gov/about/press/ 12102007_01.html.

[24] The Lobbying Disclosure Act Guidance document can be found on the Clerk of the House's website at http://lobbyingdisclosure.house.gov/ldaguidance.pdf, and on the Secretary of the

Senate's website at http://www.senate.gov/legislative/resources/pdf/S1guidance.pdf. The two documents are identical.

[25] LDA Guidance July 2008, p. 2.

[26] The LDA Guidance Document issued on June 9, 2009 provided a test for triggering registration requirements. "The registration requirement of potential registrant is triggered either (1) on the date their employee/lobbyist is employed or retained to make more than one lobbying contact on behalf of a client (and meets the 20% of time threshold), or (2) on the date their employee/lobbyist in fact makes a second lobbying contact (and meets the 20% of time threshold), whichever is earlier." See, U.S. Congress, Clerk of the House of Representatives and Secretary of the Senate, Lobbying Disclosure Guidance, 111th Cong., 1st sess., June 9, 2009. [Hereinafter, LDA Guidance June 2009].

[27] 2 U.S.C. §1602 (7) defines "lobbying activities." A "lobbyist" is someone who makes more than one "lobbying contact" and spends at least 20% of his or her time engaged in "lobbying activities" for his or her client or employer. Additionally, as a requirement to register, the lobbyist must have received at least $2,500 in a quarterly reporting period from a client, or, if an in-house lobbyist, the organization had to spend at least $10,000 on "lobbying activities."

[28] U.S. Congress, Clerk of the House of Representatives and Secretary of the Senate, Lobbying Disclosure Guidance, 111th Cong., 1st sess., December 23, 2009. [Hereinafter, LDA Guidance December 2009].

[29] Form LD-1 is the lobbying registration form used for initial registration by a lobbyist or lobbying firm. Updated copies of Form LD-1 can be found on the House of Representatives lobbying website http://lobbyingdisclosure.house.gov/help/default.htm?url= Word Documents/downloadforms.htm. Pursuant to the HLOGA amendments, form LD-1 is filed only online through the House of Representatives lobbying website Registrants no longer file separate copies of LD-1 with the Secretary of the Senate. A detailed guide to filing reports is available through the House website: http://lobbyingdisclosure.house.gov/ld_user_guide.pdf.

[30] Form LD-2 is the lobbying report form used by lobbyists and lobbying firms to fulfill their quarterly reporting requirements. Updated copies of form LD-2 can be found on the House of Representatives lobbying website at http://lobbyingdisclosure.house.gov/help/ default. htm?url=WordDocuments/downloadforms.htm. Pursuant to the HLOGA amendments, form LD-2 is filed only online through the House of Representatives lobbying website. Registrants no longer file separate copies of LD-2 with the Secretary of the Senate. A detailed guide to filing reports is available through the House website: http://lobbying disclosure.house.gov/ld_user_guide.pdf.

[31] U.S. Congress, Clerk of the House of Representatives and Secretary of the Senate, Lobbying Disclosure Act Guidance, 111th Cong., 1st sess., January 16, 2008. [Hereinafter, Lobbying Guidance January 2009].

[32] LDA Guidance June 2009, p. 17. Previous guidance documents stated: "Once an individual has met the definition of a lobbyist and has been disclosed or identified as such, he or she does not need to meet that standard every reporting period in order to trigger the required disclosure of his or her lobbying activities." This guidance has been removed in the June 9, 2009, release.

[33] LDA Guidance December 2009, p. 14.

[34] LDA Guidance December 2009, p. 17.

[35] U.S. Congress, Clerk of the House of Representatives and Secretary of the Senate, Lobbying Disclosure Guidance, 111th Cong., 2nd sess., June 10, 2010, http://www.senate.

gov/legislative/resources/pdf/S1guidance.pdf, p. 18, and http://lobbyingdisclosure. house.gov/amended_lda_guide.html. [Hereinafter, LDA Guidance June 2010.]

[36] LDA Guidance December 2009, p. 18.

[37] Form LD-203 is the lobbying report form used by lobbyists and lobbying firms to fulfill their semi-annual reporting requirement of political and other contributions and activities. On June 30, 2008, the Clerk and the Secretary released the LD-203 Contribution Reporting System. To access the system, registrants use the same ID and password required for other lobbying disclosure forms. The LD-203 form can only be viewed through the LD-203 Contribution Reporting System on the lobbying disclosure website https://lda. congress.gov/LC.

[38] All "active" registrants and individuals who are listed as active lobbyists by their employer on forms LD-1 and LD-2 are required to file form LD-203 by July 30 and January 30 (or the next business day should either occur on a weekend or holiday). A registrant or individual is "active" if the registrant has not submitted a termination form pursuant to section 8 of the guidance document. LDA Guidance June 2009, p. 18, provides additional clarification by reminding sole proprietors and small lobbying firms of their requirement to file two reports: one by the registrant and one by the listed lobbyist, even if those individuals are the same.

[39] Lobbying Guidance January 2009, p. 21. The guidance document also contains a reminder that each registrant is responsible for maintaining the integrity and use of their password. If a password is used without authorization, the registrant should immediately contact the Clerk or the Secretary.

[40] LDA Guidance June 2010, p. 19.

[41] Lobbying Guidance January 2009, p. 24.

[42] LDA Guidance December 2009, p. 20.

[43] LDA Guidance June 2009, p. 23. Further clarification on termination of a registered lobbyist was issued on June 16, 2009. See http://lobbyingdisclosure.house.gov/ amended_ lda_guide.html; and U.S. Congress, Clerk of the House of Representatives and Secretary of the Senate, Clarification of Recent Notice and Revised Guidance Regarding Conditions for Lobbyist Termination, 111th Cong., 1st sess., June 16, 2009, http://lobbyingdisclosure. house.gov/ 0615_Notice_Lobbyist_Clarification.pdf.

[44] 22 U.S.C. §611 et seq. The Department of Justice maintains the Foreign Agents Registration Unit. More information is located at http://www.usdoj.gov/criminal/fara/. Both the LDA Section 9 and the HLOGA Section 212 amended the Foreign Agents Registration Act.

[45] 26 U.S.C. et seq., as amended. The Internal Revenue Code can also be found on the Internal Revenue Service website http://www.irs.gov/taxpros/article/0,,id=98137,00.html.

[46] 18 U.S.C. §1001.

[47] LDA Guidance July 2008, p. 26.

[48] Ibid.

[49] 2 U.S.C. §1606, as amended. The HLOGA amended the LDA to establish the following penalties: "(a) Civil Penalty—Whoever knowingly fails to—(1) remedy a defective filing within 60 days after notice of such a defect by the Secretary of the Senate or the Clerk of the House of Representatives; or (2) comply with any other provision of this chapter; shall, upon proof of such knowing violation by a preponderance of the evidence, be subject to a civil fine of not more than $200,000, depending on the extent and gravity of the violation. (b) Criminal Penalty—Whoever knowingly and corruptly fails to comply with any provision of this Act shall be imprisoned for not more than 5 years or fined under title 18, United States Code, or both."

[50] The LD-203 form can be completed by logging into the Contributions Reporting System website: https://lda.congress.gov/LC/. The LD-203 form cannot be viewed without logging into the system.

[51] U.S. Congress, Clerk of the House and Secretary of the Senate, LCUserManualV1, https://lda.congress.gov/LC/help/default.htm?turl=WordDocuments%2Faccessingthesystem .htm. The user manual is also available as a PDF file at http://www.senate.gov /legislative/resources/pdf/LCUser ManualV1.pdf.

In: Lobbying Disclosure
Editor: Keri Matthews

ISBN: 978-1-63321-777-5
© 2014 Nova Science Publishers, Inc.

Chapter 4

LOBBYING DISCLOSURE ACT GUIDANCE[*]

Clerk of the House of Representatives and the Secretary of the Senate

Effective January 1, 2008
(Reviewed June 17, 2014/Last Revised February 15, 2013[†])
http://www.senate.gov/LDA

SECTION 1 – INTRODUCTION

Section 6 of the Lobbying Disclosure Act (LDA), 2 U.S.C. § 1605, provides that: The Secretary of the Senate and the Clerk of the House of Representatives shall (1) provide guidance and assistance on the registration and reporting requirements of this Act and develop common standards, rules, and procedures for compliance with this Act; [and] (2) review, and, where necessary, verify and inquire to ensure the accuracy, completeness, and timeliness of registrations and reports.

---

[*] This is an edited, reformatted and augmented version of document reviewed June 17, 2014 and last revised February 15, 2013.

[†] The Secretary and the Clerk review the Guidance semiannually. Any questions, comments, and suggestions should be directed to the Senate Office of Public Records and the House Legislative Resource Center in sufficient time for evaluation before the next semiannual reporting cycle.

The LDA does not provide the Secretary or the Clerk with the authority to write substantive regulations or issue definitive opinions on the interpretation of the law. The Secretary and Clerk have, from time to time, jointly issued written guidance on the registration and reporting requirements. This document is both a compilation of previously issued guidance documents and our interpretation of the changes that were made to the LDA as a result of the Honest Leadership and Open Government Act of 2007 (HLOGA).

This compilation supersedes all previous guidance documents. This combined guidance document does not have the force of law, nor does it have any binding effect on the United States Attorney for the District of Columbia or any other part of the Executive Branch. To the extent that the guidance relates to the accuracy, completeness, and timeliness of registrations and reports, it will serve to inform the public as to how the Secretary and Clerk intend to carry out their responsibilities under the LDA.

SECTION 2 – WHAT'S NEW

This revision has been written based upon comments received in the last six months and issues that have arisen as a result of the Secretary's and Clerk's statutory and administrative responsibilities. It also includes non-substantive grammatical changes throughout.

Updated Registration Threshold

As required by the LDA, the lobbying disclosure thresholds referenced throughout the Guidance have been updated to reflect changes in the Consumer Price Index (as determined by the Secretary of Labor) during the preceding 4-year period. After January 1, 2013, an organization employing in-house lobbyists is exempt from registration if its total expenses for lobbying activities does not exceed and is not expected to exceed $12,500 during a quarterly period. The $3,000 income threshold for lobbying firms remains unchanged. See Guidance Section 4 on "Who Must Register and When" for additional information.

SECTION 3 – DEFINITIONS

Actively Participates: An organization "actively participates" in the planning, supervision, or control of lobbying activities of a client or registrant when that organization (or an employee of the organization in his or her capacity as an employee) engages directly in planning, supervising, or controlling at least some of the lobbying activities of the client or registrant. Examples of activities constituting active participation would include participating in decisions about selecting or retaining lobbyists, formulating priorities among legislative issues, designing lobbying strategies, performing a leadership role in forming an ad hoc coalition, and other similarly substantive planning or managerial roles, such as serving on a committee with responsibility over lobbying decisions.

Organizations that, though members of or affiliated with a client, have only a passive role in the lobbying activities of the client (or of the registrant on behalf of the client), are not considered active participants in the planning, supervision, or control of such lobbying activities. Examples of activities constituting only a passive role would include merely donating or paying dues to the client or registrant, receiving information or reports on legislative matters, occasionally responding to requests for technical expertise or other information in support of the lobbying activities, attending a general meeting of the association or coalition client, or expressing a position with regard to legislative goals in a manner open to, and on a par with, that of all members of a coalition or association—such as through an annual meeting, a questionnaire, or similar vehicle. Mere occasional participation, such as offering an ad hoc informal comment regarding lobbying strategy to the client or registrant, in the absence of any formal or regular supervision or direction of lobbying activities, does not constitute active participation if neither the organization nor its employee has the authority to direct the client or the registrant on lobbying matters and the participation does not otherwise exceed a de minimize role.

Affiliated Organization: An affiliated organization is any entity other than the client that contributes in excess of $5,000 toward the registrant's lobbying activities in a quarterly period, and actively participates in the planning, supervision, or control of such lobbying activities. The 2007 amendments to the LDA did not change the way in which the LDA identified affiliates (i.e., those that in whole or in major part plan, supervise, or control such lobbying activities) are to be disclosed on Forms LD-1 and LD-2.

Client: Any person or entity that employs or retains another person for financial or other compensation to conduct lobbying activities on behalf of that person or entity. An organization employing its own lobbyists is considered its own client for reporting purposes.

Contribution Reports: Form LD-203 is required to be filed semiannually by July 30th and January 30th (or next business day should either of those days fall on a weekend or holiday) covering the first and second calendar halves of the year. Registrants and active lobbyists (who are not terminated for all clients) must file separate reports that detail FECA contributions, honorary contributions, presidential library contributions, and payments for event costs. (See discussion in Guidance Section 7 below.)

Covered Executive Branch Official: The application of coverage of Section 3(3)(F) of the LDA (who is a covered Executive Branch official) was intended for Schedule C employees only. Senior Executive Service employees are not covered Executive Branch officials as defined in the Act unless they fall within one of the categories below. Covered Executive Branch officials are:

- The President
- The Vice President
- Officers and employees of the Executive Office of the President
- Any official serving in an Executive Level I through V position
- Any member of the uniformed services serving at grade O-7 or above
- Schedule C employees.

Covered Legislative Branch Official: Covered Legislative Branch officials are:

- A Member of Congress
- An elected Officer of either the House or the Senate
- An employee, or any other individual functioning in the capacity of an employee, who works for a Member, committee, leadership staff of either the Senate or House, a joint committee of Congress, a working group or caucus organized to provide services to Members, and any other Legislative Branch employee serving in a position described under Section 109(13) of the Ethics in Government Act of 1978.

In whole or major part: The term "in major part" means in substantial part. It is not necessary that an organization or foreign entity exercise majority control or supervision in order to fall within Sections 4(b)(3)(B) and 4(b)(4)(B). In general, 20 percent control or supervision should be considered "substantial" for purposes of these sections.

Lobbying Activities: Lobbying contacts and any efforts in support of such contacts, including preparation or planning activities, research, and other background work that is intended, at the time of its preparation, for use in contacts, and coordination with the lobbying activities of others.

Lobbying Contact: Any oral, written, or electronic communication to a covered official that is made on behalf of a client with regard to the enumerated subjects at Sections 3(8)(A) of the Act (2 U.S.C. § 1602(8)(A)). Note the exceptions to the definition at Section 3(8)(B) of the Act (2 U.S.C. § 1602(8)(B)). See Discussion at Guidance Section 4 below.

Lobbying Firm: A lobbying firm is a person or entity consisting of one or more individuals who meet the definition of a lobbyist with respect to a client other than that person or entity. The definition includes a self-employed lobbyist.

Lobbying Registration: An initial registration on Form LD-1 filed pursuant to Section 4 of the Act (2 U.S.C. § 1603).

Lobbying Report: A quarterly report on Form LD-2 filed pursuant to Section 5 of the Act (2 U.S.C. § 1604).

Lobbyist: Any individual (1) who is either employed or retained by a client for financial or other compensation (2) whose services include more than one lobbying contact; and (3) whose lobbying activities constitute 20 percent or more of his or her services' time on behalf of that client during any three-month period.

Person or Entity: Any individual, corporation, company, foundation, association, labor organization, firm, partnership, society, joint stock company, group of organizations, or state or local government.

Public Official: A public official includes an elected or appointed official, or an employee of a Federal, state, or local unit of government in the United States. There are five exceptions to this definition, including a college or university, a government-sponsored enterprise, a public utility, guaranty agency, or an agency of any state functioning as a student loan secondary market. The 1998 amendments to the LDA expanded the definition of a public official in Section 3(15)(F) to add a group of governments acting together as an international organization. Its purpose was to ensure those international organizations, such as the World Bank, would be treated in the same manner as the governments that comprise them.

Registrant: A lobbying firm or an organization employing in-house lobbyists that files a registration pursuant to Section 4 of the Act.

SECTION 4 – LOBBYING REGISTRATION

Who Must Register and When

Lobbying firms are required to file a separate registration for each client. A lobbying firm is exempt from registration for a particular client if its total income from that client for lobbying activities does not exceed and is not expected to exceed $3,000 during a quarterly period.

Note: A lobbyist is not the registrant unless he/she is self-employed. In that case, the self-employed lobbyist is treated as a lobbying firm.

Organizations employing in-house lobbyists file a single registration. An organization is exempt from registration if its total expenses for lobbying activities do not exceed and are not expected to exceed $12,500 during a quarterly period.

The registration requirement of potential registrants is triggered either (1) on the date their employee/lobbyist is employed or retained to make more than one lobbying contact on behalf of a client (and meets the 20% of time threshold), or (2) on the date their employee/lobbyist (who meets the 20% of time threshold) in fact makes a second lobbying contact, whichever is earlier. In either case, registration is required within 45 days.

> Example 1: Lobbying firm "A" is retained on May 1, 2008 by Client "B" to make lobbying contacts and conduct lobbying activities. "A" files an LD-1 on behalf of "B" with an effective date of registration of May 1, 2008.
>
> Example 2: Corporation "C" does not employ an individual who meets the definition of "lobbyist." Employee "X" is told by her supervisor to contact the Congressman representing the district in which Corporation "C" is headquartered. "X" makes a lobbying contact on June 1, 2008. "X" does not anticipate making any further lobbying contacts, but spends 25% of her time on this legislative issue. No registration is required at this point. In August 2008, "X" is instructed to follow up with the Congressman again. "C" registers and discloses August 5, 2008 as the effective date of registration (the date that "X" contacted the Congressman for the second time and thereby met the definition of a lobbyist).

Preparing to File a Registration – Threshold Requirements

In order to determine the applicability of the LDA, one must first look at the definition of "lobbyist" under Section 3(10) of the Act. Under this definition, an individual is a "lobbyist" with respect to a particular client if he or she makes more than one lobbying contact and his or her "lobbying activities" (as defined in Section 3(7)) constitute at least 20 percent of the individual's time in services for that client over any three-month period. Note that a registration would not be required for pro bono clients since the monetary thresholds of Section 4(a)(3)(A)(i) in the case of a lobbying firm, or of Section 4(a)(3)(A)(ii) in the case of an organization employing in-house lobbyists, would not be met. Keep in mind that the obligation to report under the LDA arises from active status as a registrant. Therefore if a registration has been filed for a pro bono client, LD-2 and LD-203 reports would be expected to be filed until the registration is validly terminated.

More than One Lobbying Contact

"More than one lobbying contact" means more than one communication to a covered official. Note that an individual falls within the definition of "lobbyist" by making more than one lobbying contact over the course of services provided for a particular client (even if the second contact occurs in a later quarterly period).

> Example 1: Lobbyist "A" telephones Covered Official "B" in the morning to discuss proposed legislation. In the afternoon she telephones Covered Official "C" to discuss the same legislation. Lobbyist "A" has made more than one lobbying contact.
>
> Example 2: Under some circumstances a series of discussions with a particular official might be considered a single communication, such as when a telephone call is interrupted and continued at a later time. Discussions taking place on more than one day with the same covered official, however, should be presumed to be more than one lobbying contact.

Clarification of an Exception to Lobbying Contact

Section 3(8)(B)(ix) excepts from the definition of "lobbying contact" communications "required by subpoena, civil investigative demand, or otherwise compelled by statute, regulation, or other action of the Congress or an agency." The 1998 amendments to the LDA clarified that communications that are compelled by the action of a Federal agency include communications that are required by a Federal agency contract, grant, loan, permit, or license.

> Example: Contractor "A" has a contract to provide technical assistance to Agency "B" on an ongoing basis. Technical communications between Contractor "A's" personnel and covered officials at Agency "B" would be required by the contract and therefore would not constitute "lobbying contacts."

Note, however, that this exception would not encompass an attempt by "A" to influence covered officials regarding either matters of policy, or an award of a new contract, since such communications would not be required by the existing contract.

Do Lobbying Activities Constitute 20% or More of an Individual's Time?

Lobbying activity is defined in Section 3(7) as "lobbying contacts and efforts in support of such contacts, including . . . background work that is intended, at the time it is performed, for use in contacts, and coordination with the lobbying activities of others." If the intent of the work is to support ongoing and future lobbying, then it would fall within the definition of lobbying activities. Timing of the work performed, as well as the status of the issue, is also pivotal. Generally, if work such as reporting or monitoring occurs at a time when future lobbying contacts are contemplated, such reporting and monitoring should be considered as a part of planning or coordinating of lobbying contacts, and therefore included as "lobbying activity." If, on the other hand, a person reports back to the relevant committee or officer regarding the status of a completed effort, that activity would probably not be included as a lobbying activity, if reports are not being used to prepare a lobbying strategy the next time the issue is considered.

Communications excepted from the definition of "lobbying contact" under Section 3(8)(B) of the LDA may be considered "lobbying activities" under some circumstances. Communications excepted by Section 3(8)(B) will constitute "lobbying activities" if they are in support of other communications which constitute "lobbying contacts."

> Example: Under Section 3(8)(B)(v), the term "lobbying contact" does not include "a request for a meeting, a request for the status of an action, or any other similar administrative request, if the request does not include an attempt to influence a covered Executive Branch official or a covered Legislative Branch official." However, a status request would constitute "lobbying activity" if it were in support of a subsequent lobbying contact.

Please note that the 20% of time threshold applies to registration and not to the reporting section.

Is it Lobbying Contact/Lobbying Activity?

If a communication is limited to routine information gathering questions and there is not an attempt to influence a covered official, the exception of Section 3(8)(B)(v) for "any other similar administrative request" would normally apply. In determining whether there is an attempt to influence a covered official, the identity of the person asking the questions and her relationship to the covered official obviously will be important factors.

> Example 1: Lobbyist "A", a former chief of staff in a congressional office, is now a partner in the law firm retained to lobby for Client "B." After waiting one year to comply with post-employment restrictions on lobbying, Lobbyist "A" telephones the Member on whose staff she served. She asks about the status of legislation affecting Client "B's" interests. Presumably "B" will expect the call to have been part of an effort to influence the Member, even though only routine matters were raised at that particular time.
>
> Example 2: Company "Z" offers temporary employment to recent college graduates. The graduates are hired to conduct surveys of congressional staff by reading prepared questions and recording the answers. The questions seek only information. These communications do not amount to lobbying contacts.

Lobbying Contacts and Activities Using Section 15 Election (Alternate Reporting Methods)

Section 15 of the LDA permits those organizations that are required to file and do file under Section 6033(b)(8) of the Internal Revenue Code (IRC) and organizations that are subject to Section 162(e) of the IRC to use the tax law definitions of lobbying in lieu of the LDA definitions for determining "contacts" and "lobbying activities" for Executive Branch lobbying. Registrants should note that the tax definition of lobbying is broader with respect to the type of activities reported, while it is narrower with respect to the universe of Executive Branch officials who qualify as covered Executive Branch employees.

Under the 1998 amendments to the LDA, registrants making a Section 15 election must use the Internal Revenue Code definition for Executive Branch lobbying, and the LDA definition for Legislative Branch lobbying. Because there are fewer Executive Branch officials under the IRC definitions than under the LDA definitions, this may result in fewer individuals being listed as lobbyists and fewer lobbying contacts reflected on the Form LD-2.

Also note that definitions under the tax code include "grass-roots" and "state" lobbying, while the LDA excludes those types of lobbying from the definition of "lobbying activities." The LDA does not permit modification of the tax code definition to exclude such expenditures when reporting lobbying expenses.

Relationship between 20% of Time and Monetary Threshold

If the definition of "lobbyist" is satisfied with respect to at least one individual for a particular client, the potential registrant (either a lobbying firm or an organization employing the lobbyist, or a self-employed individual lobbyist) is **not** required to register if it does not meet the monetary thresholds of Section 4(a)(3)(A)(i), in the case of a "lobbying firm," or of Section 4(a)(3)(A)(ii), in the case of an organization employing in-house lobbyists. Note that the monetary exemption is computed based on the lobbying activities of the potential registrant as a whole for the particular client in question, not simply on the lobbying activities of those individuals who are "lobbyists."

Example 1: A law firm has two lawyers who perform services for a particular client. Lawyer "A" spends 15 percent of the time she works for that client on lobbying activities, including some lobbying contacts. Lawyer "B" spends 25 percent of the time he works for the client on lobbying activities, but makes no lobbying contacts. Neither lawyer falls within the definition of "lobbyist," and therefore the law firm is not required to register for that client, even if the income it receives for lobbying activities on behalf of the client exceeds $3,000.

Example 2: Employee "A" of a trade association is a "lobbyist" who spends 25 percent of his time on lobbying activities on behalf of the association. There are $6,500 of expenses related to Employee "A's" lobbying activities. Employee "B" is not a "lobbyist" but engages in lobbying activities in support of lobbying contacts made by Employee "A." There are $6,500 of additional expenses related to the lobbying activities of Employee "B." The trade association is required to register because it employs a "lobbyist" and its total expenses in connection with lobbying activities on its own behalf exceed $12,500.

Example 3: Same as Example 2, except the expenses related to the lobbying activities of Employees "A" and "B" total only $9,000, but the trade association also pays $5,000 to an outside firm for lobbying activities. Registration is still required because payments to outside contractors (including lobbying firms that may be separately registered under the LDA) must be included in the total expenses of an organization employing lobbyists on its own behalf.

Timing

The registration requirement of a potential registrant is triggered either (1) on the date their employee/lobbyist is employed or retained to make more than one lobbying contact on behalf of the client (and meets the 20% of time threshold), or (2) on the date their employee/lobbyist (who meets the 20% of time threshold) in fact makes a second lobbying contact, whichever is earlier. In either case, registration is required within 45 days of that date.

Example: Lobbying Firm "A" is retained to monitor an issue, but whether or not lobbying contacts will be made depends on future legislative developments. In another case, Corporation "B," which employs an in-house lobbyist, knows that its lobbyist will make contacts but reasonably expects its lobbying expenditures will not amount to $12,500 in a quarterly period. However, issues of interest to "B" turn out to be more controversial than expected, and the $12,500 threshold is in fact met a month later.

Lobbying firm "A" has no registration requirement at the present time. The requirement to register is triggered if and when the firm makes contacts, or reasonably expects that it will make contacts. Corporation "B's" registration requirement arose as soon as it knew, or reasonably expected, that its lobbying expenditures will exceed $12,500. "B" needs to register immediately.

Listing of Foreign Entities

Each registration must contain the name, address, principal place of business, amount of any contribution greater than $5,000 to the lobbying activities of the registrant, and approximate percentage of ownership in the client of any foreign entity that: holds at least 20% equitable ownership in the client or any affiliate of the client required to be listed on Line 13; **or** directly or indirectly, in whole or major part, plans, supervises, controls, directs, finances, or subsidizes the activities of the client or affiliate of the client required to be listed on Line 13; **or** is an affiliate of either the client, or an organization affiliated with the client identified on Line 13 or 14 of Form LD-1 and has a direct interest in the outcome of the lobbying activity. The purpose of the disclosure is to identify the interests of the foreign entity that may be operating behind the registrant.

Example: Lobbying Firm "A" is retained to lobby on behalf of Company "B," which is wholly owned by Foreign Company "C." "C" is wholly owned by Foreign Company "D," and "D" is wholly owned by Foreign Company "E." "C," "D," and "E" must be disclosed on Line 14.

SECTION 5 – SPECIAL REGISTRATION CIRCUMSTANCES

Elaboration on the Definition of Client

In some cases a registrant is retained as part of a larger lobbying effort that encompasses more than one lobbying firm on behalf of a third party. Generally, the entity that is paying the registrant is listed as the client on behalf of the third party. The third party, who is paying the intermediary (client), is listed also on Line 13 of Form LD-1 as an affiliate.

Example: Client "P" retains lobbying firm "F" for general lobbying purposes, but has a new interest in obtaining an outcome in an area new to "P." "F" realizes that a boutique lobbying firm "L" has an excellent track record for obtaining the type of outcome "P" is seeking, and talks to "P" about subcontracting. "P" agrees with "F's" strategy. "F" contacts "L" to retain the latter to do the project. "F" is responsible for paying "L." Within 45 days, "L" registers disclosing "F on behalf of P" as the client, and listing "P" as the affiliate on Line 13 of Form LD-1.

Lobbying Firms Retained under a Contingent Fee

Law other than the LDA governs whether a firm may be retained on a contingent-fee basis. There is, for example, a general prohibition on the payment of contingent fees in connection with the award of government contracts. Assuming, however, that the agreement is not contrary to law or public policy, an agreement to make lobbying contacts for a contingent fee, like other fee arrangements, triggers a registration requirement at inception. The fee is disclosed on Form LD-2 for the quarterly period that the registrant becomes entitled to it.

Example 1: On January 1, 2008, Lobbying Firm "G" agrees to lobby for Client "H" for a fee contingent on a certain result, and the agreement is permitted under other applicable law. Lobbying activities begin. "G" is required to register by February 14, 2008. The result is not obtained and "G" is not entitled to any fee during the first quarterly period. "G" must report its lobbying activities for the first quarterly period; the income reported is "Less than $5,000." The desired result does occur in the second quarterly period of 2008. In the report for that period, "G" discloses its lobbying activities for that period and the total contingent fee.

Example 2: Lobbying Firm "J" discusses an arrangement to accept stock options worth $4,500 from Client "M" in lieu of payment of a contingency fee. After determining that acceptance of a success fee is not a violation of another statute, "J" signs a contract with "M," and registers. Late in the first quarter of the lobbying activities, it appeared "J" achieved the result. "J's" initial quarterly lobbying report disclosed lobbying income of less than $5,000. "M's" stock value increased shortly thereafter to be valued at $6,000, so "J" exercised its options. "J" amended the previously filed quarterly report to reflect income of "$5,000 or more," and rounded the amount to $10,000.

Registration for Entities with Subsidiaries or State and Local Affiliates

Assuming a parent entity or national association and its subsidiary or subordinate are separate legal entities, the parent makes a determination whether it meets the registration threshold based upon its own activities, and does not include subordinate units' lobbying activities in its assessment. Each subordinate must make its own assessment as to whether any of its own employees meet the definition of a lobbyist, and then determine if it meets the registration threshold with respect to lobbying expenses.

Example: Lobbyist "Z" is an employee of Company "A," which is a wholly owned subsidiary of Company "B." "Z's" lobbying activities advance the interests of both. Which company is responsible for registering and reporting under the LDA?

The registration and reporting requirements apply to the organization of which Lobbyist "Z" is an employee. Therefore, Company "A" would register and file the quarterly reports.

If Company "B" contributes $5,000 or more to "Z's" lobbying activities during a quarterly period and actively participates in the planning, supervision, or control of the lobbying activities, Company "B" must be listed on Company "A's" Form LD-1, Line 13. A contribution may take any form, and may be direct or indirect. For example, if Company "B" established Company "A" with an initial capital contribution of $1,000,000, which "A" draws upon for employee salaries, including "Z's," and to pay for office space used by "Z," a $5,000 contribution probably has been made.

If Company "B" is a foreign entity, and the facts are otherwise the same as above, "B" would be listed on Line 14 of the Form LD-1 filed by Company "A." "B's" interests in specific lobbying issues would also be disclosed on Line 19 of Form LD-2.

The LDA does not make any express provision for combined or consolidated filings. A single filing by a parent corporation may be appropriate in some cases, especially when there are multiple subsidiaries and the lobbyists address the same issues for all and act under the close control of the parent. In this regard, note that the LDA does not contain any specific definition of "employee" (there is only the general definition of Section 3(5)), and the policy of the LDA is to promote disclosure of real parties in interest.

In circumstances in which multiple subsidiaries each have only a fraction of the lobbyist's time and little control over his work, the parent which in fact exercises actual control can be regarded as the "employer" for LDA purposes. In such cases, the parent may file a single registration, provided that Line 10 of Form LD-1 discloses that the listed lobbyists are employees of subsidiaries and the subsidiaries are identified as affiliated organizations on Line 13.

Effect of Mergers and Acquisitions on Registrations

The following examples serve to illustrate hypothetical situations regarding mergers and acquisitions:

> Example 1: Corporation "C" registered under the LDA during 2008. Effective upon close of business on December 31, 2008, "C" merged with Corporation "D." "D," the surviving corporation, had no lobbyist employees before the merger and is not registered. How and when should this information be reported? Assuming that "D" retains at least one of "C's" lobbyist employees and will incur lobbying expenses of at least $12,500 during the January – March quarterly period, Corporation "D" is required to register. The 45-day period in which its initial registration must be filed begins to run on December 31, 2008, the date "D" first had lobbyist employees, and the registration is due by February 14, 2009. On the other hand, if "D" will not be lobbying after the merger, it is not required to register. In pre-merger discussions, Corporation "C" might have agreed to terminate its registration and file its final lobbying report before ceasing its corporate existence. If, however, "C" did not do so, Corporation "D" should terminate the registration and file the outstanding lobbying report in "C's" name. "D" may simply annotate the signature block on Form LD-2 to indicate that it is filing as successor in interest to "C."
>
> Example 2: Lobbying Firm "O" is a registrant under the LDA. It merges with Lobbying Firm "P," which is also a registrant. The new entity will be known as Lobbying Firm "T." How and when should this information be reported? The answer depends on the particular facts. If Lobbying Firm "T" is a newly created legal entity, it should file a new registration within 45 days. The registrations of both "O" and "P" should be terminated by filing separate termination reports for each remaining registrant/client relationship. But if "T" is simply the new name adopted by "O" following the merger with "P," with "P" going out of existence, "O" should report its new name and other updated information (such as the names of lobbyist employees of "P" who are retained or hired by "T") on Form LD-2. "P's" registration should be terminated, and P should file termination reports for each remaining registrant/client relationship, but only after P ceases to exist.

Example 3: Corporation ".1," a registrant, acquired Corporation "K," a non-registrant. At the time of the acquisition, ".1" changed its name to ".1 & K." How and when should this information be reported? For LDA purposes, this is simply a change in the name of the registrant. The change should be reported on Line 1 of the next LD-2 quarterly report.

Associations or Coalitions

The LDA provides that "[i]n the case of a coalition or association that employs or retains other persons to conduct lobbying activities, the client is the coalition or association and not its individual members" (Section 3(2)). A bona fide coalition that employs or retains lobbyists on behalf of the coalition may be the client for LDA purposes, even if the coalition is not a legal entity or has no formal name. A registrant lobbying for an unnamed informal coalition needs to adopt some type of identifier for Line 7 of Form LD-1, and indicate "(Informal Coalition)" or another applicable description. For all coalitions and associations, formal or informal, the LDA requires further disclosures, e.g., of organizations other than the client that contribute more than $5,000 toward the lobbying activities of the registrant in the quarterly period, **and** actively participate in the planning, supervision, or control of the lobbying activities (Section 4(b)(3)). Such organizations are identified on Line 13 of Form LD-1.

Example 1: Association "A" has 20 organizational members who each pay $20,000 as a portion of their annual dues to fund "A's" lobbying activities. "E" is an employee of Organization "O," which is a member of "A." "E" serves as a member of "A's" board, as a representative of "O." While "A" carries out various functions, a substantial part of its mission is lobbying on issues of interest to its member organizations. "E's" board membership constitutes active participation by "O" in the lobbying activities of "A," and thus "O" would need to be listed as an affiliated organization of "A."

Example 2: Another association "A" has 1000 organizational members who each pay $20,000 as a portion of their annual dues to fund "A's" lobbying activities. "E" is an employee of Organization "O," which is a member of "A." "E" serves as a member of "A's" board, as a representative of "O." "A" performs numerous functions, only a modest portion of which is lobbying. With regard to "A's" lobbying activities, "A's" board is only involved in approving an overall budget for such activities, but otherwise leaves supervision, direction, and control of such matters to a separate committee of member organizations. "E's" board membership in this case does not constitute active participation by "O" in the lobbying activities of "A."

Example 3: Another association "A" has 1000 organizational members who each pay $1,000 a month in annual dues to "A." "E" is an employee of Organization "O," which is a member of "A." "E" serves as a member of "A's" lobbying oversight group as a representative of "O." The lobbying oversight group plans and supervises lobbying strategy for "A." While "E's" activities in "A" would constitute active participation, because "O" does not contribute $5,000 in the reporting quarter to the lobbying activities of "A," "O" would not need to be listed as an affiliate of "A."

Example 4: Another association "A" has 100 organizational members who each pay $30,000 a month as a portion of their annual dues to fund "A's" lobbying activities. "E" is an employee of Organization "O," and attends "A's" annual meeting/conference, informally provides "O's" list of legislative priorities to "A," and also facilitates responses from "O" to occasional requests for information by "A's" lobbyists. These activities would not make "O" an active participant in the lobbying activities of "A."

Example 5: Organization "O" joins with a group of nine other organizations to form Coalition "C" to lobby on an issue of interest to it. Each contributes $50,000 to "C's" budget. "O's" vice president for government relations is part of the informal group that directs the lobbying strategy for "C." "O" would be considered an active participant in "C's" lobbying activities and would have to be disclosed.

Note that a coalition with a foreign entity as a member must identify the foreign entity on Line 14 of Form LD-1 if the foreign entity meets the test of either Section 4(b)(3) or 4(b)(4).

Churches, Integrated Auxiliaries, Conventions or Association of Churches and Religious Orders – Hiring of Outside Firms

Although the definition of a lobbying contact does not include a communication made by a church, its integrated auxiliary, a convention or association of churches and religious orders (Section 3(8)(B)(xviii)), if a church (its integrated auxiliary, a convention or association of churches, and religious orders) hires an outside firm that conducts lobbying activity on its behalf, the outside firm must register if registration is otherwise required.

Registration of Professional Associations of Elected Officials

The Section 3(15) definition of "public official" includes a professional association of elected officials who are exempt from registration. If the association retains an outside firm to lobby, the lobbying firm must register if otherwise required to do so, i.e., the firm employs a lobbyist as defined in Section 3(10) and lobbying income exceeds $3,000 in a quarterly period.

SECTION 6 – QUARTERLY REPORTING OF LOBBYING ACTIVITIES

When and Why a Report is Needed

Each registrant must file a quarterly report on Form LD-2 no later than 20 days (or on the first business day after such 20th day if the 20th day is not a business day) after the end of the quarterly period beginning on the first day of January, April, July, and October of each year in which a registrant is registered. Lobbying firms file separate reports for each client for each quarterly reporting period, while organizations employing in-house lobbyists file one report covering their in-house lobbying activities for each quarterly reporting period. All reports must be filed electronically (with exceptions as noted below). The Secretary and Clerk do not have the authority under the LDA to grant extensions to registrants.

The obligation to report under the LDA arises from active status as a registrant (i.e., a registration on file that has not been validly terminated). Section 5(a) of the LDA requires a registrant to file a report for the quarterly period in which it incurred its registration requirement, and for each quarterly period thereafter, through and including the reporting period encompassing the date of registration termination. A timely report using Form LD-2 is required even though the registration was in effect for only part of the reporting period. So long as a registration is on file and has not been terminated, a registrant must report its lobbying activities even if those activities during a particular quarterly period would not trigger a registration requirement in the first instance (e.g., a lobbying firm's income from a client amounted to less than $3,000 during a particular quarterly period). A registrant with no lobbying activity during a quarterly period checks the no activity box on Form LD-2.

Example 1: "A" is the only lobbyist of Lobbying Firm "Z" listed in the registration filed for Client "Y" on February 14, 2008. During January – March 2008, "A" lobbied for "Y" nearly full-time. During the April – June period in 2008, however, "A" made only one lobbying contact for "Y" in April, but lobbying fees for the quarter were $10,000. For the April – June quarterly period, even though "A" had minimal lobbying activities, Lobbying Firm "Z" must report "A's" lobbying activities (due to "A's" being listed as a lobbyist) and must report the $10,000 lobbying fees.

Example 2: Lobbying Firm "Z" is retained by Client "X" on June 1, 2008 for thirty days to lobby on a particular issue that is on the legislative calendar and the issue is settled prior to the departure of House and Senate Members for the July 4th recess. Firm "Z" must file its registration by July 15, file its Q2 LD-2 Report by July 20, and, if it chooses to terminate, file its termination report by October 20.

Disclosing That a Client Is a State or Local Government or Instrumentality

If the client is a state or local government or instrumentality, check the box on Line 7 of Form LD-2.

Mandatory Electronic Filing

Section 5 of the LDA was amended to require the mandatory electronic filing of all documents required by the LDA. The only exception to mandatory electronic filing is for the purpose of amending reports in the format previously filed, or for compliance with the Americans with Disabilities Act. Each electronic lobbying disclosure form provides usability for people with vision impairments who have the appropriate software and hardware. If you have questions regarding additional ADA accommodations, please contact the Senate Office of Public Records at 202-224-0758.

Preparing to File the Quarterly Report – Income or Expense Recording

The LDA does not contain any special record keeping provisions, but requires, in the case of an outside lobbying firm (including self-employed individuals), a good faith estimate of all income received from the client, other than payments for matters unrelated to lobbying activities. In the case of an organization employing in-house lobbyists, the LDA requires a good faith estimate of the total expenses of its lobbying activities. As long as the registrant has a reasonable system in place and complies in good faith with that system, the requirement of reporting expenses or income would be met. Since Section 6(a)(5) requires the Secretary and Clerk to "retain registrations for a period of at least 6 years after they are terminated and reports for a period of at least 6 years after they are filed," we recommend registrants retain copies of their filings and supporting documentation for the same length of time.

Lobbying Firm Income

Lobbying firms report income earned or accrued from lobbying activities during a quarterly period, even though the client may not be billed or make payment until a later time. For a lobbying firm, gross income from the client for lobbying activities is reportable, including reimbursable expenses, costs, or disbursements that are in addition to fees and separately invoiced. Line 12 of Form LD-2 provides boxes for a lobbying firm to report income of less than $5,000, or of $5,000 or more. If lobbying income is $5,000 or more, a lobbying firm must provide a good faith estimate of the actual dollar amount **rounded to the nearest $10,000.**

Organization Expenses Using LDA Expense Reporting Method

Organizations that employ in-house lobbyists may incur lobbying-related expenses in the form of employee compensation, office overhead, or payments to vendors, which may include lobbying firms. Organizations must report expenses as they are incurred, though payment may be made later. Line 13 of Form LD-2 provides for an organization to report lobbying expenses of less than $5,000, or $5,000 or more. If lobbying expenses are $5,000 or more, the organization must provide a good faith estimate of the actual dollar amount rounded to the nearest $10,000. Organizations using the LDA expense reporting method mark the "Method A" box on Line 14 of Form LD-2.

To ensure complete reporting, the Secretary and Clerk have consistently interpreted Section 5(b)(4) to require such organizations to report all of their expenses incurred in connection with lobbying activities, including all payments to retained lobby firms or outside entities, without considering whether any particular payee has a separate obligation to register and report under the LDA. Logically, if an organization employing in-house lobbyists also retains a lobbying firm, the expense reported by the organization should be greater than the fees reported by the lobbying firm of which the organization is a client. An organization must contact any other organization to which it pays membership dues in order to learn what portion of the dues is used by the latter organization for lobbying activities. It is necessary for the former organization to include the portion of the dues that is designated for lobbying activities in the total of lobbying expenses reported by the former organization. A registrant cannot apportion the lobbying expense part of the dues to avoid disclosure. Dues payments for lobbying activities should be included in the estimate for the quarter in which they are paid.

All employee time spent in lobbying activities must be included in determining the organization's lobbying expenses, even if the employee does not meet the statutory definition of a "lobbyist."

> Example: The CEO of a registrant, "Defense Contractor," travels to Washington to meet with a covered DOD official regarding the renewal of a government contract. "Defense Contractor" has already determined that its CEO is not a "lobbyist," because he does not spend 20 percent of his time on "lobbying activities" during a quarterly period. Nonetheless, the expenses reasonably allocable to the CEO's lobbying activities (e.g., plane ticket to Washington, salary and benefit costs, etc.) will be reportable.

Similarly, all expenses of lobbying activities incurred during a quarterly period are reportable. The Section 3(7) definition of lobbying activities is not limited to lobbying contacts. Examples of lobbying expenses to be included are reflected below.

> Example 1: A research assistant in the Washington office of the registrant, "Defense Contractor" (described in the example above) researches and prepares the talking points for the CEO's lobbying contact with the covered DOD official. Likewise, the expenses reasonably allocable to the research assistant's lobbying activities will be included in "Defense Contractor's" expense estimate for the quarterly period.
> Example 2: Corporation "R" is a registrant that is interested in building a bypass around a city in state "S." "R's" governmental affairs team is comprised of lobbyists who are federally-focused, and lobbyists

who are state-focused. The entire staff prepares a strategic lobbying plan to support the building of the bypass. This includes both federal and state lobbying. In this example, the time spent by the state level lobbyists preparing the materials would be included in "R's" good faith estimate of lobbying expenses for the quarter because, at the time the materials were prepared, they were to be used for federal lobbying.

Example 3: Same circumstances as Example 2, but in this situation, the aforementioned strategic lobbying plan includes hiring one firm to help with the production of the plan, and another firm to place advertising in media in "S" to encourage citizens in "S" to contact their representatives about the importance of building the bypass. The total cost of producing the plan, but not the cost of the advertising media fees, must be included in "R's" good faith estimate of lobbying expenses for the quarter.

The examples below are intended to be illustrative of the possibilities of LDA expense reporting, and are not intended to require detailed accounting rules.

Example 1: An organization employing in-house lobbyists might choose to estimate lobbying expenses by asking each professional staffer to track his/her percentages of time devoted to lobbying activities. These percentages could be averaged to compute the percentage of the organization's total effort (and budget) that is devoted to lobbying activities. Under this example the organization would include salary costs (including a percentage of support staff salaries), overhead, and expenses, including any third-party costs attributable to lobbying.

Example 2: Another organization, which lobbies out of its Washington office, might avoid the need for detailed breakdowns by including the entire budget or expenses (whichever, the organization believes in good faith is closer to the actual amount) of its Washington office.

Organizations Reporting Expenses Under Section 15 (Optional IRC Reporting Methods)

Section 15(a) of the LDA allows entities that are required to report and do report lobbying expenditures under section 6033(b)(8) of the Internal Revenue Code to use IRC definitions for purposes of LDA Sections (4)(a)(3) and 5(b)(4). Charitable organizations, as described in IRC Section 501(c)(3), are required to report to the Internal Revenue Service their lobbying expenditures in conformity with Section 6033(b)(8) of the IRC. They may treat as LDA expenses the amounts they treat for "influencing legislation" under the IRC.

Section 15(b) of the LDA allows entities that are subject to section 162(e) of the IRC to use IRC definitions for purposes of LDA Sections (4)(a)(3) and 5(b)(4). The eligible entities include for-profit organizations (other than lobbying firms) and tax-exempt organizations such as trade associations that calculate their lobbying expenses for IRC purposes with reference to IRC Section 162(e) rules. We believe that this reporting option is available to include also a small number of trade association registrants not required by the IRC to report non-deductible lobbying expenses to their members (i.e., those whose members are tax-exempt).

If an eligible organization elects to report under Section 15, it must do so consistently for all reports covering a calendar year. The electing organization also must report all expenses that fall within the applicable Internal Revenue Code definition. The total that is ultimately reportable to the Internal Revenue Service is the figure that would be used for Line 13 reporting. Line 13 of Form LD-2 would require any organization to report if the amount of lobbying expenses was less than $5,000, or $5,000 or more. If the expense amount is $5,000 or more, it should be rounded to the nearest $10,000. Line 14 of Form LD-2 requires the electing organization to mark as applicable, either the "Method B" box (IRC Section 6033(b)(8)) or the "Method C" box (IRC Section 162(e)). The Secretary and Clerk are aware that the IRC and LDA are not harmonized in terms of expense reporting. Registrants are advised that if they elect to report under Section 15, they may not subtract lobbying expenses for lobbying state and local officials and grassroots lobbying from the total expenses reported under the LDA. Doing so alters the IRS reportable total, and is not permitted.

Quarterly Reporting of Lobbying Activities – Contents of Report

The two core disclosures required by Section 5(b) and 5(c) of the LDA and incorporated into Form LD-2 are: (1) lobbying income or expenses; and (2) lobbying issues. Form LD-2 has been designed to allow registrants the greatest flexibility in terms of document length to correspond with the varying amounts of information relating to the core disclosures. The following examples illustrate how the nature of the core disclosures builds the form.

Example 1: Registrant "A" represents Client "B" to monitor an issue of interest to B and make occasional lobbying contacts as necessary. During the Q1 2008 reporting period, "A" received $3,000 from "B," but had no lobbying activity because "B's" issue was dormant. "A" would complete Form LD-2, mark the box on Line 11 labeled "No Lobbying Activity," mark Line 12 as "Less than $5,000," and file the report.

Example 2: Same circumstances as above, except that "A" has two lobbyists who make lobbying contacts on a single lobbying issue with the Senate and the House. In this case, "A" will need to complete the Lobbying Activity section of Form LD-2 and file the report.

Example 3: Same circumstances as example 2, but one of the lobbyists retires during the reporting period. In this case, an update page of Form LD-2 would be required, listing the lobbyist's name on Line 23, which has the effect of reflecting the removal of the lobbyist's name (his/her retirement) from "A's" registration and reports.

Section 5(b) of the LDA requires specific information on the nature of the lobbying activities. The Lobbying Activity Section of Form LD-2 requires the registrant to:

- Disclose the general lobbying issue area code (list 1 code per page).
- Identify the specific issues on which the lobbyist(s) engaged in lobbying activities.
- Identify the Houses of Congress and Federal Agencies contacted.
- Disclose the lobbyists who had any activity in the general issue area.
- Describe the interest of a foreign entity if applicable.

When reporting specific lobbying issues, some registrants have listed only House or Senate bill numbers on the issues page without further indication of their clients' specific lobbying issues. Such disclosures are not adequate, for several reasons. First, Section 5(b)(2)(A) of the LDA requires disclosure of "specific issues upon which a lobbyist employed by the registrant engaged in lobbying activities, including ... bill numbers[.]" As we read the law, a bill number is a required disclosure when the lobbying activities concern a bill, but is not in itself a complete disclosure. Further, in many cases, a bill number standing alone does not inform the public of the client's specific issue. Many bills are lengthy and complex, or may contain various provisions that are not always directly related to the main subject or title. If a registrant's client is interested in only one or a few specific provisions of a much larger bill, a lobbying report containing a mere bill number will not disclose the specific lobbying issue. Even if a bill concerns only one specific subject, a lobbying report disclosing only a bill number is still inadequate, because a member of the public would need access to information outside of the filing to ascertain that subject. In our view, the LDA contemplates disclosures that are adequate to inform the public of the lobbying client's specific issues from a review of the Form LD-2, without independent familiarity with bill numbers or the client's interest in specific subject matters within larger bills. The disclosures on Line 16 must include bill numbers, where applicable, but must always contain information that is adequate, standing alone, to inform the public of the specific lobbying issues.

Example: Client "A's" general lobbying issue area is "Environment." During the first quarter of 2008, lobbyists for "A" made contacts concerning the Department of Defense appropriations for environmental restoration. For fiscal 2009, the Department of Defense Appropriations Act was part of the Omnibus Consolidated Appropriations Act for 2009, H.R. 3610, a lengthy and complex bill that did not have numbered sections throughout. Title II contained separate but unnumbered provisions making appropriations for "Environmental Restoration, Army," "Environmental Restoration, Navy," "Environmental Restoration, Air Force," "Environmental Restoration, Defense Wide," and "Environmental Restoration, Formerly Used Defense Sites." Lobbying contacts for Client "A" addressed all environmental restoration funding within the Defense Department bill. An appropriate disclosure of the specific lobbying issue would read as follows: H.R. 3610, Department of Defense Appropriations Act for 2009, Title II, all provisions relating to environmental restoration.

The TAR code is used for tariff bills, including miscellaneous tariff bills. Filers must use this general issue area code to report lobbying activity related to tariff issues, including miscellaneous tariff issues. For any other trade-related issues, filers should use the TRD code.

Example: Registrant "R' is retained by Client "B" to pursue a bill to provide a temporary tariff suspension for chemical X, and a separate bill to provide a temporary tariff reduction for chemical Y. During the first quarter of 2008, "R" made lobbying contacts concerning both matters on behalf of "B" and a separate bill was introduced for each matter (S.123 for chemical X and S.456 for chemical Y). "R" reports in its LD-2 filing for Q1 that the general issue area code for these bills is "TAR," and the specific issues lobbied upon were the substance of the bills, citing to the bill number, if a bill has been introduced (e.g., "temporary tariff suspension for chemical X (S.123) and temporary tariff reduction for chemical Y (S.456)"). In the Q3 reporting period, the two chemical tariff provisions are each rolled into an omnibus bill (e.g., S.789, the "Miscellaneous Tariff Bill"). If "R" had lobbying activities during the Q3 reporting period encompassing all three bills, then "R" reports that the general issue area code for these bills is "TAR" and the specific issues lobbied upon were the substance of the bills (e.g., "temporary tariff suspension for chemical X and temporary tariff reduction for chemical Y, included in the original bills (S.123 and S.456) and in the Miscellaneous Tariff Bill (S.789)"). In Q4, "R" had lobbying activities focusing on the omnibus bill which "R" then discloses on its Q4 report, using TAR for the general issue area code as well as reporting the specific issues lobbied upon ("modification focused on tariff suspension for chemical X and tariff reduction for chemical Y, included in Miscellaneous Tariff Bill (S.789)").

The Houses of Congress and Federal agencies contacted by lobbyists during the reporting period must be disclosed on Line 17 of Form LD-2, picking from the list of government entities provided on the form. If the list does not display the government entity contacted, then select the department in which the entity is housed. In the event that no lobbying contacts were made, the registrant must mark the "Check if None" box.

Previously identified lobbyists and new lobbyists for this reporting period must be listed on Line 18 of Form LD-2 if they had any lobbying activities during the reporting period, whether or not they made lobbying contacts. The Lobbying Activity Section is only intended to reflect lobbying activity by lobbyists, and not activity of those who are not lobbyists. The registrant does not report the names of individuals who may perform some lobbying activities, but who do not and are not expected to meet the LDA definition of a lobbyist.

Example: Lobbying Firm "A" filed its initial registration for Client "B" on February 14, listing Lobbyists "X," "Y," and "Z." From January through March, Lobbyists "W" (hired in February) and "X" and "Y" made contacts for "B," while Lobbyist "Z" was assigned work for other clients. Lobbyist "Z" is expected, however, to be active on behalf of Client "B" after Spring Recess until adjournment. In its Q1 LD-2 report for Client "B," filed on or before April 20, Lobbying Firm "A" lists "W," "X," and "Y" on Line 18. "W" is also identified as "new," and Firm "A" would disclose if "W" occupied a covered position within the last twenty years. "Z" is not listed on the Form LD-2 filed for Client "B" for the January – March quarterly period, but because of the current expectation that he will lobby during the

April – June quarterly period, his name is not deleted as a lobbyist for "B."

New lobbyists must be disclosed in the appropriate Lobbying Activity section for the reporting period in which the individual first meets the definition of lobbyist. Filers need to list a new lobbyist's previous covered executive or legislative branch positions held within twenty (20) years of first acting as a lobbyist for a client. Once a filer has met the previously described statutory requirement for listing a new lobbyist's previous covered position(s), then the filer does not have to list those positions again for subsequent reports concerning the same client. If a Registrant lists that lobbyist for the first time on a report/registration regarding a different client, then the Registrant must list that lobbyist's previous covered positions held within twenty (20) years of first acting as a lobbyist for the new client.

We are aware that there will be situations in which a registrant expects an individual to become a lobbyist and wishes to disclose the name of that individual as a matter of public record. Section 5 of the LDA, however, provides that updated registration information is contained in the registrant's next quarterly report. Therefore, there may be a period of time in which an individual is legitimately making lobbying contacts but is not identified on the public record until the next quarterly report is filed. In such cases, the registrant reports updated information as the LDA requires.

A foreign entity is reported on Line 19 of Form LD-2 if both of two circumstances apply: 1) the foreign entity must be an entity that is required to be identified on Form LD-1 or on the registration information update page. That, in turn, depends on whether the entity meets one of the three conditions of Section 4(b)(4) of the LDA; and 2) the entity must have an interest in the specific lobbying issues listed on Line 16. If a foreign entity has an interest in the specific issues, Line 19 requires a description of that interest. For the sake of clarity the registrant should indicate whether the foreign entity(s) is/are the same as identified on the registration. The requirement to disclose a foreign interest on Line 19 on Form LD-2 is not contingent upon the entity making a contribution of $5,000 or more to the registrant during that particular reporting period.

Example: "[Name of foreign entity], identified on Form LD-1, exports [type of product] to United States and would benefit from [specific desired outcome]."

SECTION 7 – SEMIANNUAL REPORTING OF CERTAIN CONTRIBUTIONS

When and Why a Report Is Needed

Registrants and lobbyists must file a semiannual report on Form LD-203 by July 30 and January 30 (or on the next business day should either day occur on a weekend or holiday) for each semiannual period in which a registrant or lobbyist remains active (and regardless of whether they do or do not make reportable contributions). An "active" registrant is one that has not filed a valid termination report for all clients. An "active" lobbyist is an individual who has been listed on any registrant's Form LD-1 or LD-2 and who has not been terminated by the registrant on Line 23 of an LD-2. If a lobbyist is listed as active for all or any part of a semi-annual period, he or she must file an LD-203 report for that period (see Guidance Section 8). Section 5 of the LDA states that "each person or organization who is registered or is required to register...and each employee who is or is required to be listed as a lobbyist... shall file a report." Thus, the requirement to file an LD-203 report falls upon all lobbyists who were listed on an LD-1 or LD-2 report, regardless of whether they were required to be listed (as in the case in which a registrant listed an individual as a lobbyist in an abundance of caution). Any lobbyist who is reported on Line 10 of Form LD-1 or Line 18 of Form LD-2 must file an LD-203 report, unless that lobbyist has been listed on Line 23 of Form LD-2 as removed for all clients of the registrant prior to the beginning of the relevant LD-203 filing period. The Secretary and the Clerk view Lines 10 (LD-1), 18 and 23 (LD-2) as determinative for an individual lobbyist's obligation to file an LD-203 report, rather than the mechanics of the contributions electronic filing system, which is not relevant in the determination of a filer's legal obligations.

Sole proprietors and small lobbying firms are reminded that two contribution reports are required: one filed by the registrant and one filed by the listed lobbyist (even if the lobbyist is the registrant and vice versa).

Filers are expected to use reasonable care when filling out and submitting LD-1, LD-2, and LD-203 forms.

The coverage periods for the semiannual reports are January 1 through June 30, and July 1 through December 31. The Secretary and the Clerk do not have the authority under the LDA to grant extensions for filing LDA documents.

Mandatory Electronic Filing

Section 5 of the LDA was amended to require the mandatory electronic filing of all documents required by the LDA. The only exception to mandatory electronic filing is for the purpose of amending reports in the format previously filed, or for compliance with the Americans with Disabilities Act. Each electronic lobbying disclosure form provides usability for people with vision impairments who have the appropriate software and hardware. If you have questions regarding additional ADA accommodations, please contact the Senate Office of Public Records at 202-224-0758.

It is necessary for each active lobbyist to obtain his/her individual user identification number and password in order to file semiannual LD-203 reports electronically with the Secretary and Clerk. Each and every registrant and lobbyist is responsible for maintaining the confidentiality and use of the user password and for all filings made using their assigned user ID and password. Filers should notify the Secretary and Clerk immediately upon learning of any unauthorized use of a user ID and/or password, as it is presumed that filings are made by the filer.

Semiannual Reporting of Certain Contributions – Contents of Report

The core information required by Section 5(d) of the LDA and incorporated into Form LD-203 is: (1) certain contributions that are not disclosed in the LD-2 report; and (2) a certification that the filer has read and understands the gift and travel provisions in the Rules of both the House of Representatives and the Senate, and that the filer has not knowingly violated the aforementioned Rules.

The beginning part of Form LD-203 contains identifying information. Section 5(d) requires specific information regarding certain contributions and payments made by the filer (i.e., each active registrant and active lobbyist), as well as any political committee established or controlled by the filer. In determining contributions and/or payments to report, it is important to note that, in some cases, a leadership PAC (as defined by the Federal Election Campaign Act, FECA) or a former leadership PAC (for example, in the case of a lobbyist who was previously a covered official) may be a political committee established, financed, maintained, or controlled by a lobbyist. Also, a political committee that has changed from a principal campaign committee into a multicandidate committee (defined in the FECA) could be considered to have been established by a covered official or federal candidate. Finally, the FECA defines those organizations that may establish separate segregated funds (SSFs).

The middle part of Form LD-203 requires the filer to disclose for itself, and for any political committee the filer establishes or controls:

- The date, recipient, and amount of funds contributed (including in-kind contributions) to any Federal candidate or officeholder, leadership PAC, or political party committee (registered with the Federal Election Commission), if the aggregate during the period to that recipient equals or exceeds $200. Please note that contributions to state and/or local candidates and committees not required to be registered with the Federal Election Commission need not be disclosed.
- The date, the name of honoree and/or honorees, the payee(s) and amount of funds paid for an event to honor or recognize a covered Legislative Branch or covered Executive Branch official (except for information required to be disclosed by another entity under 2 U.S.C § 434).
- The date, the name of honoree and or honorees, the payee(s) and amount of funds paid to an entity or person that is named for a covered Legislative Branch official, or to an entity or person in recognition of such official (except for information required to be disclosed by another entity under 2 U.S.C § 434).
- The date, recipient, the name of the covered official, the payee(s) and amount of funds paid to an entity established, financed, maintained, or controlled by a covered Legislative or Executive Branch official or to an entity designated by such official (except for information required to be disclosed by another entity under 2 U.S.C § 434).
  A non-voting board member (e.g. honorary or ex-officio) does not control an organization for these purposes. For purposes of the LDA, the term "designated," for instance, includes a covered legislative branch official's or covered executive branch official's directing a charitable contribution in lieu of an honoraria pursuant to House, Senate, or executive branch Ethics rules. It also includes a payment that is directed to an entity by a covered official who is also on the board of the entity. In contrast, a contribution following a mere statement of support or solicitation does not necessarily constitute a

reportable event under Section 5(d) of the LDA without some further role by a covered official.

Please note that a charitable organization established by a person before that person became a covered official and where that covered official has no relationship to the organization after becoming a covered official, is not considered to be one established by a covered official.

Please also note that a covered official's de minimis contribution to a charity (in proportion to the charity's overall receipts of contributions) is not an indication of financing, maintaining, or controlling the charity (although supplemental facts might require reporting the contribution).

- The date, the name of honoree and/or honorees, the payee(s) and amount of funds paid for a meeting, retreat, conference, or other similar event held by, or in the name of, one or more covered Legislative Branch or covered Executive Branch officials (except for information required to be disclosed by another entity under 2 U.S.C § 434). Costs related to non-preferential sponsorship of a multi-candidate primary/general election debate for a particular office do not have to be disclosed on an LD-203 report.
- The date, the name of honoree, the payee(s) and amount of funds equal to or exceeding $200 paid to each Presidential library foundation and each Presidential inaugural committee. Please note that contributions to the official Presidential Transition Organization ("PTO") of the President-elect and Vice President-elect are reportable under the Presidential Transition Act.

In the case of items 2–6 above, if a lobbyist makes a reportable payment but is reimbursed by a registrant, the Registrant reports the payment as its own, rather than the lobbyist reporting the payment.

This section of the LDA has been written broadly, and, in light of other provisions in HLOGA (P.L. 110-81), it would be prudent to consult with the appropriate Ethics Committee, as well as the Office of Government Ethics, in order to determine if any event listed above is otherwise prohibited under law, Senate or House Rules, or Executive Branch regulations. For some events, it may be prudent to consult with the Federal Election Commission as well. Please note that HLOGA and the Federal Election Campaign Act are not harmonized to contributions of exactly $200.

Example 1: In State "A," a group of constituents involved in widget manufacturing decide to honor Senator "Y" and Representative "T" with the "Widget Manufacturing Legislative Leaders of 2008" plaques. Registrant "B" is aware that "Y" has checked with the Senate Select Committee on Ethics regarding her ability to accept the award and attend the coffee, and "T" has checked with the House Committee on Ethics. "B" pays caterer "Z" $500 and Hotel "H" $200 to partially fund the event. "B" would report that it paid $500 to "Z" and $200 to "H" on November 20, 2008 for the purpose of an event to honor or recognize "Y" and "T" with the plaques.

Example 2: After checking to discover if the activity is permissible, Lobbyist "C" contributes $300 on June 1, 2008 to Any State University toward the endowment of a chair named for Senator "Y." "C" would report the information above noting that the payment was made to Any State for the endowment of "Y's" chair.

Example 3: Senator "Y" has been asked to speak at a conference held in Washington, DC, sponsored by a professional association of which Registrant "B" is a member. "B" makes a donation of $100 to Charity "X" in lieu of the association paying a speaking fee (i.e., a contribution in lieu of honoraria). "B" would disclose a contribution of $100 on the date of the payment, with the notation that the payment was made as a contribution in lieu of honoraria to an entity designated by "Y."

Example 4: There is a large regional conference on "Saving Our River," sponsored by three 501(c)(3) organizations. Senator "Y" and Representative "T" are given "Champions of Our River" awards at a dinner event that is part of the conference. Registrant "B" contributes $3,000 specifically for the costs of the dinner event, paying one of the sponsors directly. At the time of the specific or restricted contribution, "B" was aware that "Y" and "T" would be honorees. Regardless of whether "B" is a sponsor under House or Senate gift rules and although B is not listed on the invitation as a sponsor (or the like) nor is publicly held out as a sponsor (or the like), since "B" partially paid for the cost of the event, "B" would disclose a payment of $3,000 on the relevant date payable to the sponsor with the notation that "Y" and "T" were honored.

Example 5: Registrant "B," an industry organization, hosts its annual gala dinner and gives a "Legislator of the Year" award to Representative "T." Revenues from the gala dinner help fund Registrant "B's" activities throughout the year. Registrant "B" must report: 1) the cost of the event (hotel, food, flowers, etc., but not indirect costs such as host staff salaries and host office overhead); 2), the payee(s) (as a convenience to filers, separate vendors may be aggregated by using the term "various vendors"); and 3) that the event honored Representative "T." Please note that "B" must still separately report the cost of any item that "B" gave "T." The fact that the event helped raise funds for the organization does not change the reporting requirement, though it could be noted in the filing.

Example 6: Registrant "B," an industry organization, has an annual two-day "Washington fly-in" for its members. Among the events for its members is an event on "The Importance of Industry G to the U.S. Economy." Senator "T" is listed on the invitation as a speaker at the event. Based on these facts alone, Registrant "B" would not need to report the event under this section. For a covered official to speak at such an event would not, in and of itself, form the basis for concluding that the official is to be honored or recognized. Supplemental facts might require reporting the cost of the event. For example, if Senator "T" were given a special award, recognition, or honor (which may not necessarily be through the receipt of a physical object) by the organization at the event, the cost of the event would have to be reported, even if the invitation did not indicate that such would be given. Simply designating a covered official as a "speaker" at an event at which the covered official receives a special award, recognition or honor, will not permit the filer to avoid or evade reporting the expenses of the event.

Example 7: Senator "Y" and Representative "T" are "honorary co-hosts" of an event sponsored by Registrant "R" to raise funds for a charity, which is not established, financed, maintained, or controlled by either legislator. "Y" and "T's" passive allowance of their names to be used as "co-hosts," in and of itself, is not sufficient to be considered "honored or recognized." The purpose of the event is to raise funds for Charity "V," not to honor or recognize "Y" or "T." Nor are these facts (i.e. being passive honorary co-hosts), in and of themselves, sufficient to treat the event as being held "by or in the name" of "Y" or "T." Supplemental facts might require reporting the cost of the event.

Example 8: Registrant "R" sponsors an event to promote "Widget Awareness." "The Honorable Cabinet Secretary Z" is listed on the invitation as an "attendee" or "special invitee" but will not receive an honor or award at the event. Based on these facts alone, "R" would not need to include the costs of this event on "R's" disclosure under this section. Mere listing of "Z's" anticipated attendance at an event the purpose of which is to promote Widget Awareness, in and of itself, is not sufficient to be considered "honored or recognized". Use of the phrase "The Honorable" in this context is consistent with widely accepted notions of protocol applicable to referencing certain very senior government officials. Supplemental facts might require reporting the cost of the event. For instance, if "Z" received a special, award, honor, or recognition by "R" at the event, "R" would have to report the costs of the event noting that "Z" was being honored or recognized.

Example 9: Registrant "B" buys a table at a dinner event sponsored by a 501(c) organization to honor Representative "T" but Registrant "B" is not considered a sponsor of the event under House and Senate gift rules. Lobbyist "C" pays the $150 individual ticket cost to attend the dinner, but is not considered a sponsor of the event under House and Senate gift rules. The purchase of a table or ticket to another entity's event, in and of itself, is not sufficient to be considered paying the "cost of an event." Supplemental facts might require reporting the cost of the event. For example, if (1) "B" or "C" undertake activities such that "B" or "C" becomes a sponsor of the event for House and/or Senate gift rule purposes; or (2) "B" or " C" purchase enough tickets/tables so that it would appear that they are paying the costs of the event and/or would not appear to be just ticket or table-buyers (regardless of whether "B" or "C" is a sponsor under House or Senate gift rules), then "B" or "C" would need to report the costs incurred by "B" or "C" (as the case may be) for the event, noting that Representative "T" was the honoree. In the case of filers purchasing multiple tickets and/or tables to an event, a case-by-case analysis will be needed to determine if the quantity is such that it would appear that the filer is paying the costs of the event.

Example 10: Lobbyists "C" and "D" serve on the board of a PAC as member and treasurer respectively. As board members, they are in positions that control direction of the PAC's contributions. Since both are controlling to whom the PAC's contributions are given, they must disclose applicable contributions of the PAC on their semi-annual LD-203 reports. If "C" and "D" serve on the board of a Separate Segregated Fund (SSF), they may report that they are board members of an SSF in lieu of reporting the SSF's applicable contributions as long as the SSF's contributions are reported in the connected organization's LD-203 report.

Example 11: Registrant "L" holds an annual fundraising event that honors one person from each of the 50 states whom "L" deems to have played a significant role for the cause "L" supports. In 2009, four of the honorees were covered legislative and executive officials. "L" must disclose the total amount that it paid for the event, disclosing in the payee section "various vendors," and disclosing the names of the four covered officials. Although not required, and thus at its option, "L" could note in the comments section that 4 of the 50 honorees were covered officials. Section 5(d) of the LDA does not contemplate a breakdown, delineation or separation of expenses

Example 12: Registrant "O" is a university. In June 2009, in conjunction with its commencement event, "O" conferred an honorary degree upon Senator "P." "O" would report all payments relating to the commencement event (chair rental, lunch for honorees, etc.) on its LD-203 report, listing "various vendors" as the payee, and Senator "P" as the honoree. Although not required, and thus at its option, "O" could comment that "P" received an honorary degree.

The final part of the LD-203 form is a certification that the filer has read and is familiar with those provisions of the Standing Rules of the Senate and the Rules of the House of Representatives relating to the provisions of gifts and travel and has not provided, requested or directed a gift, including travel, with knowledge that receipt of the gift would violate either Chamber's Rules. The form contains a check box for the certification, and the user ID and password process will verify the filer identity. Each and every registrant and lobbyist is responsible for maintaining the confidentiality and use of the user password and for all filings made using their assigned user ID and password. Filers should notify the Secretary and Clerk immediately upon learning of any unauthorized use of a user ID and/or password, as it is presumed that filings are made by the filer.

Please note that in the case of a registrant, a signatory is an individual who is responsible for the accuracy of the information contained in the filing. In all cases an individual lobbyist is responsible for all information contained in his or her report. Under section 6 of the LDA, the Secretary and Clerk refer the names of registrants and lobbyists who fail to provide an appropriate response within sixty (60) days to either officer's written communication rather than the name of the signatory. Both signatories and any third-party preparers should retain appropriate documentation to verify report contents. Third-party preparers should also retain appropriate documentation to demonstrate that they have authorization to make such filings on behalf of all filers (including lobbyist-employees of registrants) using their services.

Each registrant and active lobbyist, regardless of any contribution activity or any lack thereof, must file Form LD203 semiannually due to the certification provision.

SECTION 8 – TERMINATION OF A LOBBYIST/TERMINATION OF A REGISTRANT

Termination of a Lobbyist

The LDA is not specific as to how far into the future the registrant should project an expectation that an individual will act as a lobbyist. It seems neither realistic nor necessary to expect registrants to make such projections beyond the next succeeding quarterly reporting period. Accordingly, if a registrant reasonably expects an individual to meet the definition of a lobbyist in either the current or next quarterly period, the lobbyist should remain in an "active" status. If a registrant does not believe this to be the case, the lobbyist can be removed from the list of lobbyists for the registrant. A registrant may remove a lobbyist only when (i) that individual's lobbying activities on behalf of that client did not constitute at the end of the current quarter, and are not reasonably expected in the upcoming quarter to constitute, 20 percent of the time that such employee is engaged in total activities for that client; or (ii) that individual does not reasonably expect to make further lobbying contacts. In order to properly terminate a lobbyist, the registrant must complete Line 23 of Form LD-2, which is used to remove names of employees who are no longer expected to act as lobbyists for the client due to changed job duties, assignments, or employment status. Amending the LD-1 or LD-2 reports to erase a lobbyist listed on lines 10 or 18, respectively, is not a proper termination.

> Example 1: Lobbying Firm "Y" registers for Client "Z" on March 15, 2008, listing employees "A," "B," "C," and "D" on Line 10 of Form LD-1. For the first quarterly reporting period in 2008, "Y" will list "A," "B," and "C" on Line 18 of Form LD-2. "D" has no lobbying activities for that quarterly period, so he would not be listed. During the second quarter of 2008, "D" leaves firm "Y" to start his own lobbying business. For the second quarterly period, "Y" will report that "D" no longer meets the definition of "lobbyist" for Client "Z" on Line 23 of Form LD-2.
>
> Example 2: Lobbying Firm "Y" registers for Client "Z" as above listing the aforementioned "A," "B," "C," and "D" as lobbyists on March 15, 2008. One month after registration, "C" and "D," who engaged in lobbying activities for "Z" as partners of "Y," decide to leave the partnership effective June 1, 2008. On the Q2 Report for 2008, "Y" would report any lobbying activity for "C" and "D" on Line 18 of Form LD-2. "Y" would also reflect "C" and "D's" departure by listing them on Line 23 of Form LD-2 in the same filing.

An individual who no longer meets the definition of lobbyist under Section 3(10) of the LDA can be relieved from having to file an LD-203 report for future semiannual periods by proper removal from the registrant's active lobbyists list. This is accomplished by the registrant listing such an individual on Line 23 of the LD-2 quarterly report for each client for which the individual was previously listed. The obligation to file an LD-203 report arises from being listed as a lobbyist and not being terminated by the registrant/employer. Thus, if a lobbyist has not been properly terminated by being listed on Line 23 of the Form LD-2 for every client for which the lobbyist was listed, the Secretary and Clerk will expect to receive a semi-annual report from him/her.

> Example: Registrant "A" employs Lobbyist "C" who has lobbying activity on behalf of Client "R" in January and February 2008. In March, Lobbyist "C" no longer expects to engage in lobbying activities for "R" or any other client in the firm, although "C" will continue to do non-lobbying consultation for numerous clients. "A" removes Lobbyist "C" as an active lobbyist by listing "C" on Line 23 of the LD-2 form for the Q1 reporting period, and "C" is not listed on subsequent quarterly LD-2 reports. However in July, Lobbyist "C" is required to file an LD-203 report due July 30 disclosing his activity from January 1 through the date of his termination.

Termination of a Registrant/Client Relationship

Under Section 4(d) of the LDA, a lobbying firm may terminate a registration for a particular client when it is no longer employed or retained by that client to conduct lobbying activities and anticipates no further lobbying activities for that client. An organization employing in-house lobbyists may terminate its registration when in-house lobbying activities have ceased and are not expected to resume. Similarly, in situations in which a registration is filed in anticipation of meeting the registration threshold that subsequently is not met, a registrant also has the option of termination. Just as we interpret that the obligation to report quarterly under the LDA arises from active status as a registrant, we believe that a report disclosing the final lobbying activity of a registrant is mandatory. In order to terminate the registration, the registrant must file Form LD-2 by the next quarterly filing date, checking the "Termination Report" box, and supplying the date that the lobbying activity terminated. A valid termination report discloses lobbying income or expenses and any lobbying activity by lobbyists during the period up to and including the termination date.

> Example 1: Lobbying Firm "A" accepted a contract with Client "B" on January 1, 2008, began lobbying activities, and timely registered on or before February 14. On March 31, the contract with "B" ended. Lobbying Firm "A" must file Form LD-2 by April 20, 2008, disclosing the lobbying income from and lobbying activity for Client "B" that took place during the period January 1 through March 31. The firm will check the "Q1" box

on Line 8, the "Termination Report" box on Line 10, and fill in "3/31/2008" in the Termination Date space (also on Line 10).

Example 2: Corporation "C" filed its registration on February 14, 2008, listing employee AE" as its only lobbyist. Through March 31, "E" spends less than 20 percent of her total time in lobbying activities. "C" would not have filed a registration if it had foreseen that its lobbying activities would be so limited, and there is no expectation that "E" or any other employee of "C" will meet the LDA Section 3(10) definition of "lobbyist" for the April – June quarterly period nor that lobbying expenses will exceed $12,500. While Corporation "C" as a registrant must file a report for January – March 2008, "C" will check the "Termination Report" box on Form LD-2, write in 3/31/08, disclose the amount of expenses for the reporting period, and "E's" lobbying activity for the reporting period.

SECTION 9 – RELATIONSHIP OF LDA TO OTHER STATUTES

LDA and FARA

The technical amendments to the LDA made in 1998 reflect a determination that the Foreign Agents Registration Act (FARA) standards are appropriate for lobbying on behalf of foreign governments and political parties, but that LDA disclosure standards should apply to other foreign lobbying. An agent of a foreign commercial entity is exempt under FARA if the agent has engaged in lobbying activities and registers under the LDA. An agent of a foreign commercial entity not required to register under the LDA (such as those not meeting the de minimis registration thresholds) may voluntarily register under the LDA. The amendments reaffirm the bright line distinction between governmental and non-governmental representations, and are not meant to shroud foreign government enterprises. Questions relating to the Foreign Agents Registration Act must be directed to the Department of Justice Foreign Agent Registration Unit at (202) 514-1231.

LDA and IRC

Restrictions on lobbying by tax-exempt organizations are governed by the definitions in the IRC, not those of the LDA. The LDA and the IRC intersect in three different ways.

First, Section 15 of the LDA defines which registrants are eligible for the "safe harbor." LDA Section 15 allows entities that are required to report and do report lobbying expenditures under Section 6033(b)(8) of the IRC to use IRC definitions for purposes of LDA Sections 4(a)(3) and 5(b)(4). Section 15(b) of the LDA allows entities that are subject to Section 162(e) of the IRC to use IRC definitions for purposes of LDA Sections 4(a)(3) and 5(b)(4).

Second, Section 15 of the LDA advises registrants regarding how they should use IRC definitions. Prior to the 1998 technical amendments, the statute was not clear as to the extent to which eligible organizations could use IRC definitions for other (i.e., non-expense) reporting and disclosure requirements of the LDA. As a result of the amendments, registrants who make the Section 15 expense election must use for other reporting the IRC definitions (including the IRC definition of a covered Executive Branch official) for Executive Branch lobbying, and the LDA definitions for Legislative Branch lobbying.

Third, Section 15 allows electing registrants to insert the amount that is ultimately reportable to the Internal Revenue Service for LDA quarterly reports.

LDA and False Statements Accountability Act of 1996

The False Statements Accountability Act of 1996, amending 18 U.S.C. § 1001, makes it a crime knowingly and willfully: (1) to falsify, conceal or cover up a material fact by trick, scheme or device; (2) to make any materially false, fictitious, or fraudulent statement or representation; or (3) to make or use any false writing or document knowing it to contain any materially false, fictitious, or fraudulent statement or entry; with respect to matters within the jurisdiction of the Legislative, Executive, or Judicial branch. The False Statements Accountability Act does not assign any responsibilities to the Clerk and Secretary.

LDA and Prohibitions on the Use of Federal Funds for Lobbying

The LDA does not itself regulate lobbying by federal grantees, or contractors, though other laws, as well as contractual prohibitions, may apply. Questions concerning lobbying activities of federal grantees or contractors should be directed to the appropriate agency or office administrating the contract or grant.

Note, however, that Section 18 of the LDA prohibits 501(c)(4) organizations who engage in lobbying activities from receiving federal funds through an award, grant, or loan.

SECTION 10 – PUBLIC AVAILABILITY

The Act requires the Secretary of the Senate and the Clerk of the House of Representatives to make all registrations and reports available for public inspection over the Internet as soon as technically practicable after the report is filed.

SECTION 11 – REVIEW AND COMPLIANCE

The Secretary of the Senate (Office of Public Records) and the Clerk of the House (Legislative Resource Center) must review, verify, and request corrections in writing to ensure the accuracy, completeness, and timeliness of registrations and reports filed under the LDA.

SECTION 12 – PENALTIES

Whoever knowingly fails: (1) to correct a defective filing within 60 days after notice of such a defect by the Secretary of the Senate or the Clerk of the House; or (2) to comply with any other provision of the Act, may be subject to a civil fine of not more than $200,000, and whoever knowingly and corruptly fails to comply with any provision of this Act may be imprisoned for not more than 5 years or fined under title 18, United States Code, or both.

For Further Information

Senate Office of Public Records
232 Hart Senate Office Building
Washington, DC 20510
(202) 224-0758
http://www.senate.gov/lobby

Legislative Resource Center
B-106 Cannon House Office Building Washington, DC 20515
(202) 226-5200
http://lobbyingdisclosure.house.gov

INDEX

A

access, 22, 76, 78, 86, 113
accommodations, 107, 117
accountability, 3
accounting, 64, 110
acquisitions, 81, 103
ADA, 107, 117
adjustment, 34, 49
agencies, 4, 7, 11, 31, 35, 48, 69, 114
Air Force, 113
algorithm, 9, 36
alters, 111
Americans with Disabilities Act, 77, 107, 117
appropriations, 113
Appropriations Act, 113
assessment, 102
Attorney General, viii, 2, 32
audit, vii, 1, 4, 6, 38
authority(s), vii, viii, 1, 3, 4, 5, 21, 23, 33, 38, 69, 77, 80, 90, 91, 106, 116

B

background information, 33, 80
board members, 104, 105, 122
breakdown, 122
buyers, 122

C

Cabinet, 121
cable television, 68
candidates, 118
certification, 59, 117, 123
challenges, vii, 1, 4, 5, 27, 32, 37
chemical, 113
children, 83
citizens, 110
City, 41
clarity, 115
cleaning, 33
clients, 4, 54, 55, 56, 60, 61, 62, 63, 64, 75, 76, 78, 92, 95, 112, 114, 116, 125
coding, 76, 78
coffee, 120
commercial, 126
communication, 7, 68, 93, 95, 97, 105, 123
community, 3, 31, 32, 56, 59, 80, 81, 83
compensation, 7, 54, 67, 68, 75, 92, 93
competition, 83
compilation, viii, ix, 90
compliance, vii, viii, 1, 2, 3, 4, 5, 6, 8, 13, 19, 22, 23, 25, 26, 27, 31, 32, 33, 37, 38, 48, 57, 59, 74, 76, 84, 89, 107, 117
computer, 59
conference, 70, 105, 119, 120
confidentiality, 117, 123
conformity, 111

D

E

F

G

Writing Local History Today

Writing Local History Today

*A Guide to Researching, Publishing,
and Marketing Your Book*

Second Edition

Thomas A. Mason and J. Kent Calder

ROWMAN & LITTLEFIELD
Lanham • Boulder • New York • London

Published by Rowman & Littlefield
An imprint of The Rowman & Littlefield Publishing Group, Inc.
4501 Forbes Boulevard, Suite 200, Lanham, Maryland 20706
www.rowman.com

86-90 Paul Street, London EC2A 4NE

British Library Cataloguing in Publication Information Available

Library of Congress Cataloging-in-Publication Data Available

ISBN 978-1-5381-8261-1 (cloth)
ISBN 978-1-5381-8262-8 (paperback)
ISBN 978-1-5381-8263-5 (electronic)

To Christine and Tara

Contents

Acknowledgments

We are grateful to all those who supported the publication of a new edition of this book. We were encouraged and kept on task by our editor at Rowman & Littlefield, Charles Harmon, and by Aja Bain, publications manager for the American Association for State and Local History (AASLH). The AASLH's anonymous outside readers offered some suggestions that enabled us to revise the manuscript in useful ways. Ray E. Boomhower, senior editor at the Indiana Historical Society, provided permission to use the organization's Author's Guidelines, and Modupe Labode, curator at the National Museum of American History, read the manuscript and provided valuable suggestions for improvement. Kristi L. Palmer, dean of the University Library at Indiana University–Indianapolis, pointed out directions for developing the manuscript. Gregory M. Britton, editorial director at Johns Hopkins University Press, also read the work and offered support, as did Mary Jo O'Rear, well-known local historian of south Texas. Colleagues at The Rowman & Littlefield Publishing Group, Inc., guided the book through its writing and publication stages. We accept responsibility for the conclusions here presented.

Finally, our wives—Christine H. Guyonneau, university archivist at the University of Indianapolis, and Tara M. Carlisle, director, Digital Information Literacy, at Texas A&M University–Corpus Christi—helped us to think like archivists and librarians and to realize the expanding range of possibilities for conducting research in the digital age. We therefore dedicate this book to them.

Introduction

> People who have cultivated new and detailed knowledge of their locality can perform a notable service by communicating that knowledge. There is great value in researching, synthesizing, and disseminating new knowledge of a community. The writing of local history has expanded its horizons in exciting ways in recent years to embrace culture broadly defined to include a wide variety of topics including music, art, and the social and ethnic composition of the community.

This is how we began the first edition of this book, which appeared in 2013. While we are from the generation that came of age in a turbulent time, and were accustomed to living amidst an accelerated pace of societal change accompanied by violence and protest, we could not have anticipated or foreseen how the events of the last decade have changed the world in which we live.

Political and economic upheavals, climate disasters, mass shootings, and virulent diseases have become the order of the day, and institutions and ideas that felt certain and decided, even boring, are now contentious and dubious. Social media products once considered a benign means of enhancing community have become vehicles for fostering tribalism, division, and hatred through sophisticated technological advancements in coding and machine learning. Surveillance capitalism targets and preys on the youngest and most vulnerable among us, cashing in on the value of our personal information and privacy.

We have become accustomed to the idea that we live in a post-truth world, and each of us chooses to follow news and information sources that tell us the things we want to hear, or, as a survival technique, we forgo paying attention to the news altogether. Years of positive change in the realms of social justice, civil rights, and women's rights have been undermined and, in some cases, reversed with orchestrated efforts to ban books and restrict teaching that deals critically with such historical issues as slavery, conquest, expansionism, and race and gender inequities.

1

The realm of publishing, long accustomed to riding the waves of social and political change, has shared in these many disruptions and dislocations and has developed contingent policies and plans for surviving the onslaught. Publishers of local history, such as university presses, historical societies, and museums, hang on tenuously (or not) as library sales continue to decline, as costs rise, as institutional support lessens, and as new forms of dissemination, such as blogs and podcasts, become consumers' preferred methods for accessing information.

Nevertheless, the desire to publish local history remains and even grows. The wish to know more about the place in which you find yourself magnifies as we become increasingly mobile and as the outward features of the places in which we live become increasingly papered over with a thin veneer of heterogeneity. Why are these streets and schools named the way they are? Who are the people and the families who fought over this contested land? At no time in the last century have the skills and instincts of the local historian been as needed, or as little valued: objectivity, lucidity, curiosity, balance. Modupe Labode, curator at the National Museum of American History, has written:

> I've noticed that a hunger for history has been one of the responses to the pandemic and the crises in democracy. Also, there have been amazing projects and resources, ranging from "History Unfolded" at the United States Holocaust Memorial Museum in Washington (https://newspapers.ushmm.org) to "Mapping Inequality: Redlining in New Deal America" (https://dsl.richmond.edu/panorama/redlining/#loc=5/39.1/-94.58) that have helped people see their local community as part of a much larger regional, national, or even global historical movements. And these resources and experiences have only raised interest in writing a book as opposed to dampening the urge to explore local history in a book-length format.[1]

The coauthors of this book began working together in the 1980s at the Indiana Historical Society. Thomas A. Mason was named director of publications in 1987; J. Kent Calder began as editor there in 1983. They would work together until 1998, when Calder left to work in the field of college textbook publishing and later served as editorial director at the Wisconsin Historical Society and executive director of the Texas State Historical Association. Mason continued as director of what became the Indiana Historical Society Press until 2006, when he stepped down to resume a career in university teaching. During the time the two worked together, they published many books on Indiana history; founded the illustrated history magazine *Traces of Indiana and Midwestern History*; and advised and edited many authors working on local history topics. In all their work, a primary goal was to broaden the audience for state and local history by presenting sound scholarship written for a general audience in a well-designed form, whether in a book or a magazine article.

In 2014, after we published the first edition of this book, coauthor Calder began an eight-year stint as acquisitions editor and ultimately editorial director for the University of Oklahoma Press, a noted publisher since 1928 of Western and local history. During his time, he acquired books dealing with various aspects of local history in states such as Oklahoma, Texas, New Mexico, Arizona, Washington, and California. We believe that the new edition of this book has benefited from that experience. As we described in the first edition, it is important for those wanting to publish a book to understand how their editor thinks. This is no small task, but we have sought to provide as much knowledge in that realm as possible to demystify the process, even though it is a constantly moving target. One constant remains: Acquisition editors at university presses and historical societies are looking for good manuscripts to fill their pipeline and bring revenue and prestige to the press, and those authors with the best understanding of editors' expectations and standards, whether they are academic authors or independent scholars, will have the greatest success in getting their manuscript accepted for publication.

The pandemic caused numerous dislocations, including rapid movement to print-on-demand, disruptions in the supply chain, closures of museums and archives, cancellations of academic conferences and other kinds of gatherings that support book publishing, and budget cuts to libraries and archives. Most of these disruptions have had the potential to hamstring authors in completing research or in securing illustrations and permissions, thereby delaying book publication. In navigating these changes and overcoming these obstacles, publishers by necessity learned to streamline their processes and procedures, primarily doing away with or significantly altering any process that involved passing paper from one person to another. This made it possible for publishers to continue operations as staff members went home to work. As a result, most publishers no longer accept hard copy submissions of proposals, manuscripts, images, or permissions, making it even more important than it was previously for prospective authors to be able to navigate the digital world. Authors without those skills are going to have a difficult time working with publishers in the twenty-first century. We acknowledge such changes and offer advice to prospective authors about the best way to navigate them.

Because, as one reader of our proposal for a second edition stated, the "boundary lines of publishing history for the public are wider now" than they were in 2013, we have updated and expanded our sections on websites, blogging, and social media. The focus of the book remains on first-time authors (in some cases, only-time authors) who aspire to write studies (whether in print or online) based on original research, intending to create new knowledge in their field, and aimed at a popular audience.

We want this guide, however, to be especially useful for nonacademic authors who want to write books. There are many guides that advise academic authors on how to navigate the publishing world and the various processes involved in revising dissertations, publishing journal articles, working with scholarly publishers, and writing for an audience beyond their academic specialty, and much of this advice is applicable to those outside the academy wishing to write and publish a manuscript on local history as well. Nevertheless, local history authors operating independently and wishing to publish a book are animated by a different set of motivations than are academics, and much of the advice and instruction in such studies, such as how to revise a dissertation, is not pertinent to nonacademic authors.

What is the purpose of a book on local history in 2024? The authors who are the audience for this book are writing to commemorate an event; document a life, a family, or a community; preserve the memory of a place; or add to or correct the historical record. To do so successfully, that is, to provide information that will be valued by others doing research on the same or similar topics over years and decades to come, they will need to navigate the standards of quality for academic research without benefiting from academic rewards such as tenure and promotion (though museum and archive professionals can certainly advance their careers through their writing). Local history authors are generally not motivated to write for strictly pecuniary reasons. If they do have dollar signs in their eyes, they are likely headed for disappointment. Since unrealistic expectations regarding sales and remuneration are the biggest cause of conflict between author and publisher, we've added a considerable amount in this edition regarding the ever-changing and evolving economics of publishing, and we deal explicitly with that topic in chapter 4.

We have also followed readers' suggestions to invite others "of different gender/color/ethnicity into this project to contribute some thoughts or ideas." We have asked local history practitioners to read and comment on the various topics covered in this book as we seek to broaden our coverage and shed new light on navigating issues of cultural sensitivity and appropriation, conscious and unconscious bias, and the need for inclusivity as these issues pertain to research and writing.

This book had its origin in a panel discussion in which the authors participated—together with Beth E. Luey, Gregory M. Britton, and Susan Walters Schmid—titled "So You Want to Publish a History Book?" at the 2006 meeting in Phoenix of the American Association for State and Local History. It was based on Thomas E. Felt's classic book *Researching, Writing, and Publishing Local History*, first published in 1976 and last reprinted in 1988. Felt clearly identified his audience: "This book is directed to anyone who has already admitted an interest in studying the past and is now considering doing something about it besides reading the works of other historians."[2] *Writing Local History Today: A Guide to Researching, Publishing, and Marketing Your Book* is intended for the same audience as it exists today.

Although many of the interests of today's readers coincide with those for whom Thomas Felt wrote, and much of his advice and wisdom is still valid, the sources for research, the opportunities for dissemination of local history writing, and the economics of book publishing have changed drastically. Felt remains a vital presence in the current work. We have sought to retain a good deal of his organizational structure, much of his advice, and some especially good examples of what William T. Alderson referred to in the original foreword as Felt's "wry humor," which serves to remind us "that we shouldn't take ourselves too seriously as we do our serious work."[3]

"The goal of the author," we often explained to local historians aspiring to publication, "is to anticipate every reason an editor might have to say 'no' to your project." To do that, authors needed to be able to put themselves in the editor's place, see their own work as an editor might see it, and understand considerations involving the size of the market for a particular work, the quality of the research and writing, and the amount of effort it would take for a project to be successful. The better an author understands editorial considerations, the more likely that author is to be successfully published. This book is intended to help local historians fulfill their publication goals.

Of course, since Felt wrote his book (and since we published the first edition of this book in 2013), the world of publishing has changed dramatically. In 2013 we wrote:

> Only a few years ago, few could have imagined how smartphones and tablets, social networking, and cloud computing would change the world. Who could have foreseen in the early 2000s, say, the extent to which e-mail would become the realm of older business people, while the younger crowd extended their social lives and careers in geometric proportions through social networks such as MySpace, Facebook, LinkedIn, and dozens of others? We cannot know with any certainty what technological advancements are on the horizon or measure with any accuracy the effects they are likely to have on society, work, and communication. All we can know is that the pace of change will continue to accelerate, and the impact of those changes for all of us will mushroom.

Now, social media (one of the most effective means of promoting books) disseminates false and misleading information that has led to undermining our very democracy, its algorithms amplifying hostility and targeting those most vulnerable. Twitter (now X) is in the control of a controversial leader, and its various communities, including writing and publishing communities, are in chaos and looking to new alternatives (such as Mastodon, Post, Bluesky, and Hive) with uncertainty and trepidation. In the future, it is not likely that any one site will ever be as dominant as Twitter once was. Thus, online audiences will increasingly splinter, and authors and marketers will need to be attentive and creative in leveraging evolving social media tools for their benefit. Moreover, artificial intelligence in the form of Open AI's chatbox, ChatGPT, and other programs has received much attention for its ability to generate text and images from language prompts, and the worlds of education and publishing are only beginning to parse the ramifications of its ongoing development and evolution. With all the big tech companies investing heavily in AI, authors and publishers will have to keep up with the rapid changes in this realm in order to maintain the integrity of their work and ensure accuracy.

We still believe there is a place amid the roar of this technology and information revolution for the local historian. In fact, we contend that an understanding and appreciation of the value of local history is an antidote to many of the ills of information overload that beset us, especially in the realm of an overabundance of information that is not based on thoughtful examination of sources, solid methodology, and unbiased presentation.

And this is where much of the work of Thomas Felt remains useful. As he explains, there are two essential standards against which the work of the local historian is measured:

> One has to do with ethics, and one has to do with competence. There is an ethical principle common to all good work in history, whether the work be collecting, analyzing, editing, or writing history. It is not just the principle of respect for the truth, but of respect for the whole truth. The distinction is real. It is not enough to avoid lies; the truths that are told must be as complete as the teller can make them.[4]

This "ethical ideal," however, is not a sufficient condition for reliable and readable history. Felt continues with characteristic wryness: "One can have the ethics of a saint and still be an unreliable historian. What more is needed is competence—and that is the proper subject of this book."[5]

Of course the number of competencies required for successful local history publishing is vast and continues to grow at an accelerating pace. Added to the nuances and complexities of researching, writing, and traditional publishing is the need to ride the wave of technology and to accommodate the changing landscape in which the local historian works. A facility with basic computer programs will allow an author to be a helpful partner to their publisher and may even be the difference between landing a contract or not. As we have mentioned, in publishing as in most businesses, the pandemic necessitated streamlining of workflow and eliminating any procedures that weren't absolutely necessary, especially those that involved moving paper or hard copy around. In this new environment, if it's not digital, it doesn't really exist from an editor's or publisher's point of view. This work offers an introduction to these topics and issues, as well as references to other works for more in-depth study. As with the acquisition of any skill, competence is a matter of study and practice as well as passion and talent. Felt saw clearly that a "serviceable memory" and a solid "general education" enhance competence. These qualities, building on what he called "a continuing curiosity and alert intelligence," enable a passionate and talented local historian to produce a successful publication.

This book is inspired by all the talented local historians we have talked to and worked with over the years, and it is written for those like them who already possess the necessary curiosity, intelligence, and passion and are seeking greater competence in crafting their work and disseminating it widely. In the midst of rapid changes in the publishing landscape and the ways that editors and publishers think, practicing local historians must think about their audience and market in rather traditional ways and shape their work accordingly. A clear understanding of one's audience will affect the depth of research and style of writing that should be applied, as well as determine the distribution models that are most appropriate for any project. It will also enable an author to create an effective proposal, which is perhaps the most important key to landing a publishing contract.

NOTES

1. Modupe Labode, communication to the authors, September 19, 2023.
2. Thomas Edward Felt, *Researching, Writing, and Publishing Local History*, 2nd ed. (Nashville, TN: American Association for State and Local History, 1981), xi.
3. Felt, vii.
4. Felt, xii.
5. Felt, xiii.

ONE

Readers

Who Is Your Audience?

Identifying an audience is the most fundamental issue that any author or publisher—large or small—must address. "Who is your audience?" should be the first question a researcher/writer/publisher should ask. The answer to that question will determine the medium (printed book or article, website, microform) and level of detail in which the writer will present the results of research. From the nature of your audience, everything else follows in terms of how you communicate your content—the historical subject matter that is the result of your research. The nature of your audience will dictate—if your publication is successful—how your publication is written, designed, formatted (in print or electronically), marketed, and sold or otherwise disseminated.

With each sentence and paragraph, an author must make decisions about what to include and what to leave out, providing enough information so the reader has a proper context for the subject at hand but not so much that the reader becomes lost or bored with information that is commonly known. Only writers who have a good understanding of their audience can make such decisions.

For example, this book is written for a specific audience: those who are passionate about local history and who would like to have a better understanding of the options available for publication of their research. Readers of this book will be involved in researching their family, their community, or a particular topic that interests them, and they would like clues about how to enhance that research and make their writing of it more effective. They will also be seeking a better understanding of the publishing process: how editors and publishers think and methods for increasing the likelihood that their manuscript or proposal will receive thoughtful consideration rather than no consideration at all. Readers will be interested in at least an introduction to the many ways in which the publishing world is changing and the impact of those changes on local history publishing.

Local history publishing has its roots in a time when there was little or no distinction between the work of amateur and professional historians and when even the best of these authors infused their work with myth and boosterism in order to celebrate a community, establish its superiority, and perhaps encourage immigration. These are the kind of men who founded the Indiana Historical Society in 1830, as one example, within the generation following statehood. That society defined its mission or "objects" of "the collection of all materials calculated to shed light on the natural, civil, and political history of Indiana, the promotion of useful knowledge and the friendly and profitable intercourse of such citizens of the state as are disposed to promote the aforesaid objects."[1] These "objects" and the language in which they are expressed reflect a patrician attitude or ideal that would be the norm as leading men formed historical societies and associations throughout the country in the nineteenth century.

The Indiana Historical Society met only twelve times between its founding in 1830 and its revitalization in 1886, when—according to former director Peter T. Harstad—a group of "lawyers, writers, professional historians, editors, librarians, and Hoosiers from many walks of life gradually transformed a state-chartered corporation that received a few small appropriations from the General Assembly into a multifaceted, privately financed twentieth-century institution."[2] Two aspects of this statement are particularly noteworthy. One is that by the 1880s, the patricians of the early nineteenth century were giving way in the local history realm to a professional class whose occupations allowed them the leisure to write history and whose writing was primarily commemorative, promotional, or celebratory. The other is the emergence in the late nineteenth century of the professional historian, and at that point the purposes of and audiences for local history began to diverge in ways that remain significant for today's practitioners.

This divergence, however, did not fully manifest itself for some time. The goals and perspectives of the academic and nonacademic historians coincided in the beginning so that they found common ground in collecting and publishing important foundational documents, establishing journals such as the *Indiana Magazine of History*, and providing necessary funding to make the partnership viable.

Other than the historical societies and associations, the most important publishers were commercial entities that created a successful formula that consisted of engaging agents, or "compilers," to solicit contributions from prominent individuals and families and asking them to pay a fee to be included in a proposed volume of local (usually county) history. The process not only funded the manufacturing of the volume but also included a built-in distribution mechanism through family and business networks, taking a good deal of the risk out of the publishing venture. Anyone who does research in the field is familiar with these volumes and with the kind of material they offered. Regardless of the location, the story that emerged was the same for all. In *On Doing Local History*, Carol Kammen refers to Indiana folklorist Richard Dorson's *American Folklore and the Historian* (1971) to explain:

> They began with a reference to Indians and the wilderness topography; hailed the first settlers; noted the first churches, the first schools, the first stores; . . . swung into full stride with the establishment of the newspaper, the militia, the fire department, and the waterworks; . . . recounted the prominent citizens of the community, and enumerated famous personages . . . who had passed through; listed a roster of Civil War dead; and rounded off the saga with descriptions of the newest edifices on Main Street.[3]

This is not a bad description of what even today's academic historians think about the worst characteristics of local history writing and publishing, but these volumes are invaluable for researchers since they preserved detailed information that in many cases is elsewhere unavailable.

This successful publishing formula declined as the forces of modernization in the twentieth century such as automobiles, new roles for women, and a more international focus derived from World War I became prevalent. Local history became old-fashioned. Local history writing and publishing nevertheless continued, supported primarily by historical societies and commercial publishers who could figure out how to make it pay, and the best way to make it pay was to continue in the celebratory vein and to ignore the impact of significant changes taking place in the world. Academic historians increasingly sought to work with the growing number of university presses, which in the beginning received significant support from their institutional hosts to further scholarly discourse. The scholarly presses had a greater impact in serving the tenure and promotion needs of the academics than local commercial publishers or historical societies, and at this point the divergence of the two modes of writing and publishing local history became pronounced, though the journals of some organizations, especially state historical societies, often took a different trajectory, publishing both local and academic historians.

Texas offers a particularly revealing landscape for studying the diverging strains of state and local history writing. This is not only because many books are published on Texas history each year by a wide range of publishers, but also because Texas is a place where the hold of a particular romantic interpretation of history continues stubbornly to survive despite the efforts of a couple of generations of academic historians to revise it, temper it, and encourage it to evolve in ways that reflect the conditions and inhabitants of a state that is rapidly changing.

Historian Walter L. Buenger, professor at the University of Texas and former chief historian for the Texas State Historical Association, has

worked for many years on defining the various approaches to Texas history and interpretations of Texas identity, along with their ramifications
for publishing. He is among a number of historians who have identified
a particularly resilient traditionalist approach in which little attention is
paid to women, and non-Anglo populations are generally not considered
as worthy or capable of controlling Texas. While such attitudes have been
tempered since the 1960s, the traditionalist approach depicting a time
when "sundrenched white men strode nobly into the frontier" is still
strong and reflects a desire to retain traditional values and identity in a
state that is rapidly growing more diverse and more urban.[4]

In his essay "Three Truths in Texas," which appeared as the introduction to the anthology *Beyond Texas through Time: Breaking Away from Past
Interpretations*, Buenger acknowledged that the competing historical interpretations of traditionalism and revisionism had evolved into three truths
that moved in "a multilinear fashion" that is "three evolving, sustained,
and only partially connected ways of seeing the past." These were what
he calls "updated traditionalists," "persistent revisionists," and a third
interpretation that he labels "cultural constructionists." Updated traditionalists celebrate and preserve the accomplishments and influence of
leaders in business, politics, and military affairs, and their work provides
moral lessons for today's readers. Persistent revisionists are intent on
broadening the definition of who is a Texan from the perspectives of gender, class, and race. While they have done great service creating a more
inclusive story of Texas, they often depict Mexican Americans, African
Americans, and Indians, as victims rather than as "agents of their own
fate." Cultural constructionists, according to Buenger, examine the interactions between cultural groups at specific places and times, especially
those that involve conflict. They are writing for a national audience of
academic and professional historians in an effort to "cross the spatial and
intellectual borders of Texas and Texas history."[5]

The point of this discussion for local historians generally is not that
one form of writing is necessarily more publishable than another (though
uncomplicated celebrations that do not account for more recent historical interpretations will likely have more difficult sledding). The point is
rather that such varieties of approaches to history writing exist, that they
appeal to different audiences and publishers, and that an awareness of
them and where one's work falls within them will help local historians
communicate with editors about their audience and find the publisher
that is right for them.

Potential audiences for local history, therefore, range widely. Genealogists and family historians write histories of particular families, which

they intend for an audience numbering in the hundreds. Authors of such micro-histories often find that the most cost-effective means of publishing their work is to have it duplicated at a quick-print company that can bind the work attractively, and the author can donate the work to family members and local and genealogical libraries. While print-on-demand technology offers new outlets for this kind of work, broad readership is generally not the primary goal of genealogists.

Graduate students often succeed in writing theses or dissertations that meet the standards and expectations of their committees of a half dozen specialist scholars. But recent alumni of graduate programs often face an awakening—if they are lucky, it is an epiphany—when they try to persuade a press to publish a book based on such a dissertation.

An old proverb about graduate education asserts that graduate students learn more and more about less and less until finally they know everything about nothing. A common misconception of first-time authors and neophyte researchers—including students at all levels—is a reluctance to give up or excise from their draft book any minute bit of detail because it took so long to discover during the course of research. The result is a dissertation or book of doorstop weight that few people will read.

If they are going to reach a nonspecialist audience, all authors have to do a crossover of sorts—they must *con*verge on their specialized subject, but they must also *di*verge to put that subject in context and provide enough background so it will be intelligible to a nonspecialist audience. Getting that balance right is the great challenge of authorship, and those authors who can do it will succeed and get their work published. Modupe Labode sheds additional light on the process of identifying an audience:

> I recently was co-facilitating an exhibition planning workshop for a community group, and when we asked who their ideal audience was, to a person they said "everyone." Or as my colleague Elee Wood used to tell museum studies students, "the general public is not an audience." I suspect that many first-time authors have the same response if someone asked who they wanted to read their book! And they might also be stumped when asked to be more specific about the audience. Identifying the audience helps the author determine how they will approach a topic. There are often concentric circles (or Venn diagrams) of audiences. For example, a book about nineteenth-century coverlets of Lancaster, Pennsylvania, might have as its primary audience specialists in Pennsylvania coverlets, but that could also be widened to include people interested in nineteenth-century coverlet design, to those interested in domestic spaces and decorative arts, to those interested in craft work in the 1800s. This audience does not equal everyone—nor does it mean the general public—but the author will have identified some specific networks of potential readers, and helped the prospective press identify their approach to the book.[6]

In his study of publishing local history, Thomas E. Felt identified five audience groups:

1. "Dedicated and knowledgeable students of your subject . . . never more than a handful."
2. "Adults with a real interest in at least some aspect of your subject"— maybe in the hundreds.
3. Adults, "sharing some interests with members of the last group," but with a more casual interest in history—who would be attracted to well-illustrated coffee-table books—a secondary market—with higher production costs.
4. "A juvenile readership"—to meet educational standards (set by state and federal education authorities)—aimed at school and library sales. The Indiana Historical Society Press has successfully published books for young (middle and high school) readers.
5. "Adults living or working outside the locality or special topic you are describing"—which requires an exemplary study by a sophisticated author.[7]

It is important to distinguish between your audience and the potential universe of people who will be willing to pay for your publication. Those two parts of your market overlap, but they by no means coincide. The Indiana Historical Society Press learned to its sorrow that the number of people who would actually pay for printed copies of conference proceedings—no matter how important to the historical field—or research tools such as cumulative indexes for historical periodicals is negligible. But when we put such publications on our website, they received tens of thousands of page views, even before they were announced, marketed, or advertised. Cases such as indexes and conference proceedings demonstrate in the starkest terms the contrast between mission fulfillment and cost recovery.

What are your options for reaching your audience—be it a book-buying audience or an audience of Web users who expect to get their information for free? The good news for authors and historical organizations is that it is easier to get published in some form today than ever before. The advent of electronic publishing has broadened the options for authors and historical organizations and revolutionized the publishing industry.

The more sobering news is that the specialized monograph that used to be the bread and butter of historical societies and university presses is much less tenable than it used to be. Specialized monographs (books focused on a particular research topic) now sell two hundred or three hundred copies if the publisher is lucky—numbers at which it is impossible to recover production cost. As a result, historical societies and university presses are seeking "mid-list" titles that will appeal to a more general, nonspecialist audience. The specialized monograph is clearly beleaguered but can be viable in the right circumstances. Publishers with title lists in specialized subject areas such as military history, especially the Civil War, and museum publishers with title lists focusing on art history—and the knowledge of how to market to their subject areas—can successfully market such monographs.

The nature of the audience will drive the shape and characteristics of your publication. If the audience is "dedicated and knowledgeable students of your subject . . . never more than a handful"—Felt's category 1—then your publication can go to extended length and into minute detail, but you should consider a bound photocopied or Web-based publication, not a printed book, the production of which would be cost ineffective. If the audience is primarily "adults with a real interest in at least some aspect of your subject" or a more casual interest in history—Felt's categories 2 and 3—then your publication can be of short or medium length and can go into some detail on the subject, always subordinating detail to a role of illustrating and substantiating the broad argument, interpretation, and narrative of the book. Once the nature of the audience has shaped the characteristics of the publication, and you have researched, written, and produced it, then you and your publisher will be ready to market your publication (topics discussed in the following chapters).

To justify the expense of a book in the twenty-first century, you need to have a potential book-buying public—not just an audience—of at least several hundred. As of 2023 the average self-published book sells 250 copies; the average self-published author makes $1,000 per year from the sale of their books; 33 percent of self-published authors make less than $500 per year; 90 percent of self-published books sell less than 100 copies; and 20 percent of self-published authors report making no income from their books.[8] While new media in various formats, including all forms of social media, provide a wide range of alternative delivery systems for historical content and may bring that content to many more individuals, the writing still may not justify the investment and risk that is the key to any book project and to understanding the thinking of editors and publishers.

CHOOSING AND WORKING WITH A PUBLISHER

For those who are writing on a subject that has appeal beyond the specific topic or locale with which they are immediately concerned (Felt's category 5), a full-service publisher will be desired. Finding a publisher that is a good fit for your project is no small task, and those who go into it without a sound understanding of how the process works will have a diminished chance for success and a greater likelihood for disappointment.

There are many kinds of publishers that might be suitable for a book-length work of local history. They range from very small to very large and from not-for-profit and mission driven to commercial and profit-driven. They operate in different ways and serve different purposes. To reach your eventual audience of readers, you will first need to appeal to an audience of prospective publishers' representatives, generally known as acquisitions editors (AEs) or sponsoring editors. An acquisitions editor, once persuaded of the value of your work and its fit for a press's list, will serve as an author's representative throughout the publishing process, making arguments for your project's success to co-workers, colleagues, and, in some cases, editorial board members.

TYPES OF PUBLISHERS

On the not-for-profit side of the publishing equation are university presses and presses affiliated with historical and educational organizations. On the commercial side are commercial scholarly publishers, trade publishers, and vanity presses. Although these publishers vary widely in terms of how they work with authors, develop manuscripts, and reach intended markets, any of them might serve the purposes of a local historian if considered rationally according to an author's audience and expectations.

Having worked for state historical societies and university presses throughout our careers, the authors of this book are partial to these outlets for serious local history that seeks a lasting impact on the field or subject areas it addresses. Local historical organizations often encompass museums and archival collections, and some have publishing operations of one kind or another. As publishers, they might have the capacity to bring books to the market independently or through partnerships with other entities. They can also serve as a conduit for grants and fundraising to help support publishing projects. Most state historical organizations have publishing departments or full-service presses, such as the Minnesota Historical Society Press, the Indiana Historical Society Press, the Texas State Historical Association Press, and many others. These presses have their own marketing departments, as in the case of Minnesota, or they partner with university presses to publish and distribute books, as the Texas State Historical Association does with Texas A&M University Press through the Texas Book Consortium.

The primary mission of university presses is to publish scholarship in particular disciplines that will bring respect and prestige to the press and its host university through awards and positive reviews, while also adding to the bottom line through sales. According to the Association of

University Presses website, "the university press's mission is to publish work of scholarly, intellectual, or creative merit, often for a small audience of specialists or a regional community of interest."[9] While university and historical organization presses receive support from their host institutions, generally in terms of salaries and benefits for employees, and are considered not-for-profit, as Beth Luey explains in her *Handbook for Academic Authors*, "That does not mean they don't need to make money. They must be responsible publishers, using limited resources wisely, and they must on balance earn more than they spend."[10] Book publishing, whether commercial or scholarly, has always been a game of small margins, and many of the trends that make publishing challenging in terms of finances were only exacerbated during the pandemic when everyone was sent home to work remotely, bookstores and libraries closed, and authors were not able to travel and do research.

Declining institutional support and library sales, along with mission-driven incentives to publish work about their particular states and regions, have led many university presses into what is called regional trade publishing—that is, publishing books about a particular region in the realms of history, geography, environment, music, and art that will appeal to an audience larger than that of the average scholarly book.

Publishing for the "trade," or the retail market, involves risks that go beyond those of scholarly publishing, and university presses must exercise caution when deciding to take on those risks. Large trade publishers such as Random House, Simon & Schuster, HarperCollins, and others publish books intended to reach large general audiences, and they sell their books through retail outlets. They compete for manuscripts by offering advances on "royalties," or future earnings. (See chapter 4 for a discussion of the "Economics of Publishing" and the glossary.) University presses are generally aiming for a sweet spot in terms of an audience that is too small for a large trade publisher to consider, yet larger than that of the average scholarly monograph. In many instances, local history about a particular region can reach such an audience. For writers of local history navigating this space, it is useful to have some knowledge of the differences between trade publishing and university press publishing.

As a general practice, acquisitions editors at trade houses deal only with agents. Manuscripts or proposals sent to trade editors directly have very little chance of ever being read, much less responded to. On the other hand, while AEs at scholarly presses will deal with agents on occasion, they generally prefer not to. Dealing with agents and the trade usually involves navigating such issues as advances to authors, royalties based on retail sales rather than net sales, higher royalty rates for e-books and subsidiary rights, lower prices with steep discounts offered to retailers, and the right of retailers to return books that don't sell. University presses and other not-for-profit publishers have a lot to consider when taking on a trade book, and it's not uncommon for any of the following to happen when they try:

- Putting significant time and energy into figuring out potential sales and making an offer to an agent that is not strong enough to be accepted and is often not even in the ballpark.
- Successfully negotiating a project with an agent and publishing a book that doesn't pay for the resources that went into it (including the advance on royalties).
- Being inundated with returns from retailers a few months after publication.
- Having a disgruntled author on hand who is disappointed in the level of sales achieved and blames it on the marketing department for not doing enough.

In every aspect of the publishing process, realistic expectations are the key to success. Local history authors who believe their project has the potential to reach an audience in the tens of thousands and the wherewithal to convince an agent to represent them should go that route. But authors working with university presses and other nonprofit presses should not expect to receive the same kinds of terms they might at a large trade publishing house.

University presses have much to offer authors wishing to publish local history, however, especially if they would like their work to be taken seriously as a historical contribution. There are around 140 university presses in North America, and, as the Association of University Presses website states, they are "at the center of the global knowledge ecosystem" that serves the university and scholarly community. They also reach beyond the academy to provide "informed and engaged peer-reviewed scholarship published to the highest standards."[11] Peer review is the practice that differentiates scholarly publishing, not-for-profit or commercial, from other kinds of publishing endeavors. It is a method for ensuring the scholarly quality of manuscripts before publication and involves securing expert readers in pertinent disciplines to review and comment on such topics as quality of research and writing, the nature of the audience, and the value to the field. We will say more about the details of the process and how to navigate it in chapter 3. Suffice it to say for now that, despite its flaws, it is the foundation of scholarly publishing, which in turn is the foundation for new knowledge. While peer review is indispensable for scholarship, it can feel intrusive and onerous to authors outside the

academy when they come upon it for the first time. The best peer reviewers are those who will offer constructive criticism in a thoughtful manner
that will encourage the authors to make any suggested revisions to improve the quality of the book. Acquisitions editors and university presses
publishing books for general audiences will seek readers who will understand the need to evaluate a manuscript for historical accuracy as well as
accessibility and appeal. The process, properly undertaken, almost never
fails in helping to make a better book.

In addition to the regional publishing efforts of university presses,
many commercial publishers of serious nonfiction have divisions, or
imprints, that publish local history. Specialized commercial local history
publishers that provide books for niche audiences in the local history
realm include Arcadia Publishing, founded in 1993, and the History
Press, begun in 2004 and acquired by Arcadia Publishing in 2014. These
presses have found ways to work with organizations and communities
to publish projects that reach a general audience and are financially viable. Driven by passion for preserving and commemorating the past and
taking advantage of new technology, such presses have played a major
role in the increase in local history publishing. According to its website,
"Arcadia has blended a visionary management approach with the in-
novative application of state-of-the-art technology to create high-quality
historical publications in small local niches." It has eight thousand books
in print and releases hundreds of new titles each year. It is best known
for its Images of America series that "celebrates a town or region, bringing to life the people, places, and events that define the community,"
primarily through historical photographs. It also has series on sports,
railroads, aviation, postcards, business, and schools. The site boasts a
series of Legendary Locals.[12]

Likewise, the History Press has found a formula for making local history publishing profitable. The guidelines for authors encourage prospective authors to spend time with the catalog and become familiar with the
twenty or so series offered by the press, including American Heritage,
American Legends, Brief History, Definitive History, Disaster, Forgotten
Tales, Vintage Images, Sports, and Wicked. Presses like Arcadia Publishing and the History Press, producing books in the traditional vein, help to
account for the continuing increase in local history publishing, and they
provide new options for those working seriously on local history topics.[13]

These books do not necessarily move the dialogue between traditionalists and revisionists forward, and they are not meant to since that is
primarily an academic exercise. Instead, they should move forward the
kind of goals ascribed generally to local historical societies by Anne W.
Ackerson in her entry for the *Encyclopedia of Local History* (3rd ed.) on

"Local Historical Societies and Core Purpose." Publications done well can connect people to the past, engage communities, and build partnerships that maximize the value and reach of a shared understanding of the connections between the past and the future.[14] Authors should also bear in mind that these kinds of presses do not engage in the practice of peer review to ensure historical accuracy. Authors who are working with presses that do not require peer review should consider building time in their schedule to secure their own readers with the necessary expertise and ability to provide honest commentary that can help avoid embarrassment when the book appears.

For many writing local history, then, a smaller scholarly press that publishes in the target area of interest is going to be the best bet for reaching the intended audience. While advances on royalties will be slim to none, books published by these presses will stay in print longer than they would with a strictly trade press, and they will carry the imprimatur of a scholarly press, even if the work itself is not intended for a strictly scholarly audience. For authors, especially first-time authors, who want to be taken seriously, publication by a university press, or other presses with rigorous peer review and editing standards, is the way to go. Acquisitions editors for these presses are accessible, and you can meet them at conferences and email them directly. It is good to do some research to discover which AEs are responsible for the local history lists and to address them by name when you are emailing them for the first time either to set up a meeting at a conference or to gauge interest in receiving a letter of inquiry or proposal.

Finally among the various types of publishers are self-publishers who offer authors a range of publishing services, from editing and design to production and marketing, for a fee. The publishers have proliferated during the digital age and serve useful purposes for authors of all kinds. Local history authors who want a book to sell for their family, business, church, or other organization, who don't have any desire to go through the peer review process, or who wish to bring out a book in a hurry might wish to consider such an outlet for their work. We will discuss them at greater length in chapter 4.

THE PROPOSAL

The vehicle (coin of realm) by which this information is communicated to an editor is the proposal. The quality of your proposal reflects the quality of your book project, your qualifications for writing it, and your understanding of your audience and how to reach it. It should be undertaken with a good deal of care and consideration, for it will serve as your primary tool for communicating with an acquisitions editor. The proposal is such an important part of the process of securing a publisher that one author has written an entire very successful book about it. Primarily meant to guide academic authors, Laura Portwood-Stacer's *The Book Proposal Book: A Guide for Scholarly Authors* provides a good deal of advice that is pertinent for independent authors writing outside the academy as well, especially those wanting to solicit university presses and commercial publishers.[15]

Most presses will have guidelines for authors on their website, and some will provide a form for providing necessary information about a project. It is important for prospective authors to pay attention to the detailed information found here. If you think of an acquisitions editor as an audience who will be judging the quality of your book project and its fit for their list, then making it clear that you have reviewed the instructions for submission is a good first step toward a positive response. Editors are always pleased to learn that prospective authors are paying attention to instructions, because that is a necessary condition for being successful at each stage of the publishing process, from putting a contract in place to submitting the manuscript to working with copyeditors and the marketing department. It goes a long way in editorial meetings when an editor seeking approval for a project can provide evidence to colleagues that an author has shown themselves to be attentive to instruction.

At the beginning of the pandemic, many presses created a proposal submission portal for receiving digital submissions. Since acquisitions editors were working remotely from different parts of the country, the online submission portal allowed proposals to be placed in a digital folder to which all editors had access. This solved several problematic issues for editors, some of which had nothing to do with remote work. All editors were notified when a new proposal was received, and the author who submitted it received an automated notice to that effect, thanking them for submitting and letting them know to allow up to two months for evaluation. Authors were told not to submit a proposal more than once, obviating the need for editors to be constantly checking with one another to see who had received what proposal before they move something forward or reject it. The website let authors know that the editors would only receive proposals sent through the online submission form and would not respond to proposals sent through the postal mail, a necessity early on when there was often no one around to check the regular mail or send hard copy proposals to AEs. In addition, the website made clear the kinds of submissions that would not be accepted, such as fiction or poetry.

Another advantage of the online proposal submission form was that the "submit" button didn't appear until the submitter had provided all the requested information in some version of the following fields (*with commentary in italics*):

- Copy of curriculum vitae or résumé, including your contact information, occupation, education, book publications (with publisher, publication date, and estimated unit sales), and journal and magazine articles.
  [*Establishing credentials for authorship.* **Note:** *Editors always like to receive sales information for previous books if possible.*]

- Length of work in words.
  [*Use your word processing program's word count tool (preferably Microsoft Word), and make sure to include word count of notes and bibliography in calculation.*]

- Number and type of illustrations to accompany the text.
  [*Specify color and/or black-and-white photographs, line drawings, maps, charts, graphs, and any other graphic images. Editors will look at this carefully since illustrations, especially color illustrations, add significant expense to a book. Authors may be asked to help find financial support, or a subvention, for a book, especially if it involves numerous photographs or artwork that is expensive to procure or reproduce.*]

- Estimated date for completing the manuscript. Percentage of manuscript currently complete.
  [*This date will help an editor who is interested in pursuing the project decide whether it would be best to discuss with the author the possibility of moving the project forward toward a contract on proposal, or advance contract, which would include the date for the final manuscript and all maps, images, and permissions to be submitted, or wait for the complete manuscript. For an advance contract, some presses will send the proposal out for review before contracting, and some will offer a contract on proposal without peer review. In either case, the final manuscript will be sent out for peer review.*]

- Five-hundred-word description of the book project, including its purpose, audience, scope, contribution to scholarship, and relationship to the existing literature on the topic.
  [*This five-hundred-word description is probably the most important part of the proposal. If the project moves past the proposal stage, editors will use this description to prepare materials that will go to necessary committees for approval along the way to a contract.*]

- Author, title, publisher, and date of publication of significant comparable or competitive books.

[*Comparable books, or "comps," should not be more than five years old. These books are the primary means, along with sales of an author's previous books, by which editors project sales for the project, another necessary step in moving it forward. This list will also indicate the extent to which authors understand exactly who their audience is. Competitive books should also be recent books dealing with the same or similar topics as the proposal. They reveal an author's awareness of where a book fits into the literature and why it is needed*].

- Table of contents, with descriptions of each chapter.
  [*This is a standard piece of the proposal package. Chapter descriptions should be brief, no more than two or three sentences, and they should be written in a fashion that will encourage an editor to want to read more.*]

- Two sample chapters, preferably including an introductory chapter that describes the work.
  [*Beyond the introduction, choose a chapter to include that has the greatest ability to stand alone and represent the overall quality of the manuscript.*]

- Sample bibliography.
  [*The bibliography doesn't have to be exhaustive, but it should represent the range of sources used in creating the manuscript. It allows editors and possibly reviewers to ensure that necessary sources have been consulted.*]

- Names and email addresses of three or more experts in your field of study who are qualified to review your manuscript and can do so objectively.
  [*This list of names can be tricky for local historians who are coming from outside the academy. The basic idea is to provide information about the highest quality readers the author trusts to provide useful and constructive criticism in evaluating the work should it go out for peer review. Editors will take the author's list of potential readers into consideration, but they have no obligation to use it in the peer review process. Authors should also let editors know if there is a particular peer reviewer who should not be considered because of some indication that the reader might not be able to provide an unbiased review.*]

- Simultaneous submission.
  [*There is nothing wrong with submitting a proposal to more than one publisher if editors are aware that it is being done. Once an editor decides to expend the time and resources of the press to find reviewers and send a project out for review, the editor and author will generally agree that the author will not move forward with another publisher until the peer review is complete and the proposal or manuscript is either accepted for publication or rejected. Authors who do wish to send out proposals to multiple presses will still need to format them to each press's standards.*]

The online proposal form ensures that the editor receives all the necessary proposal materials needed to make an informed decision about a project. A proposal is not easy to create, but it is a necessary document for any successful book publication project. Even authors whose manuscripts are complete should create a proposal to make a case for the value and importance of their work, knowing that the information will be necessary to help an editor move a project forward. Of course, after all that work, authors can sometimes be disconcerted by the short amount of time that it takes an editor to write a letter of rejection. By reviewing a proposal, an editor can tell right away if a project is not a good fit for their list. They read many submissions daily and usually can tell quickly if a project has potential for their press. Authors who receive rejections should not necessarily expect a lengthy justification for a rejection. Editors know what they are looking for, and they may say little more than that the project is "not a good fit for the list." Editors, whether they acquire a project for commercial or not-for-profit presses, are entrepreneurs whose reputation is based on the quality of their "list," or the cumulative success of the projects they sign for their press. They know what they are looking for, and if they tell you that your project is not a good fit, they are not likely to be argued otherwise. An author who received such a rejection should simply move on to the next prospective publisher, where they might find a better fit. Finally, authors should keep in mind that even a rejected proposal is not a waste of time, because it will be needed by the next publisher for consideration as well.

To lessen the likelihood of such a rejection, authors should send editors a letter of inquiry to gauge interest in receiving a full proposal. This should be a brief email that provides information about the author and the project and asks if an editor would be interested in receiving a proposal. Authors can also ask to schedule a meeting with an editor at an upcoming conference. Even when projects are not likely to be a good fit, prospective authors can learn a lot about an editor's decision-making process from an in-person meeting.

Thus, the climate for local history publishing is as promising as it was when we published the first edition of this book in 2013, with many options available. If anything, however, the need for reliable and balanced history on issues important to local communities has grown significantly in that time. As politics and media have become more heated and divided, the issues that shape the writing of local history have become more contested. In many ways, there has never been a greater need for honest, diligent, and competent interpreters with understanding and respect for their readers to help communities make sense of their history.

NOTES

1. David J. Bodenhamer and Robert G. Barrows, eds., *The Encyclopedia of Indianapolis* (Bloomington: Indiana University Press, 1994), 739–40.

2. Ibid.

3. Carol Kammen, *On Doing Local History*, 3rd ed. (Lanham, MD: Rowman & Littlefield, 2014), 13.

4. Walter L. Buenger and Arnoldo De León, eds., *Beyond Texas through Time: Breaking Away from Past Interpretations*, new ed., twentieth-anniversary ed. (College Station: Texas A&M University Press, 2011), 7–8.

5. Buenger and De León, *Beyond Texas through Time*, 3.

6. Modupe Labode, communication to the authors, September 19, 2023.

7. Thomas E. Felt, *Researching, Writing, and Publishing Local History*, 2nd ed. (Nashville, TN: American Association for State and Local History, 1981), 64–66. Felt was senior historian at the New York State Education Department.

8. Nicholas Rizzo, "Self-published Books & Authors Sales Statistics [2023]," https://wordsrated.com/self-published-book-sales-statistics; accessed February 27, 2023.

9. "About University Presses," Association of University Presses website, accessed February 17, 2023, https://aupresses.org/the-value-of-university-presses/about-university-presses/.

10. Beth Luey, *Handbook for Academic Authors: How to Navigate the Publishing Process*, 6th ed. (Cambridge, UK: Cambridge University Press, 2022), 52.

11. "About University Presses."

12. "Arcadia Publishing Series—Imprints, Arcadia Publishing," n.d., www.arcadiapublishing.com/series.html.

13. Walter Buenger found that 33 percent of the 1,600 books about Texas published between 1988 and 2009 came from commercial presses, and these commercial local history presses originated during the period of the study with strong Texas lists (Buenger and De León, eds., *Beyond Texas through Time*, 7–8). Similar growth in local history titles nationwide can be inferred from the Texas information.

14. Amy H. Wilson, ed., *Encyclopedia of Local History*, 3rd ed. (Lanham, MD: Rowman & Littlefield, 2017), 395–98.

15. Laura Portwood-Stacer, *The Book Proposal Book: A Guide for Scholarly Authors* (Princeton, NJ: Princeton University Press, 2021).

TWO

Evidence

Where Do You Find It?
How Do You Use It?

The thrill of conducting research is what draws most people to the field of local history. Discovering new facts, finding fresh sources, making new connections, and solving mysteries are the kinds of activities that drive researchers to travel to libraries and archives in search of collections that might shed new light on their topic and to sort through records in dank basements of courthouses, churches, and old businesses. Research is the exciting part of the process, and those who become good at it develop the instincts and aptitude for knowing where to look and for making sense of what they find. Like a good detective, they are aided by curiosity, persistence, and creativity in discovering clues and making sense of them to determine how the pieces of the puzzle fit together.

In his autobiographical book, *Working: Researching, Interviewing, Writing*, the journalist/historian Robert A. Caro, author of the massive and influential biographies of Robert Moses and Lyndon Johnson, revealed much about how he developed his instincts and methods for solving research puzzles. Beginning as a young reporter at *Newsday* in 1959, he was guided by a managing editor "right out of *The Front Page*" named Alan Hathaway, who told him, "Turn every page. Never assume anything." In those early years Caro discovered he had a talent for going through "raw files" and "making them yield up their secrets." Such sources were "closer to reality, to genuineness. Not filtered, cleaned up, through press releases or, years later, in books."[1]

Recalling Hathaway's advice years later, when Caro was working in the Lyndon Baines Johnson Library and Museum in Austin, Texas, on the first volume of the Johnson biography, *The Path to Power*, the author became depressed while going through the finding aids and coming to the realization that the Johnson papers consisted of forty thousand boxes and more than thirty-two million pages: "There would be no turning every page here." For Johnson's eleven years in Congress alone, Caro counted up hundreds of boxes and hundreds of thousands of pages in diverse groupings that were sometimes confusing. In addition to the general files, "JHP," which consisted of more than two hundred thousand pages, there were other collections that pertained to the same period, such as the "LBJA" files composed of numerous papers pulled out of the general files dealing with congressmen, senators, and "close associates." Since Caro was primarily interested in Johnson's life as a young congressman, he started with the collections and boxes for which he thought it would be important to "turn every page." In so doing, he noticed a change in tone among Johnson's correspondence:

> And as I was doing this—reading or at least glancing at every letter and memo, turning every page—I began to get a feeling: something in those early years had changed. For some time after his arrival in Congress, following a special election, in May 1937, his letters to committee chairmen, to senior congressmen in general, had been in a tone befitting a new congressman with no seniority or power, in the tone of a junior addressing a senior, beseeching a favor, or asking, perhaps, for a few minutes of his time to discuss something. But there were also letters and memos in the same boxes from senior congressmen in which they were doing the beseeching, asking for a few minutes of his time. What was the reason for the change? Was there a particular time at which it had occurred?

With that research question in mind, Caro figured out an answer that became a key to his understanding of Johnson's ability to accrue and wield power. By putting all his notes in chronological order, he identified October 1940 as the date when the attitude in the correspondence changed. He asked a colleague of Johnson, Thomas G. Corcoran, what changed at that point in Johnson's career, and Corcoran replied, "Money, kid, money." Going assiduously through the collections focused on the date and looking for money, Caro pieced together a scheme by which Johnson received contributions from wealthy Texans in the oil and gas industry to support Democratic candidates nationwide. The Texans each donated $5,000 to the Democratic Congressional Campaign Committee, a subsidiary of the Democratic National Committee. The Texas oilmen received assurances that the Oil Depletion Allowance and other tax breaks would not be touched, and Johnson revived what Caro calls "a previously moribund" institution allowing him to distribute wealth to fellow congressmen during the 1940 elections, ensuring their gratitude, allegiance, and respect and enhancing his personal power.[2]

Of course, in the same way that two people can experience the same event differently, researchers using the same sources can draw completely divergent conclusions. Local history organizations, like local schoolboards and libraries, have become battlegrounds over different ways of seeing and interpreting the past. In some cases, those new ways of seeing and interpreting the past are the result of newly discovered source materials, but in most cases the ostensibly new interpretations are the result of new ways of looking at facts and sources that have been known all along but now appear differently in the light of modern experience. Curricula and books that focus on the history of slavery, white supremacy, and civil rights are being outlawed and banned in some places, and history has become increasingly politicized and weaponized. Those who describe themselves as traditionalists contend they are fighting back against a rising tide of revisionist history that is demeaning the legacy of their ancestors and heroes, who once were celebrated for their ability to settle and transform a wild and uncivilized land. They want to celebrate their heroes and not be considered racist for doing so, and they don't want their children to learn a history that might cause them to feel uncomfortable or embarrassed. The revisionist history that these people complain about has been the work of generations of scholars working against the grain of the original celebratory pioneer narratives that neglected the experience of women and minorities fighting to gain the rights guaranteed in the nation's founding documents.

"At the heart of all this, it's about history—what is good history and what is not good history," Texas historian Walter L. Buenger said. "Good history is about assigning dignity to all groups, [with] accuracy, and honesty. You don't need to be afraid of certain things in the past if it happened," he added. "Get it out there. . . . Honesty is central to history."[3]

Thus, the general principles of research have remained constant, though the media and the procedures necessary to extract information from those media have altered fundamentally. Honesty and balance are necessary to turn facts into evidence. Historians of the ancient world (from which relatively few documents survive) learn that documents and artifacts alone are not evidence. They do not speak for themselves. The evidence is derived from the questions that are asked of these sources. Thus researchers who know the right questions to ask will be successful in turning documents and artifacts into evidence that is revealing and useful for understanding the past.

Computers and the internet had revolutionized the research process by the time the first edition of this book was published in 2013. During the past decade, the pace of that change has accelerated in significant, sometimes unexpected, ways. While a great deal more material has been digitized and made available to researchers in that time, a development emerged that became particularly important for researchers during the height of the pandemic, when libraries and archives shut down. Other aspects of the digital revolution revealed a dark side in terms of spreading misinformation, including suspect interpretations of history. Therefore, the researcher should combine the best of both worlds—print and electronic media—in accessing source materials, along with a refined understanding of how to assess their accuracy and value. In the electronic age as in the age of print, the researcher's most valuable ally remains the reference librarian. Excellent general introductions to research techniques include:

- Jacques Barzun and Henry F. Graf, *The Modern Researcher* (1957; 6th ed., Belmont, CA: Thomson/Wadsworth Publishing, 2004). It is no coincidence that this guide has been in print for more than half a century and has gone through six editions.
- David R. Beasley, *Beasley's Guide to Library Research* (Toronto: University of Toronto Press, 2000).
- David E. Kyvig, Myron A. Marty, and Larry Cebula, *Nearby History: Exploring the Past around You* (1982; 4th ed., Lanham, MD: Rowman & Littlefield, 2019). This book provides an excellent introduction to the variety of evidence available for the study of local history and guidance on how to deploy it. See especially chapter 2: "What Can Be Done Nearby?" (the questions to ask when constructing a local history), pages 15–34; and chapter 3: "Sources and Storytelling" (how to structure and construct a local history, and where and how to find evidence), pages 35–48.
- Thomas Mann, *The Oxford Guide to Library Research* (1987; 3rd ed., New York: Oxford University Press, 2005).
- Jenny L. Presnell, *The Information Literate Historian: A Guide to Research for History Students* (2007; 3rd ed., New York: Oxford University Press, 2019).
- Zachary M. Schrag, *The Princeton Guide to Historical Research* (Princeton, NJ: Princeton University Press, 2021).
- Ian Milligan, *The Transformation of Historical Research in the Digital Age* (Cambridge, MA: Cambridge University Press, 2022).

Historians recognize two fundamental categories of source materials. Primary sources include original records and eyewitness accounts such as government documents, diaries, letters, data sets (such as the census), images of various kinds, interviews, emails, blogs, and social media. When using photographs, researchers must beware of potential alterations, from cropping to Photoshop. Secondary sources include interpretive works written after the events they describe, such as journal articles, specialized monographs, encyclopedias, biographies, obituaries, and surveys of local, state, national, and international history. Secondary sources are based on primary sources and incorporate, in varying degrees, narrative and analytical elements. Autobiographies, newspaper articles, oral histories, and radio and television broadcasts can serve as either primary or secondary sources depending on the questions that are asked of them and the context in which they are used. Attorneys—whether prosecutors or defense lawyers—will attest that even eyewitness testimony has its problems: Eyewitnesses can have an axe to grind.

HOW TO ANALYZE EVIDENCE

When analyzing any historical document or book, regardless of whether it is in print or in manuscript, found online or in a library or archive, the researcher should address/answer the following questions:

- Who wrote this document or book? Who was the author (if known)? What was the author's personality/character/circumstances/rank/office/relationship with the intended audience/recipient? These characteristics of the writer will provide insights into why he or she wrote the document or book.
- Where (location) and when (date, as exact as possible; approximate if necessary) was the document or book created? The place/setting where the author wrote the document or book can provide an insight into his or her motivation and concerns.
- What audience/recipient did the author intend to reach with the document or book? Public? Private? In the case of a book, within the general reading audience that any author of a published book intends to reach, what specific/core audience did the author hope to reach with this book?
- Was the document or book commissioned? If so, who commissioned it? Private or public patron? Governmental entity? Religious organization? It is important to know the context of the commissioned work, since the commission might reveal some bias, influence, deference to the patron, or other limitation, whether deliberate or unintentional.
- What does the document or book tell us about the society in which it was created?
- What was the author's purpose in writing the document or book? To put it another way: Where is the author coming from? Where is he or she going with this document or book?
- How well did the author achieve that purpose?
- What are the document or book's strengths and weaknesses?
- To what extent did the author set standards for accuracy in writing history?
- To what extent are the author's expectations and standards of accuracy similar to or different from modern/current standards?

- To what extent have modern/current expectations and standards of accuracy changed since the author's time?
- How did the author deal with the challenges and dilemmas he or she encountered?

Not all evidence appears in the form of books and manuscripts. Be sure to consider the evidence provided by material culture: archaeology, art, architecture, historical geography, environment, monuments, cemeteries, tombstones, and their inscriptions. When analyzing an artifact as historical evidence, the questions you should ask are variations on those used in analyzing a document or book:

- Who created the artifact? Who was the creator/artist/craftsman (if known)?
- Where and when (date, as exact as possible; approximate if necessary) was the artifact created?
- In what medium was the artifact created? Painting (oil, tempera, watercolor, fresco)? Sculpture (bronze, marble, terra-cotta)? Drawing (graphite, print, engraving, etching, pastel)? Mosaic? Textile? Furniture (wood, metal, other material)? Photograph?
- What was the intended audience/use for the artifact? Public? Private?
- Was the artifact commissioned? If so, who commissioned it? Private or public patron? Governmental entity? Religious organization?
- If the artifact is a work of art, what is its subject? Portrait (individual, group, self-portrait)? A religious subject (representation of a scriptural or devotional subject)? Historical (history painting has been a major subject area since the sixteenth century)? Domestic (northern European artists from the fifteenth century and American painters since the nineteenth century specialized in domestic scenes)? Landscape? Townscape? Seascape?
- What does the artifact tell us about the society in which it was created?
- If the artifact is a work of art or useful, is it realistic or idealized? Is it characteristic of an identifiable style?[4]

RESEARCH

With those guidelines about how to analyze historical evidence in mind, you are now prepared to search for that evidence.

An extraordinary range of primary source and secondary source materials is available on the internet, with more being added each day. Still, what is available online is only a fraction of what can be found in physical repositories. Digital collections can lead researchers to much greater riches in archives, libraries, and museums, and these institutions in turn will often have digital collection guides (also known as finding aids) that can be examined in advance to help researchers plan how to make a visit as productive as possible.

Searching for historical materials on the internet involves a good deal more than just firing up a web browser of some kind, such as Chrome, Safari, or Firefox, and conducting a keyword search through a search engine such as Google or Bing. Doing so can provide tens of thousands of results, but if the searcher does not have at least a rudimentary understanding of how search engines such as Google or Bing work and some searching skills, those results are not likely to be very helpful.

Search engines match a search request with keywords and web pages and then post the results with URLs (uniform resource locators), which serve as the address of a website. The leading search engines use sophisticated algorithms to find websites, but such sophistication does not mean that the most relevant sites will appear at the top of the search results list. A website may be ranked higher because it is more popular, although it may not have the most useful or trustworthy content. Analyzing a website's address, as well as its content, is a necessary step in evaluating its value as a historical resource.

A URL uniquely describes how to access a specific online resource. URLs typically have the following format: protocol://computer.domain.name/pathname/file.

A domain name consists of a string of identifiers that defines a particular realm of administrative authority and control on the internet. It is very important that researchers pay attention to domain names when evaluating search results. The most prominent top-level domain names are *.com* (commercial), *.edu* (education), *.gov* (government), and *.org* (organization). Academic websites, including academic libraries, use *.edu* and can generally be trusted to provide more authoritative historical information than *.com* or *.org*, though exceptions abound. Many historical organizations use the *.org* domain name, including the Wisconsin Historical Society (www.wisconsinhistory.org), the Virginia Museum of History and Culture (www.virginiahistory.org), and the Texas State Historical Association (www.tshaonline.org). It is the mission of historical organizations like these to provide easily accessible and trustworthy information, and they can be counted on to do so. But not all organizations are equally trustworthy. Researchers should maintain a certain amount of skepticism regarding the intentions of an organization and the information on its site. Websites using the *.org* domain can have political or ideological axes to grind, and researchers should evaluate those intentions with the same care they would those of a historical document or photograph.

In a world in which blogging has begun to take the place of accurate journalism and in which historical analogies, often spurious or fabricated, are used to justify political and commercial ends, how is one to trust that the quotation or interpretation of events their browser has landed them on is worthy of being included in their work and passed on? Providers with apparent intellectual or political biases must be screened out or at least recognized and acknowledged as such.

Since its debut to the public in November 2022 and the investment by Microsoft of $10 billion in OpenAI, the technology giant that developed it, the chatbot program ChatGPT, along with many other similar artificial intelligence programs, has been widely reported with stories of amazement regarding its capabilities and concern for its potential for disruption of all aspects of our lives and work.[5] Artificial intelligence programs not only have the ability to generate text, images, and music but also can learn how to improve their output so that their products become increasingly difficult to detect. For local historians of the future, the ability to analyze evidence and the skepticism toward possible "deep fakes" will necessarily need to be enhanced. Local historians today will learn to use bots like ChatGPT and those that come after as tools in the same way they have learned to use search engines to navigate the internet. Publishers are calling for text generated by artificial intelligence to be acknowledged as such and cited, but not listed, in bibliographies.[6]

To navigate online resources successfully, researchers should begin with trusted websites that provide lists and links to other trusted websites. The Library of Congress (LOC) offers many of these. Its "American Memory" project (http://memory.loc.gov/ammem/index.html) is the longest running and most extensive digital collection in the country, providing "free and open access through the internet to written and spoken words, sound recordings, still and moving images, prints, maps, and sheet music that document the American experience. It is a digital record of American history and creativity."[7] The materials are from the collections of the Library of Congress and other institutions, and they reflect historical events, people, places, and ideas that are integral to American history. Launched in 1994 as the leading effort of the National Digital Library program, "American Memory" surpassed the library's goal of providing access to five million items by 2000. Offering the ability to browse and search by collection, topics, time period, and types of materials, "American Memory" is a critical place to begin research for almost any local history project dealing with the United States.

From the "American Memory" site researchers can link to other useful sites for primary historical materials, including the Library of Congress's "Primary Sources by State" and "State Resource Guides." Among these sites is one of the best places to begin looking for local history materials on the internet: the LOC's "State Digital Resources: Memory Projects, Online Encyclopedias, Historical & Cultural Materials Collections" (www .loc.gov/rr/program/bib/statememory). Compiled by Christine A. Pruzin, the site features an exhaustive list of digital projects from museums, libraries, archives, and historical organizations throughout the country. These projects, inspired by the American Memory project, "provide unprecedented access to materials that document local and regional growth and development as well as a look at the cultures and traditions that have made individual states and communities unique."[8] This site is a state-by-state listing of digital archives—such as the California Digital Archive, Alaska's Digital Archives, the Virginia Memory project, the Portal to Texas History, and many more—which digitize holdings of repositories in their states and make primary source materials available to researchers. Also included in these listings are digital encyclopedias that provide signed and vetted articles on states and regions. These encyclopedias, led by early efforts such as the *Encyclopedia of Cleveland History* (https://case .edu/ech/, 1998) and the *Handbook of Texas Online* (www. tshaonline.org /handbook/online, 1999) have been followed by other ambitious initiatives, including the *Tennessee Encyclopedia of History and Culture* (http:// tennesseeencyclopedia.net, 2002), *HistoryLink.org: The Free Online Encyclopedia of Washington State History* (www.historylink.org, 2003), the *New Georgia Encyclopedia* (www.georgiaencyclopedia.org, 2004), and the online version of the *Encyclopedia of Chicago* (www.encyclopedia.chicagohistory.org, 2005). They are indispensable guides to local history information that can open up directions for further research through their links and bibliographic references. A single database that brings together all these local and state digital collections is the Digital Public Library of America (https://dp.la), which includes more than forty-eight million images, texts, videos, and sounds from across the United States. The *Inclusive Historian's Handbook* (https://inclusivehistorian.com), edited by Modupe Labode, William S. Walker, and Robert Weible, supports inclusive and equity-focused historical work in public settings by sharing a knowledge base that invites more people to engage in history projects.

Many reference works are now online, but some of the best-quality reference works—peer-reviewed sources such as the *American National Biography*—are proprietary publications whose websites require a paid license or must be accessed through the network of a licensed institution such as a participating public or university library. The *Encyclopædia Britannica*—first published in 1768—ceased to publish its print edition in 2012 and is now available only online (www.britannica.com), surely a landmark in publishing history. It offers a free version, which contains advertising, and subscriptions for premium versions without the advertising at various levels.

DATABASES OF PRIMARY SOURCES
AND SECONDARY INTERPRETIVE WORKS

During the 1990s commercial publishers of scholarly journals (especially in the sciences) escalated subscription prices.[9] In an effort to circumvent this price gouging, university libraries, university presses, and nonprofit publishers formed consortia, began publishing journals online, and began creating their own digital collections, often of local and state history, and making them freely available to the world. These collections feed into state repositories like Indiana Memory and national repositories such as the Digital Public Library of America (DPLA). These consortia established databases that are accessible by subscription and by students, faculty, alumni, and community residents affiliated with institutional subscribers.

In 1993 the Johns Hopkins University Press and the Milton S. Eisenhower Library at the Johns Hopkins University founded Project MUSE (http://muse.jhu.edu; subscription required), an online database containing peer-reviewed academic journals and electronic books funded by the National Endowment for the Humanities and the Andrew W. Mellon Foundation. As a nonprofit collaboration between libraries and publishers, Project MUSE expanded in 2000 to include journals and e-books published by other academic publishers. The database now provides access to more than 550 journals and 23,000 e-books in the humanities and the social sciences from 250 university presses and scholarly societies. This database, like those described below, requires a subscription but may be accessible through academic or public libraries if the researcher is affiliated with the library.

In 1995 William G. Bowen, the former president of Princeton University, founded JSTOR (short for Journal Storage; www.jstor.org) with support from the Andrew W. Mellon Foundation. JSTOR is a digital library that provides access to 237 current and more than 1,500 archival scholarly journals, primary sources, and more than 15,000 scholarly books.

In her entry for the *Encyclopedia of Local History*, "Local History Resources Online," Virginia Cole lists a number of databases, or "a collection of information stored electronically and available online, usually accessed through the web" that are indispensable for historical research. "Many of the most powerful and largest databases and digital collections," she explains, "are produced by commercial firms and require subscription for access."[10] Among the sources she cites are the following:

- America: History and Life (www.ebsco.com/products/research-databases/america-history-and-life; subscription required) is a full-text database that indexes 1,700 journals dating from 1910, books, dissertations, and citations and links to book and media reviews relating to state, provincial, and local history of the United States and Canada. America: History and Life is run by EBSCO Publishing, an Ipswich, Massachusetts–based aggregator of full-text content.

- Google Scholar (https://scholar.google.com) is a bibliographic database and web search engine that indexes journal articles and books. In most cases the user can only access an abstract (when an article or book is still copyrighted) and can access the full text only through a licensed institution or by paying a fee. A great deal of open access scholarly content is also findable through Google Scholar.
- Google Books (https://books.google.com) is an online book search engine. The user can search the full text of the more than twenty million public domain books and magazines that Google has scanned. The user can have only limited access to books and magazines that are still copyrighted.
- The Internet Archive (https://archive.org) is a is a nonprofit library of millions of free books, historical video, and primary resources such as city directories.

Modupe Labode recommends the following research guides, which can give users a sense of their topic from a larger perspective:

For example, the Library of Congress has a strong series of research guides—https://guides.loc.gov—with topics such as African American history and women and gender. The Library of Congress also has research guides for local history and genealogy (https://guides.loc.gov/local-history-genealogy -research-guides). Some libraries and research centers also have wonderful research guides—such as the one from the Western History Collection at Denver Public Library (https://history.denverlibrary.org/research) and the New York Public Library's research guides (https://libguides.nypl.org).[11]

OPEN ACCESS VERSUS PROPRIETARY SOURCES

Open access is the latest trend that is challenging university presses and other publishers of scholarly books and journals. Open access is a mode of publishing by which the user gains free and unrestricted access through the internet to peer-reviewed scholarly journal articles. It is also being extended to books, theses, and dissertations. Open access is a classic case of the cost shifting imposed by computerization and electronic communication. Individuals and institutions pay for their subscriptions to print journals but gain free access to open access online journals. Kristi Palmer, dean of the University Library at Indiana University Indianapolis, explains further:

Open access came about in part to interrupt the massive inflation rates of scholarly published material, primarily journal articles. Articles are written by faculty authors (paid by universities) who give those articles to the publisher, signing over copyright. The editorial board and reviewers are typically comprised of faculty who are again paid by universities, not publishers. And then the publisher turns around and sells back to universities for a major profit. Open access is working to interrupt this cycle.

Both print and open access journals use peer review to accept articles, but authors must pay a heavy subsidy (often more than $1,000) to have their articles published in open access journals. As Kristi Palmer has observed, "Many researchers now write these fees into their grants that supported the research. Additionally universities, in particular academic libraries, have established funds to support faculty in paying these fees."[12] But university presses and journal publishers still more or less operate in the market economy—they recover their costs through sales and subscriptions; most history journals require subscriptions or licenses to gain access to online editions. These licenses are available through most academic and many public libraries if the researcher has an affiliation with the library.

The Directory of Open Access Journals (www.doaj.org) provides free full-text access to a multitude of scholarly and scientific journals available only online. It "aims to be comprehensive and cover all open access scientific and scholarly journals that use a quality control system to guarantee the content." The contents of many but not all open access journals are included in standard periodical indexes and are accessible from internet search engines. This is a "one-stop shop" for users of open access journals, containing thousands of academic journals from around the world.[13]

Since Jimmy Wales, Larry Sanger, and others founded Wikipedia (https://en.wikipedia.org) in 2001, it has become a mainstay and first stop for students, journalists, and researchers. Instead of peer review, Wikipedia relies on crowdsourcing (with some oversight by an editorial staff) and a gift economy. Crowdsourcing has a long history, going back to the *Oxford English Dictionary*, work on which began in 1857. But in 2006 Jeff Howe coined the term to mean "taking a function once performed by employees and outsourcing it to an undefined (and generally large) network of people in the form of an open call. This can take the form of peer-production (when the job is performed collaboratively), but it is also often undertaken by sole individuals. The crucial prerequisite is the use of the open call format and the large network of potential laborers."[14]

Users have free access to Wikipedia, which receives financial support from donations to the Wikimedia Foundation. As in any publishing venture, the Wikipedia editors wrestle with issues of accuracy, interpretation, and context; and in the process, Wikipedia has become increasingly reliable during recent decades. A Wikipedia article's source list, if provided, may offer suggestions for further research.

Because of the extraordinarily large size of Wikipedia's audience, major cultural and educational institutions such as the National Archives, the Smithsonian Institution, and the Indiana Historical Society have initiated a new form of quality control known as "open authority." These institutions regard it as part of their mission to assure the accuracy of Wikipedia articles by providing the services of Wikipedians in residence—personnel (usually working off-budget on soft-money grants) on the staffs of these institutions who write and check the accuracy and sources of articles in their fields of expertise.[15] Nevertheless, Wikipedia as a cited source still carries less credibility than the digital proprietary encyclopedias mentioned above, and researchers should be wary in using its articles as evidence in their research.

Many additional databases of primary sources and secondary interpretive works, relevant for historical research in general and local history in particular, are available. Museums, universities, colleges, and public libraries often host websites and databases on the history and primary sources (documents, visual materials, and artifacts) relating to their locality. For more information, the researcher should consult a librarian, who can help to differentiate between free and proprietary online sources.

PRIMARY SOURCES FOR LOCAL HISTORY

Despite the volume and accessibility of online records, many records are not (and probably will never be) digitized and disseminated online. Digitization is an expensive process, and archivists choose collections to digitize based on existing levels of demand (as measured by frequency of requests to access an original manuscript collection). Therefore, in the course of original research in primary source materials, a researcher will want to search not only collections available online but also collections not previously digitized. This research strategy has two advantages: It leads to materials that few if any researchers have previously consulted, and it avoids the professional pitfall of historians repeating themselves.

Most repositories in the general categories listed below have collections including manuscripts, journals, and books. Documents, and the evidence they provide for local history, can be found in:

- City and county courthouses (for land records [deeds, mortgages, and assessed valuations], probate records [wills, estate inventories, and ademptions], tax records, marriage and divorce records, civil and criminal court proceedings, and trial records [order books and case files]). Some city and county courts have turned over their historical records to state archives. For a helpful guide to research, see James D. Folts, "courts and court records," in Amy H. Wilson, ed., *Encyclopedia of Local History* (2000; 3rd ed., Lanham, MD: Rowman & Littlefield, 2017), 144–50.

- City and county health departments (for records of births and deaths). Some city and county health departments will give only transcripts, not copies, of original birth and death certificates. Some county health departments will release such certificates only to family members. In some states, the state health department issues death certificates. Before the twentieth century, churches maintained such vital records (of births [baptisms], marriages, and deaths [burials]).
- City and county public libraries often have a local history or special collections room that includes books, manuscripts, maps, and photographs relating to the locality.
- Local and county historical societies have special collections of books, manuscripts, maps, and photographs relating to the locality. These societies and their collections are often housed in local public libraries.
- State historical societies (for special collections of books, journals, manuscripts, maps, and photographs relating to the state). Some state historical societies are state agencies; some are independent membership organizations; others are public-private partnerships.
- State libraries (for special collections of books, journals, manuscripts, maps, and photographs relating to the state).
- State archives (for government documents, often manuscripts, generated by state agencies). Many state archives also include collections of private papers among their collections, as well as centralized holdings of city and county records no longer in everyday use.
- The National Archives and Records Administration (NARA; www .archives.gov). Prominent record groups that can be useful to local history include military, personnel, and pension records; land claims; federal court records (including bankruptcies); passenger lists; naturalization records; and census records. The National Archives has repositories in downtown Washington, DC (Archives I); College Park, Maryland (Archives II); twenty regional archives throughout the United States; and thirteen presidential libraries. See *Guide to Federal Records in the National Archives of the United States*, Robert B. Matchette, comp., three vols. (1974; 3rd ed., Washington, DC: NARA, 1995), also available at www.archives. gov/research /guide-fed-records, which contains the most up-to-date information. See also Loretto Dennis Szucs and Sandra Hargreaves Luebking, *The Archives: A Guide to the National Archives Field Branches* (Salt Lake City,

UT: Ancestry Publishing, 1988) and *Guide to Genealogical Research in the National Archives* (1982; 3rd ed., Washington, DC: NARA, 2000).

- Independent research libraries have special collections of books, manuscripts, maps, photographs, and historical prints that are useful for researching state and local history. The Newberry Library (www.newberry.org) in Chicago has outstanding collections on American Indian and indigenous studies, Chicago and the Midwest, and genealogy and local history. The American Antiquarian Society (www.americanantiquarian.org) in Worcester, Massachusetts, has particularly strong collections (many of which are digitized) of American newspapers and engravings, and of the history of printing. The Huntington Library (https://huntington.org) in San Marino, California, has collections of books, manuscripts, maps, photographs, and historical prints relating to American colonial history, eighteenth-century American military history, the American Revolution, the Civil War, the exploration and development of the American West, the building of the transcontinental railroad, and California from the arrival of Europeans to the present. The William L. Clements Library (https://clements.umich.edu) at the University of Michigan has major collections for the study of early exploration and settlement of North America, the American Revolution, the American Civil War, African American history, Native American history, race and ethnicity, reform movements, religion, and women's history.

Useful directories of all the above-mentioned categories of repositories include:

- Samuel J. Redman, *Historical Research in Archives: A Practical Guide* (Washington, DC: American Historical Association, 2013).
- *Where to Write for Vital Records*, published by the Centers for Disease Control's National Center for Health Statistics (www.cdc.gov/nchs/w2w/index.htm).
- Alice Eicholz, ed., *Red Book: American State, County, and Town Sources* (1992; 3rd ed., Provo, UT: Ancestry Publishing, 2004).
- *American Library Directory*, 2 vols. (1923; 75th ed., Medford, NJ: Information Today, 2022); accessible online at www.americanlibrarydirectory.com.
- *Subject Collections: A Guide to Special Book Collections and Subject Emphases as Reported by University, College, Public, and Special Libraries and Museums in the United States and Canada*, compiled by Lee Ash and William G. Miller, 2 vols. (1958; 7th ed., New Providence, NJ: R. R. Bowker, 1993).

- *Directory of Special Libraries and Information Centers: A Guide to More Than 37,500 Special Libraries, Research Libraries, Information Centers, Archives, and Data Centers Maintained by Government Agencies*, edited by Matthew Miskelly, 1 vol. in 6 parts (1963; 50th ed., Detroit, MI: Gale/ Cengage Learning, 2022).
- *Directory of History Departments, Historical Organizations, and Historians* (1976; 45th ed., Washington, DC: American Historical Association, 2019; since then published online at www.historians.org /research-and-publications/directories). The section on historical organizations (limited to institutional members of the American Historical Association) includes historical societies, archives, and historically related research libraries.
- *Directory of Historical Organizations in the United States and Canada* (1986; 15th ed., Walnut Creek, CA: AltaMira Press, 2002); published for the American Association for State and Local History. Many of the organizations listed (limited to institutional members of the American Association for State and Local History) are libraries, historical societies, and archives with collections of archives and books.
- Philip M. Hamer, *A Guide to Archives and Manuscripts in the United States* (New Haven, CT: Yale University Press, 1961); compiled for the National Historical Records Commission.
- Repositories of Primary Sources (www.uidaho.edu/special-collec tions/Other.Repositories.html): Terry Abraham of the University of Idaho Library compiled this list of links to more than five thousand "websites describing holdings of manuscripts, archives, rare books, historical photographs, and other primary sources for the research scholar." Coverage is worldwide but is especially detailed for the United States and Canada. The University of Idaho ceased to update and maintain this site in 2015.

The following directories are searchable online at Archive Finder (archives.chadwyck.com); subscription required:

- *Directory of Archives and Manuscript Repositories in the United States* (1978; 2nd ed., Phoenix, AZ: Oryx Press, 1988); published for the National Historical Publications and Records Commission; contains information on more than 5,600 repositories and 175,000 collections of primary source material in the United States.
- *National Union Catalog of Manuscript Collections* (NUCMC), 35 vols. (Ann Arbor, MI: J. W. Edwards, 1959–1993); since then also searchable on the Library of Congress website (www.loc.gov/coll/nucmc); contains more than 115,000 records.

- *National Inventory of Documentary Sources in the United States* (NIDS-US) (Teaneck, NJ: Chadwyck-Healey, 1983–present); published for the Manuscript Division Library of Congress; also searchable at www .proquest.com/en-US/catalogs/collections/detail/National-Inven tory-of-Documentary-Sources-in-the-United-States-260.shtml; sub-scription required; provides a complete indexing of more than seventy-two thousand collections. Academic and many public li-braries give access to the ProQuest database and other databases to researchers who are affiliated with those libraries.

Search engines can be used to locate source materials in several media. Bibliographical databases such as the Online Computer Library Center (OCLC)—which merged in 2006 with the Research Libraries Informa-tion Network (RLIN)—can be searched by author, title, and subject and provide access to books, manuscript collections, and other media. OCLC can be accessed publicly through WorldCat (www.worldcat.org), a union catalog that provides access to collections in 72,000 libraries in 170 coun-tries. It can also be accessed through proprietary databases, which require a license and password, FirstSearch (www.oclc.org/en/firstsearch.html), or OCLC Connexion (connexion.oclc.org). Academic and some public libraries give access to these databases to researchers who are affiliated with those libraries. Modupe Labode observes:

> There are some aggregators of metadata that allow users to search digitized material in several archives and libraries. For example, the Digital Public Library of America allows one to search several libraries/archives for digital material (https://dp.la). Umbra Search (www.umbrasearch.org) allows one to search materials related to African American history. There is Online Cali-fornia as well (https://oac.cdlib.org). There are also digitized collections that are usually available only through public or academic libraries—such as Al-exander Street—that include primary and hard-to-find secondary sources.[16]

Most libraries and archives now have online catalogs; manuscript repositories provide online access to many collection guides and other finding aids. A collection guide describes a manuscript collection and how it is organized and provides a list of containers, boxes, and fold-ers. When conducting manuscript research in an archive, the researcher should examine in advance any collection guides available—whether in print or online—to prepare ahead of the visit to maximize the productiv-ity of their time when there. Special collections (which include categories such as manuscripts, rare books, and visual collections such as prints and photographs) do not circulate—you have to consult them on-site. Always let the archives staff know in advance that you are coming and the topic you are working on—archivists sometimes have the desired materials pulled from the stacks and available for the researcher upon arrival. Always bring a photo identification with you; most archives and special collections welcome public researchers but will require you to register and provide identification on your first visit. Be prepared to use a pencil, not a pen, when taking notes; most archives and special collections also now allow the use of a personal computer for taking notes. Some archives and special collections also allow the use of a camera or cell phone to take photographs. Again, remember that the researcher's best ally is always a knowledgeable reference librarian or archivist.

Despite the widespread availability of online catalogs, collection guides, and finding aids, the researcher still must master the printed subject area bibliographies. A good place to start is Frank Freidel and Richard K. Showman, *Harvard Guide to American History*, 2 vols. (1896; revised ed., Cambridge, MA: Belknap Press of Harvard University Press, 1974). Volume 1 is organized topically, including a comprehensive section on biography; volume 2 is organized chronologically.

Another useful resource is the *American Historical Association's Guide to Historical Literature*, general editor, Mary Beth Norton, associate editor, Pamela Gerardi, 2 vols. (1927; 3rd ed., New York: Oxford University Press, 1995), particularly the following sections (all in volume 2): Section 39: Jack P. Greene, "Colonial North America," pages 1239–79; Section 40: Lewis Perry, "United States, General," pages 1280–323; Section 41: David L. Ammerman, "American Revolution and Early Republic, 1754–1815," pages 1324–60; Section 42: Thomas Dublin, "United States, 1815–1877," pages 1361–411; Section 43: Joe W. Trotter, "United States, 1877–1920," pages 1412–52; Section 44: James T. Patterson, "United States History since 1920," pages 1453–503; and Section 45: John M. Bumstead, "Canada," pages 1504–46.

TAKING NOTES

Once you have located the primary and secondary sources for your project, you will need to compile research notes. As you conduct your research in those sources, you will need to take notes, from which you will write the narrative of your publication. Tips on note taking:

- Learn to be selective—learn how to summarize in your own words. You can quote verbatim only a tiny fraction of the material on which you take notes. Thus you must learn to identify those revealing passages that are truly quotable, summarize the rest, and accurately record the full bibliographical citation in the notes (so when you reach the writing stage of your project, you can easily cite your source without having to return to it for the details). If the desired end product is an article or book, it is ultimately more efficient to take accurate summary notes than to photocopy reams of documents.

- Manuscripts and printed materials are subject to copyright laws. It is a researcher's and author's responsibility to learn how much (actually how little) he or she can quote verbatim in the finished book. Thus it is important to learn how to take summary notes, summarize details in the narrative, and quote sparingly—reserving verbatim quotations to the most telling and illustrative examples. In short, researchers and authors must learn how to shape the material with the end product constantly in mind. (See discussion of copyright and the concept of "fair use" in chapter 3.)
- A researcher must beware the fallacy that vast amounts of scanning, photographing, or photocopying equal research. Those who photocopy large numbers of documents and never seem to bring their writing projects to a conclusion are not researchers; so do not confuse verbatim copying (scanning, photographing, or photocopying) with research.
- Clearly demarcate within quotation marks material that is copied verbatim, to avoid inadvertent plagiarism later. (See discussion of plagiarism in chapter 3.)
- When quoting from primary sources or secondary interpretive works, always retain the original spelling, capitalization, and punctuation in your notes. Verbatim transcription is generally no impediment for modern readers, and you will need to state in the introduction to your publication if you have modernized your transcription of historical documents.
- Indicate deletions from quoted material by using an ellipsis: ". . .". Use an ellipsis of four periods when ending a sentence.
- Use [*sic*] to indicate a recognized error in the original sparingly.
- Be cautious in assuming that you know more about your subject than the eyewitnesses who lived through the events they and you are describing.

REFERENCE MANAGEMENT SOFTWARE

Numerous online bibliographic tools can aid researchers in managing research documents, notes, and references. For many of us who learned to store notes and bibliographies on index cards, this kind of software has helped streamline the work of managing sources. Among the most popular programs are EndNote, RefWorks, and Zotero. All of them streamline workflow by easily capturing bibliographic information from online library catalogs, bookselling sites, newspapers, blogs, and web pages. The programs can store this information and manage it in numerous ways, such as easily inserting references into the text while you write and formatting bibliographies to accommodate the common citation conventions. They can also store notes, documents, and image files to accompany each source. Most, like EndNote and RefWorks, cost money, but those working through an academic library with a license may have access to them for free. Zotero (www.zotero.org/download) is an open-source tool created by the Roy Rosenzweig Center for History and New Media at George Mason University. It is available for free, works with most browsers, and with just a little practice can become an indispensable tool for any researcher.

GENEALOGICAL AND FAMILY HISTORY RESEARCH

In recent decades, genealogy and family history have converged and cross-fertilized with social history to produce some remarkable publications. At the Indiana Historical Society, the *Hoosier Genealogist*—published quarterly from 1961 to 2005 and containing mostly lists abstracted from records—transformed in 2006 into the *Hoosier Genealogist: Connections*, which provides narrative articles placing the records in their social context. This recent synthesis of genealogy and family history has resulted in *Finding Indiana Ancestors: A Guide to Historical Research*, edited by M. Teresa Baer and Geneil Breeze (Indianapolis: Indiana Historical Society Press, 2007). The essays in this book—on topics such as internet research, oral history, photographs, and maps—range far beyond the borders of Indiana and are applicable to American family history research in general. Chapters on categories of records including census records, church records, court records, and cemeteries are particularly helpful. Another basic introduction to the field is Val D. Greenwood's *The Researcher's Guide to American Genealogy* (1973; 4th ed., Baltimore: Genealogical Publishing Company, 2017).

The National Genealogical Society (6400 Arlington Blvd., Ste. 810, Falls Church, VA 22042-2318; 703-525-0050; toll-free: 800-473-0060; fax: 703-525-0052; www.ngsgenealogy.org) has played an important role in establishing standards for the field of genealogy. It sets high standards for research, evidence, and documentation, and merged with the Federation of Genealogical Societies in 2020.

Several major databases are useful for genealogical research (at academic and some public libraries, researchers can gain free access to the proprietary databases requiring subscription if the researcher is affiliated with those libraries). Those databases include:

- PERSI (Periodical Source Index) provides searchers with access to historical information in more than three million local history and genealogical articles appearing in more than ten thousand periodicals published by local, state, national, and international societies and organizations. Indexed by the staff of the Genealogy Center at the Allen County Public Library in Fort Wayne, Indiana (the second-largest genealogical library in the United States), PERSI is the largest subject index to genealogical and historical periodical articles in the world. Accessible through the websites of the Family History Library, HeritageQuest Online, Ancestry.com, Cyndi's List, and the Allen County Public Library.
- The Family History Library at the Genealogical Society of Utah (the largest genealogical library in the United States), 35 North West Temple, Salt Lake City, UT 84150-9005; (801) 240-6996; the Family History Library website (www.churchofjesuschrist.org/learn/fam ily-history-library?lang=eng) provides step-by-step instructions on how to conduct family history research. The Family History Library, operated by the Church of Jesus Christ of Latter-day Saints (LDS Church), operates seventeen regional and thousands of local (ward, branch, and stake) Family History Centers throughout the United States and other countries.
- HeritageQuest Online (www.heritagequestonline.com/hqoweb /library/do/index; subscription required) enables searches in census, birth, death, marriage, and divorce records, as well as passport and military pension application files, passenger lists, PERSI, books, and other records.
- Ancestry.com (www.ancestry.com; subscription required): Developed as a publisher in electronic formats during the 1990s, Ancestry. com is now an internet company based in Lehi, Utah. The company provides access to more than thirty billion genealogical and historical records.
- Cyndi's List (www.cyndislist.com; free) provides access to a list of more than 325,000 links in 192 categories to genealogical and historical research websites.
- The USGenWeb Project (www.usgenweb.org): Volunteers compile this project, which contains links to genealogical websites in every state and county in the United States.
- Linkpendium (www.linkpendium.com) also provides links to more than ten million genealogical websites in all states and counties.
- Family Search (www.familysearch.org) is a nonprofit organization offering billions of ancestor profiles, photographs, and historical documents. It is operated by The Church of Jesus Christ of Latter-day Saints (LDS Church).

BROAD CATEGORIES OF RECORDS FOR LOCAL HISTORY

Newspapers

From the colonial period, newspapers have provided a detailed insight into the daily life, economy, and politics of local communities. Newspapers were the primary forum for debate on political issues. They recorded elections and the proceedings of colonial assemblies, state legislatures, and Congress. Historical and modern newspapers are available in microform and online. Those new to researching historical newspapers should be aware of the partisan press era in the nineteenth century, when newspapers were supported by and served as the voice of particular political parties and their candidates, policies, and office holders.[17] An essential guide to research in early newspapers is Clarence S. Brigham, *Bibliography of American Newspapers, 1690–1820*, 18 vols. (Worcester, MA: American Antiquarian Society, 1913–1928). Major databases providing access to historical newspapers include:

- Chronicling America (https://chroniclingamerica.loc.gov) is the best place for a researcher to find information about historical newspapers and select digitized newspapers. Produced by the National Digital Newspaper Program (NDNP), a collaboration of the National Endowment for the Humanities (NEH) and the Library of Congress (LOC), this rich and free digital resource is permanently maintained at the Library of Congress.
- America's Historical Newspapers (https://www.newsbank.com /libraries/government/solutions/americas-historical-newspapers; subscription required): The most comprehensive available collection, America's Historical Newspapers includes digital copies of thousands of newspaper titles from all fifty states published since 1690. It draws on the collections of more than ninety major newspaper repositories, including the American Antiquarian Society, the Library of Congress, and the Wisconsin Historical Society.
- ProQuest Historical Newspapers (https://about.proquest.com/en /products-services/pq-hist-news/; subscription required): A subsidiary of ProQuest LLC, an Ann Arbor, Michigan–based publisher in microform and electronic media, it provides aggregated databases including sixty-five ProQuest Historical Newspapers—mass-circulation newspapers published in the United States (forty-one, including eleven African American and four American Jewish titles), and twelve international titles.

- Newspapers.com (www.newspapers.com) is a digitized online newspaper archive established by Ancestry.com in 2012, including more than 24,500 newspapers (subscription required).

Modupe Labode observes:

> Some states have undertaken important newspaper digitization projects, including the Hoosier State Chronicles (https://newspapers.library.in.gov), Colorado Historic Newspaper Collections (www.coloradohistoricnewspapers. org), and Nebraska Newspapers (https://nebnewspapers.unl.edu/newspapers). Many historical societies have newspapers that were printed in languages other than English. These newspapers are very important for researching communities. Further, researchers should be aware that the newspapers in English printed by and for communities (such as African American, Jewish, and LGBTQ) may be an important way to get access to other viewpoints.[18]

City Directories

The larger cities of the colonial and early national periods had directories that researchers can use to locate persons, businesses, and institutions. A researcher can identify directories through Dorothea N. Spear, *Bibliography of American Directories through 1860* (Worcester, MA: American Antiquarian Society, 1961).

Religious Records

Before counties and states began keeping vital records (of births, marriages, and deaths) about a century ago, religious organizations—churches and synagogues—were the primary recorders of births (baptisms), marriages, and deaths (burials). To access these records effectively, the researcher must understand the administrative units and structures (such as congregations, parishes, presbyteries, and dioceses) that generated these records. For a helpful introduction to the field of local religious history, see James P. Wind, *Places of Worship: Exploring Their History* (Nearby History Series; Nashville, TN: American Association for State and Local History, 1990) and James D. Folts, "Religion in North America and Its Communities," in Amy H. Wilson, ed., *Encyclopedia of Local History* (2000; 3rd ed., Lanham, MD: Rowman & Littlefield, 2017), appendix B, pages 755–60. The LDS Church has microfilmed and digitized many of the local records of other denominations, thereby simplifying and expediting access to these local religious records. A useful guide to writing a congregational or parish history is Laurence D. Fish, *Writing a Congregational History* (2003; rev. ed., Swarthmore, PA: National Episcopal Historians and Archivists, 2009).

Business Records

The great tragedy of American business history is that most businesses
have destroyed their records. A few major corporations such as the Ford
Motor Company, Eli Lilly and Company, and the DuPont Company have
developed well-organized corporate archives. A useful guide is the Directory of Corporate Archives in the United States and Canada, Society
of American Archivists (www2.archivists.org/groups/business-archives
-section/directory-of-corporate-archives-in-the-united-states-and-canada
-introduction). Some smaller businesses have donated their historical
records to state and local historical societies. In the twenty-first century,
a driving force behind the destruction of business records has been the
desire to avoid legal liability. During the notorious ENRON scandal in
2001, Nancy Temple, a lawyer with Arthur Andersen (the accounting firm
representing ENRON), emailed Michael Odom, an Andersen partner in
Houston, Texas, reminding him of the Andersen document retention and
destruction policy. He forwarded the email to a coworker with the now-
infamous suggestion that "it might be useful to consider reminding the
engagement team of our documentation and retention policy."[19] As a result of such euphemisms and the desire to maintain plausible deniability,
many of the source materials for business history have been lost. Corporations (for-profit as well as nonprofit) must file annual reports—which can
be fertile sources for business history—with the secretary of state in the
state where they are incorporated. For a database of corporate annual reports since 1884, see ProQuest Historical Annual Reports (https://about
.proquest.com/en/products-services/pq_hist_annual_repts; subscription required). A useful introduction to the field of business history is
K. Austin Kerr, Amos J. Loveday, and Mansel G. Blackford, *Local Businesses: Exploring Their History* (Nearby History Series; Nashville, TN:
American Association for State and Local History, 1990).

Military Records

The local, state, federal, and independent libraries and archives described above all have military records in their collections. Those range
from personal records (diaries and correspondence) of serving personnel
(enlisted, noncommissioned officers, and commissioned officers) to government records on the colonial, state, and federal levels documenting the
armed conflicts from the colonial era to the present. Voluminous record
groups in the National Archives document each of the military services
during both war and peace. State records provide evidence of militia and
National Guard units' service in the armed conflicts in which they served.
Military pension applications in both federal and state archives provide

evidence of the military service of individual personnel. Unit diaries and after-action reports document the movements and battles of those units. Museums and monument commissions on the state and federal levels preserve artifacts such as the Civil War regimental banners. Fold3 (www. fold3.com), a subsidiary of Ancestry.com, is an online database with more than 670 million military records, including stories, photos, and personal documents (subscription required).

Travel Accounts

Travel accounts written by outsiders provide insightful perspectives for local history. The Jesuit *Relations* (1632–1673) and other missionary records, Philip Vickers Fithian (1775–1776), Charles Maurice de Talleyrand-Périgord (1794–1796), Alexis de Tocqueville (1831–1832), Frances Trollope (1832), Harriet Martineau (1834), Charles Dickens (1842), Robert Louis Stevenson (1883), and Ian Fleming (1963) contributed accounts to the growing body of travel literature on the United States and Canada. Local reaction to George Washington's Southern Tour (1791), James Monroe's two Goodwill Tours (1817), Harry Truman's Whistle-Stop Campaign (1948), and other political campaigns highlight the linkage between local and national history. Some authors not only commented on but also contributed to the social and political movements they described. Hinton Rowan Helper's *The Impending Crisis in the South: How to Meet It* (1857) provided a geopolitical analysis and itself became a catalyst in the events leading to the Civil War. Visits by prominent outsiders—such as the Marquis de Lafayette (1824–1825); Prince Maximilian of Wied-Neuwied (1832–1834); the Prince of Wales, later King Edward VII (1860); Winston Churchill (who visited the United States and Canada fifteen times between 1895 and 1961); and King George VI and Queen Elizabeth (1939)—provide a connection between local and international history. Also be alert to reportage by "internal tourists" such as Theodore Roosevelt (1888), Mark Twain (notably *Roughing It* [1872], *Old Times on the Mississippi* [1876], and *Life on the Mississippi* [1883]), Henry James (1907), and Theodore Dreiser (1916). The comments of such visitors, flattering or unflattering, welcome or unwelcome, can be a telescope (for the big picture) or a microscope (for the minutiae) focusing on the local community.

Maps, Atlases, Gazetteers, and Geographic Name Authorities

Maps provide a snapshot of geographical knowledge at the time of their creation. No more or less than any other primary source, maps convey the assumptions of their creators (often the victors in military, social, and economic contests). Among the factors to look for in maps is geopolitics—the politics of geography. The local, state, federal, and independent libraries described above have collections of maps and atlases (notably the Newberry Library [www.newberry.org] in Chicago and its Hermon Dunlap Smith Center for the History of Cartography). The last quarter of the nineteenth century witnessed an outpouring of not only county histories but also county maps, gazetteers, and atlases. David E. Kyvig, Myron A. Marty, and Larry Cebula's *Nearby History: Exploring the Past around You* (1982; 4th ed., Lanham, MD: Rowman & Littlefield, 2019), pages 65–72, provides insightful guidance on how to use maps as historical evidence. The "Getty Thesaurus of Geographic Names Online" (www.getty.edu/research /tools/vocabulary/tgn) is a structured vocabulary, including names and descriptions of places important for art and architecture. The US Board of Geographic Names (BGN), an agency of the US Geological Survey (USGS), was founded in 1890 to maintain uniform geographic name usage throughout the federal government. A researcher can search for geographic names on its website (www.usgs.gov/us-board-on-geographic-names).

Documentary Editions

Editions of primary documents loom large both in the research for and as an important part of local history publications. As you conduct the research on your local history subject, be alert for published documentary editions, which are more accessible and easier to use than archival manuscripts. Documentary editions provide transcriptions of manuscript materials and are available in print in the holdings of major university and public libraries and online.

The National Historical Publications and Records Commission (NHPRC), an agency of the National Archives and Records Administration, endorses editions that meet professional standards. For a list of such editions, see the NHPRC Publishing Projects Catalog (https://www .archives.gov/nhprc/projects/catalog). All such editions, whether focusing on the papers of an individual person or on a topic of national importance, are relevant to local history and can be accessed through their tables of contents and their item-level indexes.

Documentary editions have formed a major part of the publications of state and local historical societies from their inception two centuries ago. They constitute the seed corn or the fundamental building blocks of history writing in its local and all other subject areas. Documentary editions are crucial to the research enterprise. But because their sales potential is minimal, they are appropriate for online publication in the twenty-first century. Even volumes in the print editions of Founding Fathers projects sell only about seven hundred copies. Their viability depends on publication subventions from the National Historical Publications and Records Commission. Many of the major documentary editions are now available simultaneously in print and online at sites such as the University of Virginia Press's Rotunda Project (www.upress.virginia.edu/rotunda), which was created for the publication of original digital scholarship, along with newly digitized critical and documentary editions in the humanities and social sciences. The Rotunda Project makes accessible digital editions of the papers of, among others, George Washington, Alexander Hamilton, Thomas Jefferson, James Madison, Dolley Madison, and Eliza Lucas Pinckney and Harriott Pinckney Horry; the Adams Papers; and the *Documentary History of the Ratification of the Constitution*. Documentary editions on local as well as national topics are now often published in simultaneous print and digital formats. Some are "born digital" and available online only.

Modern American documentary editing began with Clarence Edwin Carter's *The Territorial Papers of the United States*, 26 vols. (Washington, DC: Government Printing Office, 1934–1962). Carter was a professor of history at Miami University in Ohio. From 1931 the project was housed at the State Department, which has jurisdiction over the federal territories, and from 1950 at the National Archives. Modern documentary editing came into its own with the post–World War II editions of the papers of the Founding Fathers. These modern editions were comprehensive and collected. Comprehensive editions make accessible the papers—correspondence to and from, and other documents such as speeches, essays, and reports—of a prominent person, the subject of the edition. Some editions are organized around a particular historical topic, such as the ratification of the Constitution or emancipation. Collected editions bring together the texts of original documents currently housed in collections in disparate repositories (libraries and archives) throughout the world. Many documentary editions include annotation that identifies persons and places and provides background and context for the user.

If you are planning a publication that may include both documentary and narrative elements, you will need to decide whether your publication will be a narrative history or a documentary edition. You should not consider a Victorian-style life-and-letters, which will fulfill neither function well. If you have a number of edited documents that could enhance the narrative text, you could add these verbatim as appendixes at the end of your publication. When preparing a documentary edition for publication, you should transcribe the document using the original spelling, punctuation, and capitalization. Such literal transcription is the modern standard, is the easiest to describe (you must describe your transcription method in an editorial method statement at the beginning of your edition), and is usually no impediment to a modern reader.

Standard introductions to the subject include Mary-Jo Kline and Susan Holbrook Perdue, *A Guide to Documentary Editing* (1987; 3rd ed., Charlottesville: University of Virginia Press, 2008); Michael E. Stevens and Steven B. Burg, *Editing Historical Documents: A Handbook of Practice* (Lanham, MD: AltaMira Press, 1997); and Beth E. Luey, ed., *Editing Documents and Texts: An Annotated Bibliography* (Madison, WI: Madison House, 1990).

Oral History

A quick way to get a sense of the importance of oral history to the work of the local historian is to note that the term appears more than one hundred times in the third edition of the *Encyclopedia of Local History*. Beyond the useful entry on the topic written by Michael Frisch, oral history is acknowledged throughout the volume, primarily as a means for bringing the words and historical perspectives of those underrepresented by other forms of documentation. In his article, Frisch cites two primary reasons for the growth of oral history during the last few decades: First, in a world in which letter writing has disappeared, the inability of documents to account for the richness and complexity of life is much reduced from what it was in previous eras; second, oral history has the potential to render a more democratic version of history, or history written "from the bottom up."[20] The historian Allan Nevins founded the Columbia Center for Oral History—the first organized oral history program—in New York in 1948. Acknowledging oral history's reliance on memory, which is imperfect and subjective, oral history proponents contend that these sources should be held to the same standards and scrutiny as any other form of historical evidence and, if done properly, can provide an indispensable source for understanding the past and adding new voice to it. Rigorous standards for conducting, transcribing, storing, and using oral histories have arisen since the 1960s. The quality of an oral history interview depends as much on the preparation of the interviewer—who must ask informed and leading questions—as it does on the memory and experience of the interviewee. For oral history recordings to be easily accessible, they must be transcribed. One hour of recording normally requires at least four hours of transcription, which is a labor-intensive and expensive process. Many libraries therefore will not accept oral history recordings without accompanying transcriptions. The Oral History Association (https://oralhistory.org), founded in 1966, serves as "the principal membership organization for people committed to the value of oral history" and provides guidance and programming for its members, who include "teachers, students, community historians, archivists, librarians, and filmmakers." The association provides many resources on its website, such as "OHA Principles and Best Practices," "Oral History Centers and Collections,"

"Web Guides to Doing Oral History," and much more. Its "Independent Practitioners' Toolkit for Oral Historians" (2020–2021) will be especially useful for those working as independent contractors, offering advice and accepted rates for various tasks such as interviewing, narrator compensation, interpretation, transcription, interview indexing, translation, project design, project management, and promotion.

ILLUSTRATION RESEARCH

Well-chosen illustrations enhance a publication. They supplement and amplify the text and provide the author with a medium, in addition to the text, to communicate and engage with the reader. An author can also increase the likelihood that an editor will favorably consider an article or book for publication if the author has identified potential illustrations. Many of the categories of repositories listed above under the section "Primary Sources for Local History"—state and local libraries, archives, museums, and historical societies—have visual collections (prints, photographs, postcards, paintings, sculpture, and artifacts) and finding aids to facilitate research in those collections. David E. Kyvig, Myron A Marty, and Larry Cebula's *Nearby History: Exploring the Past around You* (1982; 4th ed., Lanham, MD: Rowman & Littlefield, 2019), pages 109–29, helpfully explains how to analyze photographs as historical evidence. Local newspapers often maintain photographic archives; some have transferred their historic photographs to a local library or historical society. Stock photography is a large potential source for the licensing of historic images. The largest stock photography agencies are Getty Images (www.gettyimages.com) and Corbis (www.corbisimages .com; managed by Getty since 2016).

PastPerfect-Online (http://pastperfect-online.com) is a database of artifact collections at more than 600 museums, libraries, and archives containing more than 7.5 million records. The researcher can locate images and information using Artifact Search or browse through the collections, filtering by region or specialty to narrow the list.

Several federal agencies have collections that are relevant to local history, including:

- The Library of Congress's Prints and Photographs Division (www .loc.gov/rr/print) has a collection of more than fourteen million images with an online catalog, collection guides and finding aids, and guidelines for obtaining reproductions and permission to publish.
- The National Archives' Still Picture Branch (www.archives.gov /research/guides/still-pictures-guide) maintains a collection of

approximately six million photographs and graphics with an online collection guide and an archival research catalog.

- The National Portrait Gallery has a collection of twenty-one thousand works of art (paintings, sculpture, prints, drawings, and photographs) focusing on images of famous and not-so-famous Americans from all regions of the country. See *National Portrait Gallery, Smithsonian Institution: Permanent Collection Illustrated Checklist*, Dru Dowdy, comp., photographs by Eugene Mantie and Rolland G. White (1973; 25th Anniversary ed., Washington, DC: published by the National Portrait Gallery in association with the Smithsonian Institution Press, 1987). The researcher can search the National Portrait Gallery's collection at https://npg.si.edu/portraits. The National Portrait Gallery's Portal to American Portraits (https://npg.si.edu/portraits/research/search) is a database that provides access to more than one hundred thousand records from the Catalog of American Portraits (CAP), a survey of American portraits in public and private collections across the United States and other countries.

The rules of copyright and acknowledging authorship of written records (manuscript or print, published or unpublished) also apply to visual materials such as prints, photographs, paintings, and sculpture. If the author has commissioned such a visual work, if the creator is alive, or if the work is otherwise protected by copyright (see the discussion of copyright in chapter 3), the author will need to obtain permission to publish the work from the copyright owner and probably pay a usage fee (see also appendix 4: "Sample Contract with a Photographer"). Even if the work itself is in the public domain, if it is in the collection of an institution (such as a library, archive, museum, or historical society), the author/user will need to obtain a publication-quality print or digital file of a photograph of the work and permission to publish it (and pay required fees) from the institution that owns the work. The University of Chicago Press has excellent author's permission guidelines, a discussion of art permissions, and downloadable permission request templates (for text and art, copyright, and use) at https://press.uchicago.edu/resource/permissions.html.

Captions should concisely describe an illustration and not repeat information already covered in the text of a publication. A caption description should include the name of the creator (photographer or artist) of the work in the illustration, the name of the institution that owns the work, and the name of the collection of which the work is a part. By providing such caption information, an author not only complies with legal requirements and professional courtesy but also provides background and contextual information on the illustration that will be useful to the reader. Beware of errors in captions, which are sometimes written by persons other than the author of the text of a publication. Also beware of flopped (left to right) images, a common error in publishing illustrations.

THE TRANSITION FROM RESEARCH TO WRITING

The research and writing phases of a publication project (be it of article or book length) will overlap. An essential first step in planning a project is to develop a précis that will include a chapter outline of the entire project. The chapter outline will then be your guide through both the research and the writing phases of your project. The chapter outline will help give you a sense of where you are going, where you have come from, and what remains to be done on the project. It is also a required component of any book proposal. As you conduct your research, you will inevitably find that you have reached a critical mass or a point of diminishing returns, beyond which you should start writing. As the next chapter (on writing) will make clear, the process of writing will expose to the author the gaps and loose ends in the research that may require a return to the sources. "Research is the process of trying to make sure that you know what you are saying is correct," wrote Thomas E. Felt. "You may write as fluently and publish as handsomely as the best, but weaknesses in research have ways of resisting every treatment except one, which is better research. *Better* does not always mean *more*; it does always mean alert, intelligent compilation and analysis of fact. Historical scholarship is quality, not quantity."[21] In this chapter we have sought to provide suggestions and guidelines for conducting quality research along lines that Felt would have approved and that will allow sources to reveal their secrets to you.

NOTES

1. Robert A. Caro, *Working: Researching, Interviewing, Writing*, Kindle edition (New York: Alfred A. Knopf, 2019), 10, 11.

2. Caro, 84–92.

3. Josephine Lee, "Those Who Don't Know the Past," in *Texas Observer*, May 15, 2023, https://www.texasobserver.org/those-who-dont-know-the-past. See also Carlos Kevin Blanton, "Trouble in Texas: Culture Wars, the Meaning of History, and Academic Freedom," in *Perspectives on History: The Newsletter of the American Historical Association*, 61 (November 2023), 8–10.

4. For guidelines on how to analyze artifacts as historical evidence, see E. McClung Fleming, "Artifact Study: A Proposed Model," in *Material Culture Studies in America*, ed. Thomas J. Schlereth (Nashville, TN: American Association for State and Local History, 1982), 162–73; Cary Carson, "Doing History with Material Culture," in *Material Culture and the Study of American Life*, ed. M. G. Quimby

(New York: W. W. Norton, 1978), 41–64; Jules David Prown, "Mind in Matter: An Introduction to Material Culture Theory and Method," in *Winterthur Portfolio* 17 (1982): 17–37; David E. Kyvig, Myron A. Marty, and Larry Cebula, *Nearby History: Exploring the Past around You* (1982; 4th ed., Lanham, MD: Rowman & Littlefield, 2019), 131–45; and the *Oxford Handbook of Material Culture Studies*, ed. Dan Hicks and Mary C. Beaudry (New York: Oxford University Press, 2010).

5. Cade Metz and Karen Wise, "Microsoft to Invest $10 Billion in OpenAI, the Creator of ChatGPT," in the *New York Times*, January 23, 2023.

6. "Citation, Documentation of Sources," in *Chicago Manual of Style Online*, https://www.chicagomanualofstyle.org/qanda/data/faq/topics/Documentation/faq0422.html (accessed March 27, 2023).

7. "Mission and History (American Memory from the Library of Congress)," n.d., http://memory.loc.gov/ammem/about/index.html.

8. Christine A. Pruzin, "State Digital Resources (Virtual Programs & Services, Library of Congress)," n.d., www.loc.gov/rr/program/bib/statememory. Another valuable resource is Dennis A. Trinkle and Scott A. Merriman, eds., *The American History Highway: A Guide to Internet Resources in U.S., Canadian, and Latin American History* (Armonk, NY: M. E. Sharpe, 2007), which provides extensive annotated lists of historically related websites.

9. Albert N. Greco, Clara E. Rodríguez, and Robert M. Wharton, *The Culture and Commerce of Publishing in the 21st Century* (Stanford, CA: Stanford Business Books, 2007), 76.

10. Virginia Cole, "local history resources online," in *Encyclopedia of Local History*, ed. Amy H. Wilson (2000; 3rd ed., Lanham, MD: Rowman & Littlefield, 2017), 398. For a useful analysis of the strengths and weaknesses of online source materials, see Jeffrey G. Barlow, "Historical Research and Electronic Evidence: Problems and Promises," in *Writing, Teaching, and Researching History in the Electronic Age: Historians and Computers*, ed. Dennis A. Trinkle (Armonk, NY: M. E. Sharpe, 1998), 194–225.

11. Modupe Labode, communication to the authors, September 19, 2023.

12. Kristi Palmer, communication to the authors, September 18, 2023.

13. "DOAJ—Directory of Open Access Journals," https://doaj.org.

14. Jeff Howe, Crowdsourcing Blog, "Crowdsourcing: A Definition," June 2, 2006, https://crowdsourcing.typepad.com/cs/2006/06/crowdsourcing_a.html (accessed January 6, 2013).

15. Lori Byrd Phillips and Dominic McDevitt-Parks, "Historians in Wikipedia: Building an Open, Collaborative History," in *Perspectives in History: The Newsmagazine of the American Historical Association* 50, no. 9 (December 2012): 55–56.

16. Labode, communication to the authors, September 19, 2023.

17. D. W. Bulla, "party press era," *Encyclopedia Britannica*, December 29, 2015. https://www.britannica.com/topic/party-press-era.

18. Labode, communication to the authors, September 19, 2023.

19. "Andersen's Share of Enron Scandal Grows," *CNN Money*, January 15, 2003, http://money.cnn.com/2002/01/15/news/andersen/index.htm (accessed July 18, 2011).

20. Michael Frisch, "Oral History," in *Encyclopedia of Local History*, 3rd edition, 538–41.

21. Thomas E. Felt, *Researching Writing, and Publishing Local History* (1976; 2nd ed., Nashville, TN: American Association for State and Local History, 1981), 3.

THREE

Communication

How Do You Shape a Specialized Subject for a Nonspecialist Audience?

Let's just say it flatly at the very beginning: There is nothing easy about writing. While research can involve the excitement of the hunt and the pleasure of discovery, writing entails the more mundane task of sorting through everything you've found and marshaling it effectively as evidence to inform, persuade, and entertain a particular audience. Of course some have a greater facility for writing than others, but that facility is only acquired through the conscientious application of diligent effort over a lifetime. As one of our mentors in Indiana history used to say, writing mainly consists of "applying the seat of the pants to the seat of the chair." Those who write well are those who have worked at writing well. They have been inspired to write by reading authors they admire and studying their examples. They have had some good teachers and mentors along the way. They have learned how to respond to criticism and take full advantage of it without letting their egos get in the way. They have something to say, and they have a solid understanding of to whom they want to say it. Finally, they know that good writing involves constant revision, and they are able to put their feelings aside when necessary to respond to constructive criticism for the sake improving their work.

Research and writing *con*verge on the specialized topic but *di*verge to provide context and background sufficient to make that topic intelligible to a nonspecialist audience. Research and writing are not clearly compartmentalized phases; they inform and reinforce each other. Writing will reveal gaps and loose ends that will require a return to research. Research is not conducted randomly or in a vacuum; the researcher needs a précis that will include a chapter outline and a concept of the finished product to give direction to the research. The researcher needs to have some idea of where the research is going. But research often leads to unexpected surprises (pleasant and otherwise).

A writer of history (whether academic or popular) has an ethical obligation to seek the whole truth. According to the American Historical

Association's Statement on Standards of Professional Conduct, historians "should respect and welcome divergent points of view even as they argue and subject those views to critical scrutiny."[1] In pursuit of the whole truth, a writer of history needs certain core competencies. Notable among those core competencies is the ability to assess evidence and to ascertain cause and effect. A writer of history must also be free to pursue and publish the results of research wherever the evidence may lead.

History at its core and at its best is a study of cause and effect. During the ancient and medieval periods, the best historians—those still read today—rose above mere chronicle and provided explanations for the course of events. A chronicle is a historical account of events arranged in order of time, often devoid of analysis or interpretation. Or, as they say in the Marine Corps, "Two hundred years of tradition, unhampered by progress." Ancient and modern times have their chronicles and lists of rulers, events, dates, and ancestral lines. An occupational hazard of history writing is antiquarianism—the compilation of minute data with little or no analysis, explanation, or narrative. If you seek to engage an audience, in whatever medium, you must provide that analysis, explanation, and narrative. More than half a century ago, Christopher Coleman observed, "Waste of effort on nonessentials is easily prevented by keeping before one the question: What would an intelligent outsider want to know about this community, or about this subject? . . . The goal of all historical effort," noted Coleman, is "the understanding of the world in which we live."[2]

Experience is the best teacher of writing. A previously unpublished author should gain experience writing and getting article-length studies published. The discipline of seeking publication outlets, soliciting publishers, dealing with and responding to editors, and receiving critiques and feedback from knowledgeable colleagues in the field will provide valuable lessons. Through such experience, a writer of local history will learn what has already been done and who is currently doing what in the subject field. Writing and publishing are integral parts of networking—processes by which you can get to know and become known by colleagues. Newspapers, magazines, and newsletters of local historical organizations can provide outlets for book reviews, columns, and features on local history topics. Also, peer-reviewed state historical journals can provide opportunities for local history writers engaged in substantive research to respond to criticism and contribute to their field. The experience gained in writing and publishing article-length studies serves a writer well before tackling the large-scale task of organizing and writing a book.

Regardless of whether one is writing an article or a manuscript to submit for book publication, successful authors carefully study the information provided by the prospective publishers for their benefit.

They are familiar with each specific publisher's list or, in the case of a journal, the kind of articles that have appeared in the journal over the past year at least. These days, publishers' recent catalogs can generally be found on their websites, and it is easy to review the last few seasons of a publisher's list and to get a sense of the nature of its titles and how it might be changing over time. Nothing is more irritating to an editor than receiving a call or query from authors who are obviously not familiar with the previous work the publisher has done, or who do not show knowledge of significant work already done in the field in which they are working. Authors should also be aware that acquisitions editors manage their own lists and are judged by the prestige of their authors and titles as well as by the revenue their lists generate. While it is the job of editors to find suitable material for publication, and while the best of them are open and curious, they can nevertheless quickly shut down when they realize for any number of reasons that an author's work is not in their ballpark. The author's job is to keep the editor and the reader interested, and that is done through the quality of the writing one submits. Good writing can sometimes overcome a lack of familiarity with a publisher's work, but most often poor writing and lack of attention to author's guidelines go hand in hand. Even perfectly drafted proposals, however, can be rejected quickly for lack of good fit with an editor's list. As Laura Portwood-Stacer explains in *The Book Proposal Book*, "If an editor has no experience working with books like yours, and their press has no experience marketing books like yours, your book simply won't be a sensible investment for them. An editor who rejects your proposal based on fit is doing you a favor."[3] A quick rejection might be irritating to an author, but it serves them well in allowing them to move on to another publisher sooner rather than later.

In his chapter "Writing," Thomas Felt asked his readers to consider the writing they have done in their lives, including letters of all kinds, articles, and school assignments, and to think about when that writing was most effective. He asserted that any effective communication is the result of feeling or emotion that "fuels the curiosity" of an author. "It matters little what the emotion is—affection, amusement, awe, indignation, or even disgust," he wrote. "The stimulus is what counts. Nothing good has ever been written out of boredom."

While such passion is a necessary condition for effective communication, it is not a sufficient one. Writing ability is also the result of a lifelong "involvement in the craftsmanship of writing," and a dedication to mastering the conventions and expectations of the craft. As with any craft, one does not acquire proficiency overnight. Improvement is a gradual process that is the result of one's own experience, as noted above, and learning from the work of others. Felt identified a couple of ways that a writer can learn from the experience of others, which we will explore here: models and conventions.[4]

Models are simply examples of good writing that one can seek to emulate. To do so involves analysis of what makes the writing model effective. When the authors of this book were editing the Indiana Historical Society's magazine, *Traces of Indiana and Midwestern History*, we encouraged prospective authors, especially in the early years, to look at examples of successful articles that had been previously published in the magazine and, regardless of the topic, try to match them in terms of language, length, structure, style, use of illustrations, and documentation. We were looking for a melding of journalistic style and historical accuracy that would appeal to a broad audience of intelligent readers. We were not asking scholars to "dumb down" their work; we were asking them instead to present their research in a way that would be accessible to a general audience. Conversely, we encouraged journalists to use sources beyond telephone interviews, to write paragraphs that were longer than one or two sentences, and to follow the style conventions for scholarly publishing (*Chicago Manual of Style*) rather than those of newspaper journalism (*Associated Press Stylebook*). All authors were asked to tell a story scrupulously based on evidence that would engage a reader.

Because many publishers of books and journals on local history are also looking for this ideal synthesis of journalism and scholarship, it is worth describing in some detail. Most important, it involves the ability to recognize and effectively use the different modes of writing—narration, description, and exposition—in presenting well-researched information that is interesting to read. Historical narrative involves relaying a sequence of events, usually in the order in which they happened. Good narrative history appears to be easy to write because it is easy to read, but like pleasing music that is easy to listen to, it is the result of a good deal of experience, training, and talent. Just as musicians claim that the most important notes are often the ones not played, the key to telling an interesting story for a writer is knowing what to include and what to leave out.

In *A Short Guide to Writing about History*, Richard Marius and Melvin E. Page write, "A good narrative begins by establishing some sort of tension, some kind of problem that later development of the narration should resolve." Narrative also has a climax that comes near the end, ties up all its strands, and "embodies the meaning the writer wants readers to take from the story."[5] All who watch movies or read novels are familiar with this narrative arc, but presenting history as narrative, with dialogue, action, suspense, and resolution, involves special skills because the historian cannot embellish for the sake of enhancing the drama but must adhere to what is known and can be proved.

MODELS

There are many historians whose work offers especially good models for narrative history, and they have been rewarded with large audiences of readers and many awards. In the first edition of this book we focused on the work of David McCullough, Pulitzer Prize–winning author for both his *Truman* (1992) and *John Adams* (2001), to provide a model to emulate. McCullough, who began his career as a magazine journalist, and who died in 2022, mastered a popular style of history writing based on rigorous research that we encourage.

And here is the brief beginning to *John Adams* that we used as a model in the first edition of this book:

> In the cold, nearly colorless light of a New England winter, two men on horseback traveled the coast road below Boston, heading north. A foot or more of snow covered the landscape, the remnants of a Christmas storm that had blanketed Massachusetts from one end of the province to the other. Beneath the snow, after weeks of severe cold, the ground was frozen solid to a depth of two feet. Packed ice in the road, ruts as hard as iron, made the going hazardous, and the riders, mindful of the horses, kept at a walk.
>
> Nothing about the harsh landscape differed from other winters. Nor was there anything to distinguish the two riders, no signs of rank or title, no liveried retinue bringing up the rear. It might have been any year and they could have been anybody braving the weather for any number of reasons. Dressed as they were in heavy cloaks, their hats pulled low against the wind, they were barely distinguishable even from each other, except that the older, stouter of the two did most of the talking.
>
> He was John Adams of Braintree and he loved to talk. He was a known talker. There were some, even among his admirers, who wished he talked less. He himself wished he talked less, and he had particular regard for those, like George Washington, who somehow managed great reserve under almost any circumstance.
>
> John Adams was a lawyer and a farmer, a graduate of Harvard College, the husband of Abigail Smith Adams, the father of four children. He was forty years old and he was a revolutionary. . . .
>
> As befitting a studious lawyer from Braintree, Adams was a "plain dressing" man. His oft-stated pleasures were his family, his farm, his books and writing table, a convivial pipe and cup of coffee (now that tea was no longer acceptable), or preferably a glass of good Madeira.
>
> In the warm seasons he relished long walks and time alone on horseback. Such exercise, he believed, roused "the animal spirits" and "dispersed melancholy." He loved the open meadows of home, the "old acquaintances" of rock ledges and breezes from the sea. From his doorstep to the water's edge was approximately a mile.
>
> He was a man who cared deeply for his friends, who, with few exceptions, were to be his friends for life, and in some instances despite severe strains.

And to no one was he more devoted than to his wife, Abigail. She was his "Dearest Friend," as he addressed her in his letters—his "best, dearest, worthiest, wisest friend in the world"—while to her he was "the tenderest of husbands," her "good man."[6]

We praised much about this example, including the way McCullough established the tensions that would be resolved throughout the rest of the book and his execution of the modes of writing that are necessary tools of the historian's craft, such as description, exposition, and the use of quotations. Description is all about presenting sensory experience—what things look, feel, and taste like—in an effort to provide the reader with an understanding of what it was like to be with a particular person at a particular time and place. Exposition is writing that explains and analyzes. In narrative writing it provides the background upon which the story is told. It is perhaps the most prevalent form of historical writing, consisting, as Marius and Page explain, of "philosophical ideas, causes of events, the significance of decisions, the motives of participants, the working of an organization, the ideology of a political party."[7] The best historical writing reflects a balance of narrative, description, and exposition, as reflected in McCullough's example. While we are feeling the winter chill and the uncertainty of the journey along with visualizing the protagonist's physical characteristics, we also learn that he dressed plainly, relished long walks, was prone to melancholy, loved his wife, and much more. Description properly administered can add interest to exposition, while exposition is necessary to provide meaning to the narrative.

This model provides an excellent example of using quotations effectively in historical writing. Perhaps the most important thing to note in this regard is that the primary sources have been digested so thoroughly by the writer that they seem to appear almost effortlessly in support of the story. Drawn from writings done throughout Adams's life, they are offered in the beginning of the story as an introduction to his ways of thinking and writing and to his character. They reflect McCullough's proficiency in the material, leaven the narrative with a personal touch in much the same way that quotations are used in journalistic writing, and provide the reader with trust by signaling that this story is based on exhaustive research in primary sources.

Left unaddressed in our previous edition, however, was the extent to which even an author as celebrated and proficient as David McCullough can provide cautionary examples that are equally as useful for a writer of local history. In his final book, *The Pioneers: The Heroic Story of the Settlers Who Brought the American Ideal West,* published in 2019, the author tells the story of the pioneers who settled Marietta, Ohio, in the newly created Northwest Territory after the Revolutionary War, focusing on stalwarts the Reverend Manassa Cutler and Rufus Putnam. Though the story is told with a masterful command of all the elements of good writing that McCullough wields so well, it is a strictly traditionalist tale, told from a white man's perspective, of heroic idealists wresting the land from its unworthy inhabitants. Despite the quality of the storytelling on the surface, *Pioneers* ignores decades of historical commentary placing such settlement in the realm of conquest, expansionism, and what is known in academic circles as "settler colonialism," or the study of how settlers displace and marginalize native populations. Even though the portraits of Cutler and Putnam, and many others, are drawn with the same care and skill as that of John Adams, McCullough falls into a common pitfall among local historians of reflecting the attitudes and perspectives of his much-admired historical subjects. He seemingly unwittingly adopts their language regarding the land being "unsettled wilderness" and natives being "savages":

> The year before, on the morning of March 1, 1786, the Reverend Cutler and ten others gathered in Boston at the famous Bunch of Grapes tavern, at the corner of King and Kilby Streets. Their purpose was to launch a highly ambitious plan involving the immense reach of unsettled wilderness known as the Northwest Territory.

Of course, it wasn't unsettled. While most usages of these terms and others are placed in quotations from contemporaneous actors, some are not. The times when they are not belie the author's prejudices and lack of objectivity.

> Exposed as to a crossfire, men and officers were seen falling in every direction. The distress, too, of the wounded made the scene such as can scarcely be conceived. A retreat had to be called. The battle had become a one-sided slaughter. A few minutes more and it would be too late. In Denny's words, "Delay was death." The only hope was that the savages would be so taken up with plunder of the camp as not to follow after. No preparation could be made. Numbers of brave men must be left a sacrifice, there was no alternative.[8]

Even the most celebratory of pioneer histories must acknowledge recent scholarship to be taken seriously as a work of history that will stand as a reliable resource for future researchers. Reviewers, both academic and nonacademic, reacted negatively to McCullough's unbalanced depiction of historical events. After acknowledging that there is a great deal to admire about the Northwest Ordinance and the ideals of the Ohio settlers, Joyce E. Chaplin, writing in the *New York Times*, stated they could also "withstand some criticism" and denoted instances where the Ohioans didn't always live up to the high ideals proclaimed in the Northwest Ordinance regarding the treatment of African Americans and Native people. McCullough's "fondness for the sweetly evoked Midwest," she concludes, "betrays an ahistorical vision. Cutler's plan had not prevented a violent preference for white-dominated society."[9] Likewise, in the *Washington Post* Andrew C. Isenberg writes, "The fortitude of the settlers McCullough describes was quite real. So too was land fraud, racial hierarchy and the ousting of Native Americans from their homes. McCullough so blithely ignores these less-attractive aspects of the settler narrative that he could have written this book in 1893, when the historian Frederick Jackson Turner published his famous 'frontier thesis.'"[10] Rebecca Onion in *Slate* slams McCullough's lack of interest in Native strategy in resisting pioneers: "In taking a side, narratively speaking, McCullough makes sure their narrow perspective on the matter also becomes ours." In her lengthy review of *Pioneers*, Onion raises the issue of the shortcomings of popular history. "We're always told that the virtue of the popular history book is that it's 'a good story'—that it has narrative value academic history lacks. I disagree with the idea, having read many academic history books that were full of good stories, as well as popular histories that manage to combine critical analysis and storytelling."[11] This statement evokes the perfect synthesis of reliable and informed research combined with deft storytelling and a balanced presentation that all history writers are striving for, whether they are writing from within the academy or outside it.

We have focused on the work of McCullough here because he was well regarded as a nonacademic historian who wrote for a large general audience and because we want to update what we said in the previous edition of this book. Of course many historians within the academy are writing to large audiences outside it about issues of racial identity and social injustice and adapting their language and methods accordingly. Emulating such authors as Henry Louis Gates Jr. in works like *Stony the Road: Reconstruction, White Supremacy, and the Rise of Jim Crow* and *The Black Church: This Is Our Story, This Is Our Song* will serve writers of local history well.

Biased Language

As reflected in the *Pioneers* example, biased language in historical writing can be inadvertent, even for an author as successful and respected as David McCullough. Describing historical events with terms like "savages" and "barbaric" reveals a Eurocentric bias on the part of the author. Such bias is also evident in the cherry-picking of facts to support a particular interpretation by focusing on one group and marginalizing another. Authors betray biases with generalizations based on limited or anecdotal evidence that represents a single perspective as representing an entire group. Authors must strive for objectivity in not only their writing by not using loaded terms but also in the sources they use to arrive at their conclusions. What is considered biased or inappropriate language is a rapidly moving target, and authors should be aware that even historical examples of what are now considered slurs included in quotations can be considered unacceptable. Publishers may reject a manuscript outright or ask for significant editing when coming across the use of language that is insensitive and shows a lack of knowledge of evolving standards.

Peer Review, Revision, Developmental Editing, Length

Authors as renowned as David McCullough who are writing for large trade publishers are not subjected to the kind of peer review that an author writing a history for a university press or a scholarly commercial press is required to undergo. If his work had gone through a peer review process, the worst instances of an imbalanced approach to his material would likely have been purged in revision. Editors sending manuscripts out for peer review seek manuscript readers who could be potential reviewers for a work after it is published. Generally, reviewers will know the identity of authors, but an author will only learn readers' identities if they give consent and if the editor sees that revealing them will benefit the author and the work. This process can often be painful for the author, but it can help avoid some embarrassment down the road for both the author and the publisher. Peer reviewers comment on all aspects of a manuscript, including use of sources, cogency of the argument being made, quality of writing, and where a book fits within a particular field. Readers are specifically asked to cite any examples of inappropriate or biased language or places where an argument or conclusion does not hold up to scrutiny. While it is always good to have trusted readers review a manuscript and revise according to their comments before submitting it to a publisher, the peer review process almost always requires further revision before a manuscript is accepted for publication. Editors generally need two positive reader reports to move a proposal or a manuscript to the contract phase, and the positive recommendation, or endorsement for publication, is often contingent on the author's willingness to undertake certain revisions, which could require additional research, restructuring of the work, or additions or subtractions of material. When two readers disagree as to the nature of revisions that are needed or whether the work should be published, the acquisitions editor will decide whether to seek a third reader, ask the author to revise before sending back to a dissenting reader in an effort to get that reader on board, or reject the manuscript outright. Authors will write a formal author's response to the reviewers, which consists of thanking them for their time and comments and then acknowledging the concerns they will accommodate and justifying their reasons for those they will not. Good editors will advise authors about how best to navigate the peer review process. Authors should know that their response to the readers' reports will not be seen by the readers. They will only be seen as part of the package an editor puts together to present to committees for contract approval. This usually includes an in-house committee composed of representatives from different departments such as editorial, marketing, and EDP (editing, design, and production) and then, for university presses, a faculty advisory board that includes university faculty from a wide range of disciplines reflecting a press's publishing areas. An attitude of gratitude and accommodation is always useful in these situations, even if it must be convincingly feigned. The peer review process can sometimes take a long time, especially at times that are extremely busy for prospective readers, such as the beginning and end of semesters and holidays. Also, a reader may submit a "revise and resubmit" judgment, requiring the author to revise and the editor to send back out to the reader for an endorsement. This can lengthen the process and be discouraging, but authors who are patient and can keep ego out of the publishing equation with an eye to accommodating the readers' comments, especially first-time authors, will have the greatest chance for success. On occasion, an author will be asked to work with a developmental editor at the author's expense to alleviate problems with a manuscript that authors might not be able to rectify on their own. Most presses have developmental editors they can recommend to authors to help with knotty problems of language, structure, length, and more.

In terms of length, publishers most often believe that a manuscript of around eighty thousand words, including notes and bibliography, is the optimum size for appealing to general readers. Publishers and editors believe that once a manuscript gets to be more than one hundred thousand words or so, the readers lost because of the size of the work will not justify the added expense of producing it. Because authors often find it difficult to cut down their manuscripts, or "kill their darlings," the work of a developmental editor, who can look at the manuscript objectively, can be useful in helping the author with such a revision. Most often such cutting involves getting rid of long block quotations and ancillary characters and stories that get in the way of the overall effectiveness of the work.

CONVENTIONS

Studying models, both positive and negative, is a fundamental key to becoming an effective writer of local history who is successfully published. Just as important, as Thomas Felt acknowledged, is an awareness and proficiency in conventions, including various style manuals and generally accepted standards for good writing. It is not unknown for a busy editor to reject a proposal or a submission based simply on the recognition in the cover letter or the first few pages of a manuscript that the author has little understanding of certain basic conventions of the writing trade.

Prescriptions for Good Writing

Prescriptions for good writing abound, and aspiring authors will make themselves familiar with the best of them. Preeminent twentieth-century English essayist George Orwell concisely declared six rules for writers in his "Politics and the English Language," first published in the journal *Horizon* (1946):

- Never use a metaphor, simile, or other figure of speech which you are used to seeing in print.
- Never use a long word where a short one will do.
- If it is possible to cut a word out, always cut it out.
- Never use the passive voice where you can use the active.
- Never use a foreign phrase, a scientific word, or a jargon word if you can think of an everyday English equivalent.
- Break any of these rules sooner than say anything outright barbarous.

Teachers who have read quantities of student writing will detect variations on Orwell's appeal for simplicity in language:
Inexperienced writers:

- use large and obscure words.
- use impersonal ("it was" or "there were") constructions.
- rely (with brain unengaged) on a spell-checker, which will not alert the user when he or she is using a real word that is the wrong word in the context.

Experienced writers:

- use common words in uncommon ways.
- use personal constructions and strong verbs.
- follow Mark Twain's advice: "As to the adjective: When in doubt, cut it out."[12]
- know that brevity and conciseness are harder—but more desirable— to achieve than verbosity and vagueness.
- proofread their writing.
- quote sparingly, reserving verbatim quotations to the most telling and illustrative examples.
- revise and rewrite, understanding that more than one draft will be a necessary and normal part of the analytical and writing process.

One of the most valuable guides to basic writing skills is William Strunk Jr. and E. B. White, *The Elements of Style* (1918; 4th ed., New York: Longman, 1999). Strunk, the sole author of the first edition of this book, taught English at Cornell University. One of his students, E. B. White (author of books ostensibly for children such as *Charlotte's Web* and *Stuart Little*), revised the book, and it has deservedly become a classic. Widely known simply as Strunk & White, this style guide is available in many forms, both print and online, including a 2005 edition that is illustrated. While some of its admonitions may strike modern ears as out of date, most still have value, especially for editors of a certain vintage for whom the improper use of "less" and "fewer" or "literally" can be tantamount to a declaration of illiteracy.

Style

Two major style conventions—for the presentation of punctuation, abbreviations, and source citations—are available in the field of history. The nature of your audience will determine which style convention you should use. If your article or book will be published by a full-service publisher that provides a copy editor, ask your publisher what style convention to use. If you hope to engage a popular, mass audience, the *Associated Press Stylebook and Briefing on Media Law*, edited by Daniel Christian, Sally Jacobsen, and David Minthorn (1953; rev. new ed., New York: Associated Press, 2012) will be appropriate. Used by broadcast and print journalists, the latest edition of the *Associated Press Stylebook* has expanded chapters on social media and broadcasting, including online video.

If you intend to reach a specialist, scholarly audience, you will want to use *The Chicago Manual of Style* (1906; 17th ed., Chicago: University of Chicago Press, 2017). Serious authors will need to become thoroughly familiar with *The Chicago Manual*. Authors and editors refer to it for questions and answers concerning style (see especially part II: "Style and Usage" and part III: "Source Citations and Indexes," especially chapter 14: "Notes and Bibliography"). Both first-time and experienced authors can benefit from examining part I: "The Publishing Process," chapter 1: "Books and Journals" ("The Parts of a Book," "The Parts of a Journal," and "Considerations for Electronic Formats"). Authors of all levels of experience or none need to be thoroughly familiar with chapter 2: "Manuscript Preparation, Manuscript Editing, and Proofreading" and chapter 16: "Indexes."

Manuscript Preparation

Before contacting a publisher, an author needs to conduct some due diligence. An author needs to find out if a publisher responds to email (as opposed to surface mail), requires the use of certain word processing programs, or wants to see a full manuscript or a proposal. An author needs to examine the publisher's guidelines for authors, which all publishers have. Keep in mind, during preliminary manuscript preparation, that an author should not submit to a prospective publisher a manuscript that looks like a book—that is, margins should be unjustified, end-of-line words should be unhyphenated, and type should not appear in bold. On all these matters, consult the publisher's guidelines for authors. The move to remote work during the pandemic caused many publishers to streamline procedures and do away with anything that involved work with hard copies that had to be sent through the mail. Unsolicited proposals and manuscripts sent through the mail would often land in a mail bin that was seldom if ever checked. Thus, even a publisher you have worked with in the past may have updated the guidance they provide to authors on its website. Check the website before you call an editor or put anything in the mail.

Authors will find especially helpful the discussion of preliminary manuscript preparation in Robert Lee Brewer, ed., *Writer's Market* (1922; 100th ed., Cincinnati, OH: Writer's Digest Books, 2021). This is an annual publication. In the 1931 edition, H. L. Mencken, as editor of the *American Mercury*, famously explained his criteria for publishing articles. Particularly useful for first-time authors are the sections on "Finding Work" (and within it, "Query Letter Clinic" and "Publishers and Their Imprints"), "Managing Work" (and within it, the chapters on contracts and "Time Management and Organization for Writers"), "Promoting Work," and "Markets" (and within it, "Book Publishers"). The latter section is highly serviceable for contact information and subject areas on which publishers seek manuscripts. See also the section on "Consumer Magazines" (especially the part on "History"). Another helpful title from the same publisher is Wendy Burt-Thomas, *The Writer's Digest Guide to Query Letters* (Cincinnati, OH: Writer's Digest Books, 2009). Another useful annual directory with contact information and subject areas on which publishers seek manuscripts is Karen Hallard, Mary-Anne Lutter, and Vivian Sposobiec, *Literary Market Place: The Directory of the American Book Publishing Industry with Industry Yellow Pages*, two volumes (1940; 70th ed., Medford, NJ: Information Today, 2011).

Annotation should document your sources and not be discursive. If discursiveness is necessary, integrate it into the text or move it to an appendix. If your publication is a documentary edition, consider a glossary of personal and place names to reduce the burden on the annotation.

Copyright

Copyright is a large and complicated subject on which many books have been written and many courses taught. It is the means by which creators of original works are allowed to benefit from their creations. One of the best books for the purposes of a layperson who wants to understand the history, development, and intricacies of copyright, and be entertained as well, is *The Illustrated Story of Copyright* by Edward Samuels, which deals not only with books but also includes issues and examples that cover the entire entertainment industry, including music, movies, and the internet.[13] The website of the US Copyright Office (www.copyright.gov) provides a great deal of information about copyright, including copyright law, copyright basics, frequently asked questions, and various publications, reports, and studies that delve into the nuances and complexities of copyright protection. The site also allows searching copyright records from 1978 and access to online registration. Another useful introduction is Michael Les Benedict, *A Historian's Guide to Copyright* (Washington, DC: American Historical Association, 2012).

While it behooves authors of all kinds to understand the history and development of copyright law, the basic concerns of the author involve managing your own rights, as well as managing the rights of copyright holders whose material—literary or visual—may be included in your work. The first thing to know is that copyright protection now begins at the time the original work is created in a "fixed tangible form of expression." Registration is not required but is recommended in order to be eligible for compensation should infringement, or the unauthorized use of your work, occur. Copyright protection gives the owner the exclusive right to reproduce the work, create derivative works, distribute copies, and perform or display the work publicly. A copyright owner can transfer any or all of his or her exclusive rights, but the transfer must be done in writing and signed by the copyright owner. As mentioned in the next chapter, authors will likely want to consult with an attorney who specializes in intellectual property law when making decisions about managing rights in a publisher's contract.

The duration of copyright varies according to the date of a work's creation. A work created on or after January 1, 1979, is protected from its creation until seventy years after the death of the creator. Works created before 1926 are in the public domain and are copyright free, as are works published between 1926 and 1963 for which copyright registrations were not renewed. Works created between 1926 and 1963, however, may have been renewed and may still be protected. Works in this category must be considered individually. Unpublished works, such as manuscripts, letters, diaries, and photographs created before 1979, may also be problematic in terms of determining whether they are protected or in the public domain. Archivists and librarians can tell you whether their institutions have copyright to the materials in their collections. This would involve a written agreement of transfer signed by the copyright holder. Often, however, archival collections have not been formally transferred to the institutions in which they are held. In that case it is the author's responsibility to investigate the copyright status of materials he or she wishes to use. When using such materials, efforts to seek out copyright holders should be made and documented, should unknown rights holders surface after publication.

Fair Use

According to the US Copyright Office, "the doctrine of fair use has developed through a substantial number of court decisions over the years and has been codified in section 107 of the copyright law." It provides for various uses for which reproduction without seeking permission may be fair and lists the factors to determine if a particular use is fair. These include:

- The purpose and character of the use, including whether such use is of commercial nature or is for nonprofit educational purposes
- The nature of the copyrighted work
- The amount and substantiality of the portion used in relation to the copyrighted work as a whole
- The effect of the use upon the potential market for, or value of, the copyrighted work

There is no easy or foolproof way to determine what is fair use, and no safe amount of text or use of a photograph that clearly falls within its parameters. Moreover, acknowledgment of copyrighted material does not replace the need to obtain permission. Litigation is the ultimate determiner of what is fair use and what is infringement. When in doubt, consult an attorney.[14]

Plagiarism

Plagiarism is the use of another writer's words as your own. It does not necessarily involve copyright infringement, since the question of whether a work is protected by copyright does not matter. Recent scandals involving prominent historians have helped to bring attention to the issue and the importance of historical documentation. In his interesting and useful look at the topic, *The Little Book of Plagiarism*, Richard A. Posner distinguishes between fair use and plagiarism:

> The fair-use doctrine permits quotation of brief passages from a copyrighted work without the copyright holder's permission. . . . But the fair user is

assumed to use quotation marks and credit the source; he is not a plagiarist. . . . The law does not excuse copyright infringement, no matter how fulsome the infringer's acknowledgment of his copying; but the acknowledgment will exonerate him of any charge of plagiarism. . . . Concealment is at the heart of plagiarism.

While careful note taking and accurate documentation may prove no ultimate protection for copyright infringement, they can provide protection against charges of plagiarism, which is an even surer destroyer of reputations and careers.[15]

Lifelong Learning

Historical writing, like any other skill, requires dedication, study, and diligent practice. It also demands continual learning to stay updated and informed on the newest information and practices in the field. Like John Adams's journey to the Continental Congress, it is not for the weak of heart or mind. And like David McCullough's *Pioneers*, it can lead to problems when not constantly engaged with new sources and practices in the field. As with any endeavor that is worthwhile, the successful writer of local history will be amply rewarded for overcoming the obstacles and challenges of effective communication, primarily with the deep learning and understanding that accompanies research and writing. English author E. M. Forster is often quoted as asking, "How can I tell what I think till I see what I say?"[16] Only by fully engaging in the research and writing process can one ever come close to knowing what one thinks, understanding the past in any profound way, and attaining the kind of knowledge that is truly its own reward.

NOTES

1. The American Historical Association's Statement on Standards of Professional Conduct, www.historians.org/jobs-and-professional-development/statements-standards-and-guidelines-of-the-discipline/statement-on-standards-of-professional-conduct#Profession (accessed September 29, 2023).

2. Christopher B. Coleman, preface to Donald Dean Parker, *Local History: How to Gather It, Write It, and Publish It*, rev. and ed. Bertha E. Josephson for the Committee on Guide for Study of Local History of the Social Science Research Council (New York: SSRC, 1944), x. Coleman was director of the Indiana Historical Bureau; Parker was head of the Department of History and Political Science at what is now South Dakota State University at Brookings; Josephson was on the staff at what is now the Ohio History Connection and a member of the AASLH's editorial board.

3. Laura Portwood-Stacer, *The Book Proposal Book: A Guide for Scholarly Authors*, Kindle edition (Princeton, NJ: Princeton University Press, 2021), 14.

4. Thomas E. Felt, *Researching, Writing, and Publishing Local History* (1976; 2nd ed., Nashville, TN: American Association for State and Local History, 1981), 68–69.

5. Richard Marius and Melvin E. Page, *A Short Guide to Writing about History* (1989; 8th ed., Boston: Pearson, 2012), 116.

6. David McCullough, *John Adams* (New York: Simon and Schuster, 2001), 17–18.

7. Marius and Page, 119–20.

8. David G. McCullough, *The Pioneers: The Heroic Story of the Settlers Who Brought the American Ideal West*, Kindle edition (New York: Simon & Schuster, 2019), 6, 109.

9. Joyce E. Chaplin, "David McCullough's Idealistic Settlers," in *New York Times*, May 13, 2019, digital edition, https://www.nytimes.com/2019/05/13/books/review/david-mccullough-pioneers.html.

10. Andrew S. Isenberg, "Hailing the Fortitude of Early American Settlers—and Ignoring Their Failings," in the *Washington Post*, May 10, 2019, digital edition, https://www.washingtonpost.com/outlook/hailing-the-fortitude-of-early-american-settlers-and-ignoring-their-failings/2019/05/10/04e948a0-660a-11e9-82ba-fcfeff232e8f_story.html.

11. Rebecca Onion, "No Man's Land," in *Slate*, May 10, 2019, digital edition, https://slate.com/culture/2019/05/pioneers-mccullough-frontier-history-book-review.html.

12. Mark Twain, *The Tragedy of Pudd'nhead Wilson* (Hartford, CT: American Publishing Company, 1894), 130.

13. Edward Samuels, *The Illustrated Story of Copyright* (New York: Thomas Dunne Books, 2000).

14. "U.S. Copyright Office: Fair Use Index," https://www.copyright.gov/fair-use (accessed November 15, 2022).

15. Richard A. Posner, *The Little Book of Plagiarism* (New York: Pantheon, 2007), 16–17.

16. E. M. Forster, *Aspects of the Novel* (New York: Harcourt, Brace and Company, 1927), 101.

FOUR

Economics, Design, and Production

How Do You Produce and Market a Book That People Will Pay For?

Little did we know when we published the first edition of this book in 2013 how hard the twenty-first century was going to come down on us. It has not been easy on anyone and has changed the tenor of our lives completely from what we knew before. The pandemic drastically accelerated changes already rapidly taking place in all areas of society, including publishing, and we saw them sprout and bloom and grow in unexpected directions that are only beginning to become apparent.

Of course the publishing industry has been dealing with a rapidly changing environment for decades, if not centuries. In *The Book Publishing Industry* (3rd edition, 2014), Albert N. Greco put it this way:

> Although it is easy to say that publishing is in a state of uncertainty because of the shifting patterns of readers, technological innovations, and the impact of intense competition for media usage (i.e., time) and media expenditures from other more seductive media formats, publishing has been in such a predicament since 1641 when the first book was published in what is now the United States.[1]

While predictions early in this century correctly envisioned a world and media environment transformed by the internet and digital revolution, they were not so accurate as to the details of those transformations. Printed books aren't dead; enhanced digital books with audio and video have not become a widespread phenomenon; brick-and-mortar bookstores have not disappeared; electronic self-publishing has not replaced traditional publishers and distributors; sales of e-books have not met expectations; traditional publishers have not gone away; and the internet has not had a wholly beneficent effect on our lives.

Most people have given up on predicting the future at this point, as well they should. What we do know is that the rapidity of change is only going to accelerate. Nevertheless, we can now see the directions of some of the changes and trends wrought by the digital revolution and the pandemic. People work from home; workflow is completely digital; print-on-demand publishing has improved dramatically, giving publishers a wider range of less-risky options and providing readers with a variety choices; e-books have not replaced print books but serve as an additional option for readers and an additional source of revenue for publishers; and self-publishing has become what John B. Thompson calls, "a world unto itself—a parallel universe of publishing" that is "part and parcel of a burgeoning domain of what could be called 'non-traditional publishing'—the many forms of publishing books and other content that do not fit within the traditional model of book publishing."[2]

The best we can do is keep our minds open, pay close attention, and use what we know to navigate the varied options available for providing honest, accurate, and resilient history to our families and communities. Publishing and marketing your book effectively are the final steps to bringing your work to the audience you envisioned when you began your project and to realizing its anticipated impact as a contribution to the history of your topic.

Publishing and marketing processes overlap in the same way as those of research and writing. From the moment you began identifying your audience and drafting a proposal, you have been putting together materials that will eventually be used to craft a marketing plan for your published book. Publication is a multifaceted and complex process involving at least seven major elements: acquisition, editing, design (including composition), dissemination or distribution (print or electronic), storage and order fulfillment (if your publication is printed), marketing (promotion and publicity), and sales. At any given moment, these activities are all happening simultaneously in a publishing house: acquisitions editors acquiring books for future publishing seasons, production and design staff preparing books for the next season, and marketing and sales promoting the books that have recently been published in the current season along with those from previous seasons—that is, for both the frontlist and the backlist, respectively. For authors, the better they understand the process, the more likely they will be to work with the press staff as part of a team to maximize limited resources, avoid frustration, and enhance opportunities for the success of their book. For those who aren't primarily publishers, but who are thinking about undertaking a publishing project, a clear-eyed knowledge of the economics and risks involved can help them avoid potential pitfalls and disasters.

ECONOMICS OF PUBLISHING AND THE PUBLISHING CYCLE

One of the first things to understand about the economics of local history publishing is that it is an activity that is not going to make anyone rich.

Margins are slim, discounts are large, production costs continue to grow, and sales are generally counted in three or four figures rather than in six or seven. This all adds up to an equation that can be very costly for a publisher and for the reputation of an editor if a book does not perform in line with expectations. As a result of the risks inherent in the process, editors and publishers put a good deal of effort into forecasting the likely sales performance of a prospective book. The goal of the publishers is to produce an award-winning work that will be a lasting contribution to the subject without losing their shirts. What Greg Britton of Johns Hopkins University Press writes about scholarly publishing is appropriate for other kinds of publishing as well: "What we mean by 'publishing' . . . is selecting, shaping, vetting, and producing books and then connecting them with the readers . . . in a way that is responsible and sustainable. This is harder than it sounds because as important as this work may be, it rarely reaches an audience big enough to support its publication." Editors and publishers, therefore, "need to be creative, strategic, and opportunistic."[3]

John B. Thompson defines publishers in *Books in the Digital Age* as follows: "Publishers today are essentially *content-acquiring and risk-taking organizations oriented towards the production of a particular kind of cultural commodity.*" Note Thompson's emphasis on "risk taking." The four stages of a book's life cycle for Thompson are all points that involve a decision to incur or to avoid financial risk for the publisher: (1) deciding to take on a project, (2) setting prices and print-runs, (3) determining whether to reprint or bring out a paperback edition, and (4) deciding when to take a title out-of-print. To make such decisions, publishers have developed tools for rationalizing the risk associated with any project and ensuring that it is kept to a minimum. While it is true, as Thompson explains, that for publishers generally "20 percent of the titles will account for around 80 percent of the revenue," it is not always clear which titles will fall within that magical 20 percent. Those that do and those that do not are often surprises, despite the tools and methods publishers use to hone their forecasts. Because the publishing cycle is long, knowing how a book is going to perform in the marketplace can take three or four years from the time of signing the contract. Forecasting sales performance, therefore, remains as much art as science, as much instinct as intellect.

The forecasting model is based on calculating a gross profit margin for every title published; that is revenue minus costs divided by revenue, expressed as a percentage:

$$\text{Gross Margin } (\%) = \frac{\text{Revenue} - \text{Cost of Goods Sold}}{\text{Revenue}}$$

If cost of goods sold is $10,000 and revenue is $20,000, then the gross margin would be 50 percent. In most cases, a potential project needs to be able to forecast a gross margin in the 50 percent range to be considered viable. (This is the equation that is likely floating through an acquisitions editor's head when you are making your elevator pitch and it seems that he or she is distracted and not paying attention.) Cost of goods comprises not only the fixed costs, or costs that do not increase according to the number of books printed, but also variable costs, or costs that fluctuate according to the size of the print run. Fixed costs include research, writing, editing, design, and composition. Design and composition are now called "prepress" in the electronic age. Fixed costs are present for both electronic publications and printed books. Design includes composition (typesetting and page layout [composed of aspects such as the sizing and placing of graphic elements—illustrations, maps, and charts]). Variable costs depend on the number of copies printed (printing, paper, binding, shipping, and storage) or the number of copies sold (royalties to the author). Other costs include discounts offered to retailers and wholesalers, free copies for promotion, and expenses for illustrations, maps, and permissions. The only savings that electronic publishing (such as on the Web) can realize (assuming that the electronic publication is well designed) are the variable costs of printing, paper, binding, and storage. These savings are often offset by the costs of data conversion to files appropriate for e-readers. The gross margin for each title contributes to the gross margin of the firm, from which it must pay overhead costs for such items as space, utilities, and staffing. "What I think surprises most people," wrote Greg Britton in an email to the authors, "is that most of the costs of publishing happen well before printing/binding. In fact, I think PPB—paper, printing, and binding—only make up about 10 percent of the total cost of our books."[4]

Publishers must make educated guesses at the number of books they expect to sell at a price that is consistent with the market for similar books to predict whether a project will break even, lose, or make money. As Thompson explains, "Publishers aim for the price that will maximize revenue over cost, where cost and revenue are dependent on price per copy, on the total number of copies printed, and on the total number sold. By increasing the print run, one can lower the unit cost and thereby bring down the price per copy while achieving a reasonable margin; on the other hand, if the extra copies printed are not sold, the potential gains will turn out to be illusory and the publisher will have to write off unsold stock."[5] This happens often, and as a result publishers often find themselves with a warehouse full of printed books that will never sell and that will eventually have to be pulped.

The profit and loss statement (P&L) is the primary decision-making tool that publishers and editors use. A P&L can take many forms to accommodate the requirements of specific projects and presses. Most presses have a proprietary version that they keep confidential. Authors will never see it, but as it evolves it will become the basis for making final decisions on price, print run, and format. With a basic knowledge of spreadsheets and some examples to follow, P&L statements are easy to create. By searching on the internet for "sample publishing P&L," you can find downloadable examples that have the formulas built in. We will provide links and downloadable examples at the companion website for this volume (www.writinglocalhistorytoday.com). Here is a template for a basic P&L that you can adapt for the purposes of your project:

Author/Title
Binding: cloth or paper
Page Count: 300

		Budgeted	
	SALES INCOME		
A	list price	**$29.95**	
B	quantity	2,000	
C	discount	**46%**	
D	avg. receipts	$16.17	price × discount
E	comps and frees	200	
F	copies to sell	1800	
G	TOTAL INCOME	$29,111	receipts × copies to sell
	COST OF GOODS SOLD		
H	PPB costs	$8,800	paper, printing & binding
I	editorial costs	$2,300	copyedit, proof, etc.
J	prepress costs	$5,050	prepress costs
K	PPB unit cost	$4.40	PPB/F
L	mfc. unit cost	$8.08	H+I+J/F
M	subsidy		Any grant income goes here
N	royalty rate	**8.0%**	
O	royalty expense	$2,329	GxN (calculated on net)
P	unit cost to prog.	$10.27	H+I+J+O/F
Q	TOTAL COST	$18,479	
R	**GROSS MARGIN**	**$10,632**	income-cost (G-Q)
S	**% MARGIN**	**36.5%**	margin/income
T	**MULTIPLIER**	**3.7**	price/mfc unit cost (A/L)
U	**BREAK EVEN**	**1,143**	cost/ave. receipt (Q/D)

In this example, the P&L begins with the revenue generated from book sales. The book is priced at $29.95, and there is a discount of 46 percent applied. Discounts are an estimated average of the various discounts that may be applied to books sold through different channels. Books sold through bookstores usually require what is considered a trade discount of 40 to 50 percent or more. Books sold through a publisher's website will be discounted less, generally in the 30 percent range. Academic books usually command a smaller discount in the range of 20 percent or so, known as a short discount. Publishers rely on historical sales information to make educated guesses regarding discounts, price, and print run. Books printed offset, or through the traditional ink-on-paper method, can be less expensive per unit than books printed digitally at certain quantities. Short-run digital printing is more cost-effective for print runs under 500 or so; offset printing, which requires a good deal of setup of printing plates, is more effective for press runs of 1,500 or more. Print-on-demand is a form of digital printing that has improved greatly since its inception and involves printing individual books upon purchase. The unit cost of a print-on-demand or a short-run digitally printed book will be higher than a book printed offset, but the choice to print digitally can lessen the risk to the publisher, since the overall costs for short-run digital will be less than printing offset for small print runs, and for print-on-demand the manufacturing costs are spread out over the life of the title rather than paid up front. Heavily illustrated books and books printed with color are generally printed offset, though in some cases it makes sense to use digital short-run printing for color projects. For many smaller publishers, the pandemic accelerated the move toward print-on-demand publishing, decreasing the risk involved in offset printing at the expense of higher unit costs. They found, also, that print-on-demand allowed them to print split runs, offering hardback and paperback versions simultaneously to give customers a greater choice without increasing up-front costs.

The revenue per book, according to the example above, then, would be calculated as ($29.95 × 0.46= $13.78) resulting in an average net price of $16.17. If the print run is 2,000 with 200 copies designated to be given away for promotional purposes, then the net revenue generated if all the remaining 1,800 copies are sold is $29,111. The next section of the P&L deals with the cost of goods, which includes print, paper, and binding (PPB), shipping, and other editorial and manufacturing costs, as well as royalties. For this example, the total costs are $18,479, which creates a 36.5 percent gross margin with net income of $10,632, which would not likely be enough in most publishing houses to get a book across the finish line to a contract. Such a book would likely need a subsidy or subvention from a grant or an individual to make it financially viable. This is the case for many books published by nonprofit publishers, including university presses. In this case a $2,000 subsidy increases the gross margin to 43.4 percent; a $5,000 subsidy, to 53.7 percent. Of course, as we mentioned above, you can also adjust the price or print run to improve the gross margin, but it should always be done with a rational understanding of what the market will bear. Subsidies are not counted in the income section of the P&L because author royalties are based on income, and publishers do not want to increase income with subsidy dollars.

	Author/Title		
	Binding:	cloth or paper	
	Page Count:	300	

		Budgeted	
	SALES INCOME		
A	list price	**$29.95**	
B	quantity	2,000	
C	discount	46%	
D	avg. receipts	$16.17	price × discount
E	comps and frees	200	
F	copies to sell	1800	
G	TOTAL INCOME	$29,111	receipts × copies to sell

	COST OF GOODS SOLD		
H	PPB costs	$8,800	paper, printing & binding
I	editorial costs	$2,300	copyedit, proof, etc.
J	prepress costs	$5,050	prepress costs
K	PPB unit cost	$4.40	PPB/F
L	mfc. unit cost	$8.08	H+I+J/F
M	subsidy	$5,000	Any grant income goes here
N	royalty rate	8.0%	
O	royalty expense	$2,329	GxN (calculated on net)
P	unit cost to prog.	$7.30	H+I+J+O/F
Q	TOTAL COST	$13,479	

R	**GROSS MARGIN**	**$15,632**	income-cost (G-Q)
S	**% MARGIN**	**53.7%**	margin/income
T	**MULTIPLIER**	**3.7**	price/mfc. unit cost (A/L)
U	**BREAK EVEN**	**833**	cost/ave. receipt (Q/D)

Author royalties are typically a percentage of the net revenue received: net revenue after deducting the cost of goods sold. In this case, the author royalties would be 8 percent, which is standard for this kind of book, resulting in $2,329. First-time authors are often required to receive a reduced royalty of 4 to 6 percent or to waive royalties entirely on sales of the first five hundred to one thousand copies. Advances on royalties, royalties paid to the author in advance and then recouped through sales, are rare in the local history publishing realm. While understanding the costs and risks involved in taking on a publishing project does not eliminate the risk entirely, it can keep it to a minimum, increasing the likelihood of success for the publisher and curtailing unrealistic expectations on the part of the author.

When selecting a printer, an author or publisher should solicit multiple bids by means of a request for proposal (RFP). (Sample requests for proposals appear in appendixes of this book.) A long-standing dictum of the printing trade is that a printer can offer three desiderata: quality, punctuality, and a good price. Of those three, the client may choose two.

Another custom of which the client should be aware (read the "conventions of the printing trade" that are often printed on the reverse side of contracts): Most printing contracts allow the printer to supply 10 percent over or 10 percent under the number of copies specified in the contract, and the client is obligated to pay for the number of copies delivered. This is a vestige of the days when printing presses were difficult to stop. But in the twenty-first century, pressruns are more easily controllable, underruns are rare (but do occasionally occur), and overruns are common. If you require an absolute minimum number of copies (for instance, to supply subscribers or members of your organization), you should order a bit more than you need to allow for the possibility of an underrun, or have a candid conversation with your customer service representative about the number of copies you actually need.

ACQUISITION

Acquisitions editors (AEs) serve as the front door to the press. They are known by other names, such as sponsoring editors or acquiring editors, but what they all have in common is that they are entrepreneurs, deciding on which projects to reject and which to move forward based on their perceptions of a book's potential to contribute to the status and revenue of both the editor and the press. In making these decisions, AEs are balancing many factors that will determine their success in both the short and long term. They likely manage a few lists in different disciplines, many of which will have had a history before it was theirs, and some of which they started on their own, believing that publishing in that area will provide an opportunity for the press to grow in a new direction. Other times an inherited list might be discontinued because it is not performing well, either in terms of generating manuscripts or revenue. For an author who submits a manuscript in an area that appears to be a good fit, it can be frustrating to learn that a press has changed direction.

Because of the overlapping nature of the elements of publishing, we have already discussed a good deal about the acquisitions function in this book. In the first chapter we mentioned how choosing a press and choosing an editor corresponds with understanding your audience, and we offered suggestions about putting together a book proposal that would command attention from an AE. We also mentioned "peer review" as the acquisitions practice that distinguishes university presses and other scholarly publishers from those publishing primarily for general audiences, or the trade. We said more about peer review in chapter 3, the chapter on writing, to remind authors working with the peer review process to keep in mind that responding to peer reviewers will likely involve revision of some sort, as well as some patience and humility. Nevertheless, the process, if carried out properly, will lead to a more successful book, both critically and financially.

Once the AEs have completed all vetting processes, including peer review if necessary, and received required committee approvals, they are ready to put a contract in place with an author. AEs can offer contracts based on a proposal or a complete manuscript. Some presses that require peer review allow an editor to offer a contract on proposal without sending it to readers for review; others require review and committee approval for proposals. In both cases, the full manuscript will be sent out for peer review when it is received. Each method has its advantages and disadvantages. While a contract can be put in place more quickly if a proposal does not first have to be peer reviewed, the author will not receive the kind of constructive criticism that could be useful while completing the manuscript.

The legal liabilities of author and publisher are sufficiently complex that a contract, or publisher's agreement, needs to define their relationship. The basic issues to be agreed upon include acceptance; compensation in terms of a lump-sum payment, royalties, advances on royalties, free copies, and / or discounts for additional copies; warranties that the author's work is original, that it has not been published before, and that the author has the right to assign copyright in the work (including responsibility for acquiring necessary permissions for any use of the work of others, i.e., third-party content, that appears in the work); assignment of copyright; assurance that the author will not be publishing another competing book; and designation of the period following formal acceptance by which the book will be published. (Sample publishing agreements appear in the appendixes.)

Negotiations sometimes break down over the indemnification clause, whereby the author indemnifies and holds harmless the publisher in case of lawsuits that involve a breach of the author's warranties and representations—notably the warranty that the work is original—in other words, in case of infringement of copyright. An author needs to understand that this is a standard contract feature that provides one more incentive to avoid infringement of copyright and plagiarism.

Whether you are an author or a publisher, you may benefit from the advice of a lawyer. You will need not just any general practice lawyer but a lawyer who specializes in intellectual property and copyright law. The Authors Guild (https://authorsguild.org) also offers contract review as a service at certain levels of membership, which might be a valid consideration for serious authors of local history. A state or local historical society that acts as a publisher, or a small press, will have frequent recourse to a boilerplate (standard or sample) contract and, in consultation with an intellectual property lawyer, should work out such a boilerplate contract to use with authors.

A fundamental early decision in the publication process is who shall own the copyright of the publication. A publisher who wants to own all rights to the publication should be ready to pay more, in either a lump sum or royalties, to an author. The publisher will thereby assume the accompanying responsibilities, including placing the copyright notice in the book, registering the publication with the US Copyright Office, and supplying necessary copies for deposit. Publishers are often in the best position to manage subsidiary rights, such as foreign, translation, serial, paperback, motion picture, and electronic rights. While local historians working with small publishers are not likely to be concerned to a significant degree with subsidiary rights issues, movie options and translations are sometimes desired, and authors should be aware of the possibilities. With the rise in popularity of e-books, electronic rights are increasingly considered as basic publishing rights and subject to primary royalty.[6]

An author who wants to retain copyright, and a publisher who wants to reduce payments to an author, can agree on a license (exclusive or nonexclusive) to publish. An agreement whereby an author grants to a publisher a license to publish that is exclusive for a certain period or for so long as the publisher keeps the publication in print and then converts to a nonexclusive license can be mutually advantageous. The website of the Copyright Information Center at Cornell University provides a good list of the options available to authors confronted with these choices, as well as sample language and video tutorials that provide advice.[7]

For an author or a publisher embarking on a first-time or only-time publication, acquisition is a one-off prospect. But for authors and publishers for whom publishing will be a long-term enterprise, acquisition becomes an activity requiring a long-term commitment of time and resources. In the case of the publisher, that commitment becomes a responsibility carried out by editors. Acquisition is essentially a networking activity—authors seeking a publisher and acquisitions editors seeking authors, networking through professional societies. In the field of local history, networking takes place through state and local historical societies and professional organizations such as the American Association for State and Local History.

GENERAL CONTENTS OF BOOK CONTRACT

Rights of the publisher:

- Author usually assigns all publication rights to the publisher.
- Publisher will also generally desire copyright.

Rights of the author:

- Author will be offered royalties (a percentage of publisher's sales) as payment for those rights. Royalty percentages may vary on different kinds of sales (foreign distributors, book clubs, remainders, translation rights).
- Publisher will indicate if any other payments are to be made: advances against royalties, editorial stipends, payments to contributors.
- Authors will be given a fixed number of free copies of the book, and the option of purchasing others at a discount.
- Publisher will indicate how often and when royalties are to be paid.
- If it's not here in writing, the publisher doesn't plan to pay you for it!

The manuscript and publication:

- Author agrees to deliver a manuscript "in content and form satisfactory to the publisher."
- Contract establishes a length and delivery date for the manuscript, usually previously negotiated between parties.
- Indicates who is responsible for proofreading, indexing, preparation of artwork, copyright permissions (usually the author).
- Publisher reserves the right to determine design and publication processes.

Future considerations:

- A clause defines when the book is considered out of print and establishes procedures for returning publishing rights and copyright to the author.
- Author promises to revise the book for a new edition according to a schedule set by the publisher (standard in textbooks, rare in professional books).

Legal responsibilities:

- Publisher is protected against not publishing the book in cases of war, fire, natural disaster, or other situations beyond their control.
- Author is asked to warrant that the book is not plagiarized, libelous, nor that publisher's rights are in any way restricted. Obligates author to indemnify publisher in case of a lawsuit.
- Publisher is given the option of assigning rights to the book elsewhere.

Special provisions:

- Publication of a paperback edition, or within a series, should be indicated.
- The rights and responsibilities of contributing authors in case of edited books are recognized. Often a sample contributor contract will be attached as an appendix to the main contract.
- Contract will specify any special requests of the author that the publisher has agreed to.
- Occasionally there will be a "noncompetition" clause, restricting the author from writing competing books, or a "right of first refusal" promise for the author's next book.

What is usually not in the contract:

- A promise that the publisher will ever publish the book.
- A description of the publisher's production process or timetable.
- Promises concerning the amount and nature of marketing the book will receive.
- An indication of the book's price or size of print run. [8]

EDITING

Every author needs an editor. Every manuscript can be improved by the application of another set of eyes. The publication process is not only a networking but also a collegial activity. An author should ask trusted colleagues in the field to read and critique a draft publication. Readers who serve as representatives of the intended audience can also provide useful commentary. After publisher and author agree to publish, and the text more or less ceases to be a moving target, the publication is ready for copyediting. Since smaller independent publishers generally do not supply rigorous copyediting, authors may need to secure readers with copyediting experience to read their manuscripts.

Just as an author's best ally is a knowledgeable archivist or reference librarian during the research phase of a project, during the publication phase, an author's most valuable ally is a skilled copy editor. Ideally the copy editor will be knowledgeable in not only language and style conventions but also the historical content of the publication. Marshall Lee, in his excellent in-depth treatment of all phases of publishing, *Bookmaking: Editing/Design/Production*, details the various functions of copyediting, including correcting typographical errors, errors of fact, errors of grammar, improving awkward sentences, enforcing conformity to the house style, and marking the manuscript for composition and design. "Copyeditors often go well beyond these efforts," he explains, "revising the structure and even sequence of chapters. . . . There is nothing wrong with this provided that the author and the editor are willing, and the copyeditor is competent."[9] An author will be lucky if the publisher can provide copyediting service. No press that we are aware of today provides source checking; few publishers today provide fact checking. When published reviews expose errors in a publication, the publisher's response is usually that factual accuracy is the author's responsibility.

Whether or not a copy editor will be available to work on a publication, authors should immerse themselves during the writing phase in the style convention (for example the *Chicago Manual of Style* or the *Associated Press Stylebook*; see chapter 3) that will be used in editing the publication. The cleaner the author can make the manuscript before editing, the less editing the manuscript will require, and fewer disagreements between author and editor will ensue. In the memorable words of *The Economist Style Guide*: "Scrupulous writers will also notice that their copy is edited only lightly and is likely to be used. It may even be read."[10] During the editing and production phases, beware of typographical errors in unexpected areas of a publication where a proofreader's guard may be down, such as the cover, the spine, and the title page.

The University of Oklahoma Press provides an excellent overview of the editing and production process for its authors on its website.[11] Once authors have signed a contract and completed their manuscript, they will prepare the manuscript for transmittal according to precise instructions from their AE. All images, permissions, maps, tables, graphs, and charts must be gathered and prepared in the manner prescribed by the press. The cost of these items is usually borne by the author, unless contracted otherwise. Most publishers (online or in print) prefer digital scans of images and have standard formats and dpi (dots per inch) for those images, especially since the pandemic drove workflow in that direction. Maps should be prepared by a qualified cartographer who has experience preparing maps for book publication. Maps can often be a sticking point when authors submit scanned images of historical maps that editors know will not reproduce well in a book. Presses can usually recommend cartographers they have confidence in for authors to consult and contract with. Maps and images should be numbered to correspond with callouts in the text to make it easy for copy editors and designers to match them up (e.g., <fig 1 about here>, <map 1 about here>). The AE will prepare the materials to transmit to what is often called the Editorial, Design, and Production department, where it will be assigned to a manuscript editor (ME) to send out to a freelance copyeditor. Manuscript editors will not accept a transmittal from Acquisitions unless all materials are together and prepared according to their standards. Often they will accept a transmittal with some pieces still to come, as long as they are identified clearly and have realistic dates for submittal.

Once the transmittal has been accepted, the ME will contact the author to set up a schedule for reviewing the copyedited manuscript. This is all done electronically now, using the track changes function in Microsoft Word. The author will work with the freelance copyeditor directly. The copyeditor will edit for clarity and content and ask questions the author will need to respond to. The author usually has the prerogative to accept or reject changes to the manuscript. The ME will also notify Marketing that a project has been transmitted, which will be their cue to send the author a marketing questionnaire (MQ) with a deadline for returning. It is very important to fill out the MQ fully and promptly. It will become the basis for the press's marketing plan and will be used in what is called a "launch meeting" to determine the final specifications of the book, including price and print run, title, discount, and schedule. This is also the point at which cover design and catalog copy are discussed. The more thoroughly the authors complete the MQ, the more input they have in these matters.

When the copyediting is complete, Manuscript Editorial will transmit to Production for design, composition, and manufacturing. The ME will let the author know when to expect page proofs for review. At this point, the author will put together an index. The cost of the index is usually the author's responsibility. Authors often choose to pay for a professional indexer who is experienced at providing professional indexes quickly. The cost of the index can sometime be taken from the author's royalties.

DESIGN

Computers have revolutionized all phases of publication, not least in the area of design. In all publication areas, computerization has forced onto authors and publishers activities formerly performed by contractors, none more so than in the areas of composition and design. The good news is that opportunities for publishing are greater now than at any time during the past. If authors or publishers choose to take on themselves the tasks of composition and design, they can dramatically reduce the costs of publication. The more sobering news is that these tasks are labor intensive and time-consuming.

The term "desktop publishing" is a misnomer: It should more accurately be called "desktop composition." Authors or publishers who choose to do design themselves can apply QuarkXPress or Adobe InDesign. These are sophisticated software programs intended for professional book designers and run on Macintosh or Microsoft Windows operating systems.

Electronic publishing has opened wide possibilities for authors and historical organizations and transformed the publishing industry. But a computer, with its unlimited options for fonts and visual effects, will not turn a user who knows little about design into a talented and effective designer of books or websites. Good design is an important component of a successful publication, and authors working with commercial presses or university presses will have opportunities to suggest possible cover ideas and to comment on the suitability of cover and page design. The ultimate decision in these matters, however, lies with the publisher, who will likely have the best understanding of how to reach the book's intended market. Many presses will have a style and format already developed for a series, and authors will need to work within the parameters already established by the publisher. Local historical organizations seeking to bring out a book for commemorative or other purposes should seek a designer with some experience in book design. Designers will charge a rate based on a per-page cost and determined by the use of color and the number of illustrations. From authors, publishers want files in Word for Windows or application files they can edit and manipulate, not as PDF (portable document format) files, before sending them to the compositor. When a publication is ready, the publisher sends the made-up pages to the printer from an FTP (file transfer protocol) site.

With the dramatic rise in the ownership of electronic devices for reading e-books, including smartphones, tablets, and dedicated e-book readers, e-books have become a commonplace and expected piece of the publishing equation. While the variable costs of print, paper, binding, and storage are not necessary for e-book production, other production costs for converting print files to standard e-book files come into play. Many conversion services exist to accommodate the growing demand, and rates and quality can vary widely. Conversion houses can accommodate a wide variety of files, including Microsoft Word, PDF, QuarkXPress, InDesign, and many others. They can also scan printed books and provide digital files for e-book distribution. The ePub format is a standard for the industry maintained by the International Digital Publishing Forum, a nonprofit organization composed of publishers and technology companies.[12]

DISSEMINATION (PRINT OR ELECTRONIC)

If your publication is a bound photocopy, for instance a family history, the audience for which is immediate family members and, somewhat more broadly, genealogical researchers, you can donate copies to interested family members and genealogical libraries such as:

- The Family History Library at the Genealogical Society of Utah (the largest genealogical library in the United States), 35 North West Temple, Salt Lake City, UT 84150-9005; (801) 240-6996. The Family-Search Library website (www.churchofjesuschrist.org/learn/family -history-library?lang=eng) provides step-by-step instructions on how to conduct family history research. The FamilySearch Library, operated by the Church of Jesus Christ of Latter-day Saints (LDS Church), operates seventeen regional and thousands of local (ward, branch, and stake) Family History Centers throughout the United States and other countries.
- The Allen County Public Library (the second-largest genealogical library in the United States), 900 Library Plaza, Fort Wayne, IN 46802-3699; (260) 421-1320; https://acpl.lib.in.us; email: ask@acpl.info.
- Your state library and your local public library.
- Your state historical society and your local/county historical society.

Be aware that most repositories have formal processes and guidelines for adding materials to their collections. Your manuscript may not fit within the parameters of a particular collection. As with editors, always ask librarians and archivists if they are interested before sending them a manuscript or book for acquisition.

STORAGE AND ORDER FULFILLMENT

The requirements of storage are one more incentive to contract with a full-service publisher or an order-fulfillment company. Order fulfillment can be contracted out to a company that will warehouse the books and process and ship orders. The Chicago Distribution Center (CDC; 1427 East 60th St., Chicago, IL 60637-2902; 773-702-7700; https://press.uchicago.edu/cdc.html) is a major storage and order-fulfillment facility. The CDC maintains an inventory of 12 million books in a 270,000-square-foot facility and ships 19,000 units daily. Some self-publishing companies also provide storage and order-fulfillment services. But given the thin margins on which a small press operates, the fees for contracting out those services can possibly eliminate any chance of cost recovery without careful consideration of such factors as press run, the number of units printed, and pricing.

SELF-PUBLISHING

Self-publishing used to be a marginal activity, dismissed as "vanity publishing," even though university presses for many decades often imposed author subventions (or financial support) for books that might be expensive to produce because of the need for additional pages, color, or illustrations. But recently, self-publishing has become a force driving growth in, and has entered the mainstream of, the publishing industry. The overall number of new self-published books grew from 600,000 in 2014 to 1.7 million in 2019, an increase of 283 percent, and accounted for 43 percent of the total new books published during that five-year period.[13]

Before the advent of the digital age and the development of the current plethora of publishers working through Web interfaces and producing digital print-on-demand copies in low quantities and e-books, self-publishing was an expensive and labor-intensive exercise that often resulted in a garage full of books that never saw the shelves of a bookstore or the light of day. *The Culture and Commerce of Publishing in the 21st Century* offers a useful "Analysis of the Economics of Self-Publishing," which looks at the cost of producing 500 paperback copies of a 362-page, black-and-white book that used royalty-free art for a color cover. Costs were as follows: $5,000 for a commercial printer using traditional lithographic equipment ranging down to $1,875 for a digital printer who specializes in books. Self-publishers in the past also had to bear the cost of creating relationships with booksellers, purchasing ISBNs (International Standard Book Number, a unique number required for books to be ordered by bookstores or libraries), handling fulfillment, and creating promotional materials.[14]

The new crop of self-publishers, however, offers a wide range of packages to suit the needs and the budgets of a diverse array of authors. On the low end, the publishers will produce a certain number of books based on the files an author submits. In addition, publishers offer packages that can include all the tasks that were so formidable for self-publishers in the past, such as ISBN registration, copyediting, proofreading, cover design, page layout, distribution, marketing, and management of sales and returns. "In self-publishing, many of the roles and responsibilities of publishers are reversed," writes John Thompson in *Book Wars*. In the traditional model, publishers acquire the rights, pay the author a royalty, take on all the risk, and make all the decisions. Self-publishers decide how best to present their material, take all the risk, and pay for necessary services. "If the book does well, the author reaps the rewards, but if the book doesn't sell, the author absorbs any losses."[15]

Authors and small presses can self-publish through manufacturing-on-demand publishers such as:

- CreateSpace, 7290 Investment Dr., Unit B, Charleston, SC 29418-8305 (for books); (843) 760-8000; www.createspace.com. A subsidiary of Amazon.com (through Kindle Direct Publishing), CreateSpace is a manufacturing-on-demand publisher of books, DVDs, video downloads, and MP3s.
- Ingram Lightning Source, Ingram Content Group, 1 Ingram Blvd., La Vergne, TN 37086-3629; (615) 213-5815; www.lightningsource.com; email: inquiry@lightningsource.com.
- The subsidiaries, all at 1663 South Liberty Dr., Bloomington, IN 47404-5161, of Author Solutions, Inc., the largest self-publishing company in the world:
  - AuthorHouse; (833) 262-8899; www.authorhouse.com; email: authorsupport@authorhouse.com.
  - iUniverse, Inc.; (844) 349-9409; www.iuniverse.com.
  - Xlibris Corporation; (844) 714-8691; www.xlibris.com; email: publishtoday@xlibris.com.

The enhanced standing of self-publishing was demonstrated in 2012 when the Penguin Group (a subsidiary of Pearson, based in London) purchased Author Solutions. The purchase is evidence of a new direction in the publishing industry. Tony Cook, business correspondent for the *Indianapolis Star*, predicts that mainstream publishers will use self-publishing subsidiaries "as a kind of screening process funded by the writers." Michael Norris, a senior analyst at Simba Information, a market research firm, observes, "I think that Pearson is going to go through this with a fine-tooth comb and identify the ones that are going to appeal to a wider audience." But authors and small presses considering self-publishing should do so with their eyes open. Self-publishing companies do not disclose the sales records of their titles. Throughout the publishing industry, only about 7 percent of all book titles and about 5 percent of self-published book titles sell more than a thousand copies.[16]

WRITING AND PUBLISHING LOCAL HISTORY ON THE WEB

Websites provide a cost-effective means for distributing various kinds of historical content, including family histories, conference proceedings, and research tools such as cumulative indexes for historical periodicals and primary sources. They can also accommodate multimedia, such as film, video, audio recordings, and music, in ways that are impossible in a printed book. Users interact with websites or navigate in individual ways along paths that correspond to their interests and inclinations and not in a linear fashion as they might with a print publication. Moreover, the majority of visitors are likely to be directed to a part of the site from a search engine and not necessarily to a home page, or landing page, of the site. Therefore, website architecture and navigation are primary considerations that must be planned carefully. As Jenny L. Presnell explains, "Architecture in this sense is not the programming of the website but, rather, how it is laid out, labeled, and organized, as well as how visitors will navigate through it."[17]

There are many books available as guides to commercial website design, such as Patrick J. Lynch and Sarah Horton's *Web Style Guide*; Louis Rosenfeld, Peter Morville, and Jorge Arango's *Information Architecture: For the Web and Beyond*; and Steve Krug's *Don't Make Me Think, Revisited: A Common Sense Approach to Web Usability*.[18] These books are useful for historians seeking advice about how to make their websites user-friendly. One of the most important books dealing specifically with presenting history on the Web is Daniel J. Cohen and Roy Rosenzweig's *Digital History: A Guide to Gathering, Preserving, and Presenting the Past on the Web.* The book exists in both a print version and a digital version that can be accessed for free and is the first book to be consulted by those wanting to enter the field of digital history.

Cohen and Rosenzweig take readers on a tour of the "History Web," discussing its development and highlighting the different genres of sites that exist, along with significant examples. "From the perspective of those who are thinking about creating their own website, probably the most helpful way to classify history websites is by the types of materials they provide and the functions and audiences they serve," the authors explain. "The past decade has seen the emergence of five main genres of history websites that follow preexisting patterns and categories: archives (containing primary sources); exhibits, films, scholarship, and essays (that is, secondary sources); teaching (directed at students and teachers); discussion (focused on online dialogue); and organizational (providing information about a historical group). Yet these categories are often loosely followed and frequently blurred." For example, organizational sites often contain primary sources, interpretative essays, and teaching materials along with information about the hours they are open and explanations of mission and programs. Despite the fact that websites seldom conform to one genre, thinking about genres helps one consider "how what you are doing relates to the audience you are hoping to reach."[19]

Creators of sites should review examples that reflect the type of site they wish to emulate, examining the nature of the page design, navigation, organization, and the text. How easy is it to move around in the site without getting lost? Is navigation logical and intuitive? Are the same buttons on every page in the same place? Is the design inviting or distracting? For large sites, is there a "breadcrumb trail" to help visitors see where they are in the site and find their way back to where they came from? Are the hyperlinks obvious, or are they difficult to detect? All of these considerations and more must be taken into account to build a website that users will want to return to and that others will link to, thereby increasing the likelihood of showing up high on search results pages.

In *The Information-Literate Historian*, Jenny L. Presnell provides a list of necessary components for a website to be taken seriously:

- Biographical information about the author—a component of establishing a site's credibility.
- Statement of purpose—very helpful in evaluating the authority and usefulness of a site.
- Contact link for questions—to enhance discussion and to identify errors and broken links.
- Last updated date—to identify how active a site is and how well it is maintained.
- A title—at the top of each page so visitors will know where they are.
- Metadata—terms that describe the site so visitors can find it.[20]

In addition to titles mentioned above, the following publications provide excellent discussion of encoding and design for electronic publications:

- Elizabeth Castro, *EPUB, Straight to the Point: Creating eBooks for the Apple iPad and Other eReaders* (Berkeley, CA: Peachpit Press, 2011).
- Cyndi Howells, *Planting Your Family Tree Online: How to Create Your Own Family History Web Site* (Nashville, TN: Rutledge Hill Press, 2004); www.cyndislist.com/planting.

- Jakob Nielsen, *Designing Web Usability: The Practice of Simplicity* (Indianapolis, IN: New Riders Publishing, 1999); https://www.nngroup .com/books/designing-web-usability/.
- Bob Trubshaw [R. W. Trubshaw], *How to Write and Publish Local and Family History Successfully: Books, Booklets, Magazines, CD-ROMs, and Web Sites* (1999; rev. ed., Loughborough, UK: Heart of Albion Press, 2005).

BLOGS AND SOCIAL MEDIA

"Blog," a term derived from the conflation of "Web log," is an online journal to which the "blogger" contributes regularly, offering opinion and commentary and often including multimedia components. Blogs began appearing in the late 1990s but really became prevalent in the 2000s, having a major impact on journalism, politics, and scholarship. According to Cohen and Rosenzweig, John Barger, the proprietor of the *Robot Wisdom Weblog*, originated the term in 1997, and the blog as personal journal became popular among young people working in technology companies in the late nineties. As blogs became more popular, software packages arose that greatly simplified the task of creating and maintaining a blog.[21] Current popular blog services include WordPress, Blogger, Xanga, and Live-Journal, among many others. The best are user-friendly and inexpensive, often offering packages that are free. Blogs are generally written in an informal tone and should be updated frequently to be effective. According to Tim Grove, writing in the *Encyclopedia of Local History*, "the first requirement of a successful blog is commitment. . . . A blog that does not show recent activity will lose readers very quickly."[22] For authors, blogs can be a powerful tool for promoting books and ideas, bypassing the traditional gatekeepers of journalism and scholarship. But those that reflect the standards of careful writing along with creativity and timeliness will attract the most readers.

Blogs and social media can work together to build communities around and increase sales of printed books. Jerry Apps of Wisconsin, the author of more than thirty books on local history, is a deft manager of a variety of social media tools to promote his speaking engagements and printed books. His website (www.jerryapps.com) provides links to his blog and his social media accounts on Facebook and X (formerly Twitter) along with contact information and a great deal of information about his life and work. He provides an example to emulate for all aspiring local history authors.

In her article on social media for the *Encyclopedia of Local History*, Linda Norris gives this succinct definition: "Social media is Web-based technology designed to turn the Internet from a one-way form of communication into a dialogue."[23] She acknowledges that it "is constantly changing, and the use of it by local history organizations continues to evolve."[24] The primary social media sites relevant to local historians as of this writing, in addition to the blog services previously mentioned, are Facebook and X, though there are many more, and their numbers continue to proliferate. Wikipedia lists more than two hundred.[25] The social media landscape has entered a period of rapid change, with users adjusting by leaving older sites for new options. It is not yet clear how these sites will evolve, but for authors of local history, these platforms will continue to offer effective ways to communicate with audiences of all ages and interests, and sites like Facebook and LinkedIn remain an absolute necessity for promoting books.

MARKETING

If your publication is Web-based, you should take steps to publicize its availability. Logical media are newsletters, periodicals, email list management software (LISTSERV), websites of sponsoring organizations and affinity groups such as state and local historical societies, and the Networks of H-Net, Humanities and Social Sciences Online (www.h-net.org).

If you have self-published a book—whether produced by a traditional printer, an electronic printer, or a print-on-demand company—you will need to market and sell the book yourself. One method of marketing and selling—whether a book is published by an individual or a state or local historical society or other small press—is by subscription in advance of publication. A number of companies—"packagers," as they are known in the book trade—work with local historical organizations to research, write, design, print, and sell books on local history topics. Often these are photo books with minimal text beyond caption information on the photos. Examples of such packagers include:

- Arcadia Publishing Company, 420 Wando Park Blvd., Mount Pleasant, SC 29464-7845; (843) 853-2070; www.arcadiapublishing.com. Arcadia Publishing acquired the History Press in 2014; its website is now www.arcadiapublishing.com/imprints/the-history-press.
- Donning Company Publishers, 731 South Brunswick St., Brookfield, MO 64628-2403; (800) 369-2646, ext. 5573; www.donning.com.

You can do the marketing and selling yourself. These tasks are labor-intensive and time-consuming. But whether your book is self-published or published by a state or local historical society or a small press, sales cannot be cost-effectively subcontracted or outsourced to a distributor. State and local historical societies and small presses have found that marketing and/or distribution agreements with larger publishers are rarely cost-effective. "In the field of local history publishing," notes Bob Trubshaw, "the publisher *must* be the salesperson."[26] Distributors simply do not have the detailed knowledge of the contents of your book or of its likely market, nor do they have the financial incentive (no matter how high the percentage of net revenue received) to represent your book to retailers and individual book-buyers as effectively as a state or local historical publisher.

Marketing and sales tasks include communicating with and making personal visits to managers of bookstores and other retailers, who will expect you to discount the book to them at rates of 40 to 50 percent or more off the list (retail) price of the book, whether those bookstores and other retailers are for-profit or not-for-profit, such as museum stores. A retailer may be willing to sell your book on a consignment basis. You should be aware of the convention of returns in the book trade: An order is not a sale, and retailers reserve the right (often exercised) to return unsold books. In 2005 book-return rates were 35 percent for adult trade hardcovers, 22 percent for adult trade paperbacks, 17 percent for university press hardcovers, and 15 percent for university press paperbacks.[27] Retailers will sometimes accept books on a no-return basis, which requires a much deeper discount.

When self-publishing your book, you will need to advertise it in "earned" (free) media when you can get it, paid when you have to. Likely advertising media include the same newsletters, periodicals, email list management software (LISTSERV), and websites of sponsoring organizations and affinity groups such as state and local historical societies that you considered as venues to announce the availability of your publication. Consider paid advertising in newspapers local to the topic of your book and periodicals with readers likely to be interested in your book.

A good form of "earned" (free) media is a book review. You will need to send review copies of your book to the book review editor (addressed by name, when possible, which will involve research) of local newspapers and periodicals publishing in the field of your book. The Networks of H-Net, Humanities and Social Sciences Online (www.h-net.org) publish online reviews, so get to know the Networks of H-Net in your field. H-Net has individual networks for twelve states, the District of Columbia, and the following specialized topics relevant to readers and authors interested in local history (some of these networks appear in multiple categories):

- American History / Studies: H-Amstdy (American Studies), H-CivWar, H-Early America, H-US 1918–45
- North American History / Studies: H-Canada
- Oral History: H-Biography, H-OralHist

- Public History: H-Public
- Rural History / Studies: H-Rural (Rural and Agricultural History)
- State and Local History: H-Local (State and Local History; Museums)
- Urban History / Studies: H-Urban
- US Regional Studies: H-Appalachia, H-Borderlands (Spanish/Mexican Borderlands of the American Southwest and Northern Mexico), H-Midwest, H-New England, H-South, H-West

To reduce the possibility of wasting review copies, always check to make sure that a newspaper or periodical reviews books (a declining feature) in your field. Newspapers review books quickly, but academic journals can take a year or more to publish a review, by which time such a review will have minimal effect on sales unless yours is a book that academic libraries will purchase. Most books—except for the fortunate few perennial sellers—sell as much as 90 percent of their lifetime sales during the first year following publication.

Before the book goes to the printer:

- Apply for an International Standard Book Number (ISBN) from R. R. Bowker, the official US ISBN agency (www.isbn.org). The ISBN is a unique thirteen-digit commercial book identifier. The single most important thing to do in publishing today is getting accurate, thorough, and timely metadata (the unique descriptors of a publication, such as the ISBN and the Cataloging-in-Publication record) to online vendors, wholesalers, and distributors. This is the publisher's responsibility, but self-publishers are at a distinct disadvantage if they do not heed this. This is how Amazon.com gets a book and detailed description into its system.
- Apply for a Cataloging-in-Publication (CIP) record from the Library of Congress (www.loc.gov/publish/cip). When the book is published, the publisher includes the CIP data on the copyright page, thereby facilitating book processing for libraries and book dealers.
- Register the copyright with the US Copyright Office (https://copyright.gov/registration/). This involves, among other things, sending copies for deposit. Without registration, you can successfully defend your rights of authorship against an infringer in court, but with registration, you will have an open-and-shut case.

About the time that the book goes to the printer:

- Compile a review media list with the name, address, and other contact information of the book review editor for each newspaper, periodical, or broadcaster.

- Compile a list with addresses and other contact information of book-stores, convention and visitors associations, chambers of commerce, and museums local to the subject of your book. See the *ABA Bookseller Member Directory*: www.bookweb.org/member_directory/search/ABAmember?utm_source=BookWeb-Nav. This is a directory of the bookseller members of the American Booksellers Association; it is a database, searchable by location and specialty categories.
- Prepare press releases. The press release should include full details on the author, title, summary of contents, size of the book, number of pages, number of illustrations, type of binding, ISBN number, name of the imprint, how to order, and price.
- Send press releases to your list of bookstores, convention and visitors associations, chambers of commerce, and museums local to the subject of your book.
- Allow four to six weeks between the delivery date promised by the printer and scheduling the launch date, especially if you plan a launch party, to allow reviews to appear in newspapers and to allow for late delivery of books from the printer.

At least three months before launch:

If your book has a chance of national sales, send advance page proofs of the book to prepublication book trade review media:

- *Booklist*, American Library Association, 225 North Michigan Ave., Ste. 1300, Chicago, IL 60601-7616. For submission guidelines, see www.booklistonline.com/get-reviewed.
- *ForeWord*, Book Review Editor, 413 East 8th St., Traverse City, MI 49686-2626. Reviews independently published books. Submission guidelines: https://publishers.forewordreviews.com/reviews/.
- *Kirkus Reviews*, 479 Old Carolina Ct., Mount Pleasant, SC 29464-7823 (for adult nonfiction). Submission guidelines: www.kirkusreviews .com/about/publisher-submission-guidelines. If your book is self-published, see information on the Kirkus Indie Program at www. kirkusreviews.com/indie-reviews.
- *Library Journal*, Book Room, 123 William St., Ste. 802, New York, NY 10038-3822. Submission guidelines: www.libraryjournal.com/page /Review-Submissions.
- *Midwest Book Review*, 278 Orchard Dr., Oregon, WI 53575-1129. Submission guidelines: https://midwestbookreview.com/get_rev.htm. A list of book review media: http://midwestbookreview.com/links /magazine.htm#librarians.

- *Publishers Weekly,* Nonfiction Reviews, 49 West 23rd St., 9th Floor, New York, NY 10010-4225. Submission guidelines: www.publishers weekly.com/pw/corp/submissionguidelines.html. If your book is self-published, see information on the BookLife by *Publishers Weekly* program at https://booklife.com.

Two months before launch:

- Write/publish promotional articles about the book.
- Excerpt chapters from the book in periodicals.

On delivery of books from the printer:

- Carefully inspect several sample copies to ensure that there are no unpleasant surprises.

One month before launch:

- Make sure that bookstores have copies before articles/interviews about the book appear in local media.
- Send press releases to monthly and weekly periodicals.
- Send out review copies, together with a press release and a personalized cover letter, to review media.
- Schedule interviews with the author(s) in local media (daily newspapers and radio and television stations) to coincide with launch.
- Organize launch party.

One week before launch:

- Send press releases to media (daily newspapers and radio and television stations).

At the time of launch:

- Interviews (previously scheduled) with the author(s) in local media (daily newspapers and radio and television stations).

At a launch party:

- Have photographs taken for later publicity use.

After the launch:

- Follow up with local media (daily newspapers and radio and television stations).
- Arrange author talks and book signings.
- Arrange follow-up, spinoff, and promotional articles related to the subject of the book to appear in specialist periodicals.

SALES

The decline and demise of independent bookstores pose a challenge to publishing in the field of local history. Mass-market online and chain bookstores have squeezed and driven many independent bookstores out of business. Even Borders, a major mass-market bookstore, went bankrupt and out of business in 2011. The chains demand and get high discounts and often pay invoices after ninety days or more. A small local history publisher is at the mercy of the retailer (whether independent or mass-market chain), who will allocate little shelf space to local history titles. So encourage retail bookstore sales in any way you can, but the bulk of sales for a self-publishing author, a state or local historical society, or a small press will come from direct orders.

Self-publishing authors can list and sell their books on Amazon.com, and a small press can become an Amazon affiliate. As soon as the book appears on Amazon.com, the author should set up an Amazon author page. Amazon allows customers to preorder books and to "like" a forthcoming book. Because books with high numbers of "likes" can affect Amazon's initial purchasing of the book, authors might encourage friends and colleagues to do so. Authors can also promote this on their Facebook or X accounts. Since the author is driving attention to the book, this is an acceptable—even desirable—practice. This should not be confused with anonymously reviewing one's own book, which is unethical and violates Amazon's rules. Encouraging others to post reviews on Amazon is perfectly acceptable. Here too, books with heavy review traffic are treated more favorably by search engines and appear higher up on those searches.

Sales to libraries account for a significantly large share of the market for local history books. Libraries multiply the readership of books beyond the number of purchasers.

THE ATTRACTIONS OF A FULL-SERVICE PUBLISHER

The foregoing sketch of the labor-intensive process of marketing a self-published book contrasts with the several advantages of contracting with a full-service publisher, who will do many of the marketing, advertising, distribution, and sales tasks, in addition to handling editing and production (design, composition, printing, and binding). Small presses are ideal for local-history subjects, but authors should know that their marketing resources are limited. Even small presses have the necessary infrastructure to make sure the book appears in bookstores and online sales platforms and to send out review copies and copies for awards, but they most likely will not be able to set up readings and events, though they can help promote them once they are set up and make sure that books are available. Some full-service publishers encourage authors to sell copies themselves (copies purchased by the author at the author's cost). Other publishers do not want the author to compete with the publisher's retail operation, and so arrange for the authors to sell copies for the publisher's retail operation. An author who is a self-starter and good promoter, and who works with the press marketing team cooperatively with reasonable expectations, will have the best chance for success.

THE GOAL

You have researched, written, published, and marketed your book. If you have accomplished these tasks well, you will have fulfilled the valuable service of creating new knowledge of local history and communicating it to your audience. The technical aspects of publishing—acquisition, editing, design, dissemination, storage, order fulfillment, marketing, and sales—all serve the ultimate goal of communicating new knowledge of history. Historical knowledge grows incrementally, and writers of history build on the foundations created by their predecessors. Each new generation discovers new evidence, asks new questions, and creates opportunities for a fresh look at perennial topics. New perspectives provide new insights about the past.

Thomas Felt closed his book *Research, Writing, and Publishing Local History* with this observation: "Fortunately for this world, those who write local history are usually content with the self-rewarding love of seeing a job well done. I have assumed that to be your motive at the start, and hope the assumption remains good at the end."[28] In this culture of divisiveness, such altruistic motives on the part of the local historian are magnified in importance. History now often serves as a weapon in an arsenal of propaganda used to bludgeon one another. Mild-mannered local historians now find themselves placed in the middle of heated disputes involving the removal of statues, the banning of books, the renaming of buildings, the determination of whether someone once revered in the community is no longer to be admired because they owned slaves or committed violence on indigenous people. Conflicting sides produce facts to justify their viewpoints with analysis that is either too simple or too complex to persuade the other of its veracity. What should not be lost in all this is that veracity is the point: an honest effort to get at the truth of the past and to present it in a way that will make it a reliable source of knowledge in an unpredictable future. This book is about how to produce local history in a way that will be recognized as honest, balanced, truthful, persuasive, inclusive, and lasting.

NOTES

1. Albert N. Greco, Jim Milliot, and Robert M. Wharton, *The Book Publishing Industry*, 3rd ed. (New York: Routledge, 2014), 283–84.

2. John B. Thompson, *Book Wars: The Digital Revolution in Publishing*, paperback edition (Cambridge, UK/Medford, MA: Polity Press, 2022), 217.

3. Gregory M. Britton, "Thinking Like a Scholarly Editor: The How and Why of Academic Publishing," in Peter Ginna, ed., *What Editors Do: The Art, Craft, and Business of Book Editing*, Chicago Guides to Writing, Editing, and Publishing (Chicago: The University of Chicago Press, 2017), 40.

4. Gregory M. Britton, email message to authors, September 8, 2023.

5. John B. Thompson, *Books in the Digital Age: The Transformation of Academic and Higher Education Publishing in Britain and the United States* (Cambridge, UK/Malden, MA: Polity Press, 2005), 17.

6. *The Chicago Manual of Style* (1906; 17th ed., Chicago: University of Chicago Press, 2017), 171–219.

7. "Copyright Services: Copyright 101," https://guides.library.cornell.edu/copyright/copyright-101 (accessed December 4, 2022).

8. From a workshop given by Mitch Allen, former publisher of AltaMira Press, https://www.scholarlyroadsideservice.com/about.

9. Marshall Lee, *Bookmaking: Editing/Design/Production* (1965; 3rd ed., New York: W. W. Norton, 2004), 99–100.

10. www.economist.com/styleguide/introduction (accessed July 14, 2012).

11. "The Editing and Production Process: An Overview," University of Oklahoma Press, https://www.oupress.com/resources/for-prospective-authors/for-authors/ (accessed July 20, 2023).

12. "eBook Architects—eBook Formats," http://ebookarchitects.com/conversions/formats.php#mobi (accessed January 13, 2013).

13. Chris Kolmar, "23 Gripping Book Industry Statistics [2022]: Facts About the US Book Industry," zippia.com, August 17, 2022, www.zippia.com/advice/us-book-industry-statistics (accessed December 4, 2022).

14. Albert Greco, Clara Rodríguez, and Robert Wharton, *The Culture and Commerce of Publishing in the 21st Century* (Stanford, CA: Stanford Business Books, 2006), 154–55.

15. Thompson, *Book Wars*, 217.

16. Tony Cook, "Self-Publishing Comes in from the Cold with Sale," *Indianapolis Star*, July 20, 2012, A-5.

17. Jenny L. Presnell, *The Information-Literate Historian: A Guide to Research for History Students* (2007, 2nd ed., New York: Oxford University Press, 2013), 301.

18. Patrick J. Lynch and Sarah Horton, *Web Style Guide: Foundations of User Experience Design* (1999; 4th ed., New Haven, CT: Yale University Press, 2016); Louis Rosenfeld, Peter Morville, and Jorge Arango, *Information Architecture: For the Web and Beyond* (1998; 4th ed., Sebastopol, CA: O'Reilly Media, 2015); Steve Krug, *Don't Make Me Think Revisited: A Common Sense Approach to Web Usability* (2000; 3rd ed., Berkeley, CA: New Riders, 2014).

19. Daniel Cohen and Roy Rosenzweig, *Digital History: A Guide to Gathering, Preserving, and Presenting the Past on the Web* (Philadelphia: University of Pennsylvania Press, 2005); "Digital History: A Guide to Gathering, Preserving, and Presenting the Past on the Web," https://chnm.gmu.edu/digitalhistory (accessed January 13, 2013).

20. Jenny L. Presnell, *The Information-Literate Historian: A Guide to Research for History Students* (2007; 3rd ed., New York: Oxford University Press, 2019), 296.

21. Cohen and Rosenzweig, *Digital History*, 41.

22. Amy H. Wilson, ed., *Encyclopedia of Local History* (2000; 3rd ed., Lanham, MD: Rowman & Littlefield, 2017), 77.

23. Carol Kammen and Amy H. Wilson, *Encyclopedia of Local History* (2000; 2nd ed., Lanham, MD: AltaMira Press, 2013), 504–506.

24. Wilson, *Encyclopedia of Local History*, 3rd ed., 624.

25. "List of social networking services—Wikipedia, the Free Encyclopedia," https://en.wikipedia.org/wiki/List_of_social_networking_services (accessed December 5, 2022).

26. Bob Trubshaw, *How to Write and Publish Local and Family History Successfully: Books, Booklets, Magazines, CD-ROMs, and Web Sites* (Loughborough, UK: Heart of Albion Press, 2005), 241.

27. Greco, Rodríguez, and Wharton, *The Culture and Commerce of Publishing in the 21st Century*, 48.

28. Thomas E. Felt, *Researching, Writing, and Publishing Local History* (1976; 2nd ed., Nashville, TN: American Association for State and Local History, 1981), 150.

Appendix 1

Sample Author's Guidelines

Published with permission of the Indiana Historical Society Press

AUTHOR GUIDELINES

All prospective authors should read the Guidelines for All IHS Press Publications below, then refer to the author guidelines for the category or categories that best suit your work.

Guidelines for All IHS Press Publications

The following policy statement is intended to provide guidelines for potential authors and to set out the criteria used by IHS Press editors.

IHS Press publishes three to five new book titles per year, four issues of the popular history magazine *Traces*, two issues of the family and social history journal *Connections*, and two installments of articles or longer pieces in the Family History Resources section of the IHS website.

The IHS Press will issue a standard contract to an author on acceptance of a book-length manuscript or article for the magazines or the Family History Resources section. Submission of a manuscript by an author or receipt of a manuscript by IHS Press shall not in any way be construed as an obligation by IHS Press to publish a manuscript.

IHS Press can make no commitment to publish until its editors can examine a completed manuscript with all notes and bibliography. The editors initially review manuscripts submitted for publication, then send suitable ones to appropriate outside readers for evaluation. Authors should allow 90 days or more for the evaluation process. The editors make the final decision for or against publishing a manuscript and reserve the right to edit accepted manuscripts to conform to IHS Press's style and usage.

Most acceptances are conditional on an author's revisions. After acceptance, the author is responsible for obtaining permission to reproduce any illustrations and for providing captions and credit lines for them. The author is also responsible for obtaining permission to publish any material copied from the work of another.

The editors expect all manuscripts to be submitted as an electronic Word document. Authors should submit one copy of the manuscript for books and one copy of manuscripts for articles on standard 8½-by-11 inch paper, double-spaced throughout, with the author's name on the title page only. They should follow the guidelines of *The Elements of Style* by William Strunk Jr. and E. B. White and consult the latest editions of the *Chicago Manual of Style* and *Merriam Webster's Collegiate Dictionary*.

Authors should insert note numbers in the text, with notes appearing at the end of the complete text, not at the bottom of the page. This should be done manually, not with the automatic endnoting function of Word software. The endnotes should document the sources on which a manuscript is based. For its children's books for the schools and for its family and social history offerings, IHS Press's staff carries out its long-standing tradition of checking text and notes for accuracy of facts and citations in manuscripts accepted for publication. Authors are responsible, however, for their own statements of fact or opinion.

The editors will consider manuscripts submitted by members of the IHS Board of Trustees or by IHS committee members, but such manuscripts will be treated as those received from any other source and are subject to the criteria and procedures outlined in this policy statement. A trustee or committee member may be paid like any other author. An employee of IHS may be paid for a publication that is not written within the scope of his or her employment. A publication written by an employee within the scope of his or her employment by IHS—or written by a nonemployee who is paid by IHS for the creation of the publication—will be considered a work made for hire for which there is no additional compensation. All authors—whether employees or nonemployees—shall sign a contract.

IHS Press does not publish fiction except historical fiction for children's books for schools.

A rejected manuscript will be returned to the author upon request.

Author Guidelines for Books for Adults

IHS Press seeks book-length publications about Indiana on topics such as—but not limited to—biography, personal narrative, immigration, family, community development and social history, ethnic and cultural heritage, women, literature, folklore, music, the visual arts, politics, economics, industry, transportation, sports, geography, and military, medical, archaeological and agricultural history.

The editors require that manuscripts for potential publication be written in clear and appealing prose and in complete sentences free of jargon and undefined technical terms. Authors should avoid passive voice, lengthy quotations and one-sentence paragraphs.

The IHS Press will issue a standard contract to an author on acceptance of a book-length manuscript. The IHS Press shall own the copyright for books or book-length material that it finances and/or publishes. Submission of a manuscript by an author or receipt of a manuscript by IHS Press should not in any way be construed as an obligation by IHS Press to publish a manuscript.

Please address all correspondence to: IHS Press

Attn: Senior Editor
450 West Ohio Street
Indianapolis, IN 46202-3269
rboomhower@indianahistory.org

Author Guidelines for Children's Books for Schools

IHS Press will consider manuscripts of well-researched nonfiction, biographies, and manuscripts of fact-based historical fiction for children that are written in an engaging style with age-appropriate language and subject matter.

The main audiences for IHS Press children's books are students in grades 4 through 12—and their educators and media specialists. Book selections for the children's book publishing program will provide content-rich resources related to Indiana history and the state's role in national and world events, identifying IHS Press as a reliable provider of excellent Indiana-related social studies literature.

Selections will be made based on the following general criteria: imaginative and engaging content, sound historical research, effective literary style and appropriateness for the audience. Ideally, the book will provide new knowledge about the topic or subject for students, incorporate a variety of primary and secondary sources and support the national and state educational standards for language arts and social studies.

The topics listed below are derived from curriculum standards for language arts and social studies. Manuscripts will be evaluated according to how well they fit within the time periods listed with the topics.

TOPICS FOR GRADES FOUR AND FIVE

Indiana Territory, 1770s to 1816; Indiana statehood and development to the 1850s; Indiana in the Civil War era; Indiana growth and development, 1880 to 1920; Indiana life, 1920 to the present. Topics with a focus on Indiana and the Midwest may also provide information on: America before and after the arrival of Europeans; American Indigenous Peoples and arrival of Europeans to 1770; American colonization and settlement;

the American Revolution; Creation of the United States Constitution and establishment of the Federal Republic, 1783 to 1800s.

TOPICS FOR GRADE EIGHT

The following should be adapted with a focus on Indiana: Historical Time Period, 1750 to 1877: American Revolution and founding of the United States, 1754 to 1801; National Expansion and Reform, 1801 to 1861; Civil War and Reconstruction, 1850 to 1877.

TOPICS FOR HIGH SCHOOL

Early National Development, 1775 to 1877; Development of Industrial United States, 1870 to 1900; Emergence of Modern United States, 1897 to 1920; Modern United States, Prosperity and Depression, 1920 to 1940; United States and World War II, 1930 to 1945; Post-War United States, 1945 to 1960; United States in Troubled Times, 1960 to 1980; Contemporary United States, 1980 to present.

The IHS Press will issue a standard contract to an author on acceptance of a book-length manuscript. The IHS Press shall own the copyright in books or book-length material that it finances and/or publishes. Submission of a manuscript by an author or receipt of a manuscript by IHS Press should not in any way be construed as an obligation by IHS Press to publish a manuscript.

Address all correspondence to: IHS Press
                              Attn: Managing Editor
                              450 West Ohio Street
                              Indianapolis, IN 46202-3269
                              tbaer@indianahistory.org

Author Guidelines for Traces *Magazine*

The editors of *Traces* seek nonfiction articles that are solidly researched, attractively written and amenable to illustration, and they encourage scholars, journalists and freelance writers to contribute to the magazine. Accepted articles usually are a good mix of academic writing and magazine journalism.

IHS Press will issue a standard contract on acceptance of an article. IHS Press will hold a royalty-free exclusive license to publish the article in *Traces*—which converts to a royalty-free nonexclusive license six months after publication—and the right to permit Indiana newspapers to reprint the article. IHS Press owns the copyright in *Traces*, but the author owns the copyright in the article and is free to reprint the article after it is published in *Traces*. IHS Press is free to reprint the article at a future time.

MANUSCRIPT GUIDELINES

Traces seeks articles and essays on topics such as—but not limited to—biography, personal narrative, immigration, family, cultural heritage, women, literature, folklore, music, the visual arts, politics, economics, industry, transportation, sports, geography, and military, medical, archaeological, architectural and agricultural history. In addition, the magazine seeks essays from historians discussing their personal interest in the field of Indiana history.

In general, articles should be narrative in structure, have strong introductions and conclusions, and weave analysis into the larger framework. Essays should have a history component, preferably one that helps explain present practices, incidents and behaviors. The editors give priority to submissions that meet standards of research and presentation and also display a direct Indiana connection. Prospective authors should be familiar with the magazine before they submit articles or proposals.

Feature articles and essays should be 2,000 to 4,000 words in length. The editors primarily seek newly written material, although they will consider material that has been previously published. The editors will also respond to proposals submitted with writing samples and an indication of the means and costs of illustration.

Articles and essays should be written in clear and appealing prose that is free of jargon and undefined technical terms. Authors should avoid passive voice, lengthy quotations and one-sentence paragraphs. They should follow the guidelines of *The Elements of Style* by William Strunk Jr. and E. B. White and consult the latest editions of the *Chicago Manual of Style* and *Merriam Webster's Collegiate Dictionary*.

Authors should submit a copy of each article or essay on standard 8½-by-11 inch paper, double-spaced throughout, with the author's name on the title page only. They should provide brief suggestions "For Further Reading" at the end of articles and document in endnotes the sources on which articles are based. The editors will decide the form and extent of published documentation. The editors also accept manuscripts via e-mail.

Authors are responsible for providing illustrative material—in black-and-white or color—and captions that do not duplicate information in the text. IHS Press will provide staff assistance in locating—and will assume the cost of reproducing—photographs, maps and documents in the IHS collections. The quality and cost of potential illustration are major criteria by which the editors evaluate articles.

The editors initially review manuscripts submitted for publication, then send suitable ones to appropriate outside readers for evaluation. The editors make the final decision for or against publishing articles. Authors should allow 90 days or more for the evaluation process.

The editors reserve the right to copyedit accepted manuscripts to conform with the style and usage of *Traces*. The editorial staff checks the sources of articles to ensure accuracy of facts and citations. After editing an article, the editors will issue a standard contract and pay a negotiated honorarium to the author.

At the end of each volume year, the editorial board grants the Jacob Piatt Dunn Jr. Award, which includes a $500 prize, to the author whose article has best fulfilled the magazine's mission.

Manuscripts will be returned to authors if they are accompanied by a self-addressed envelope stamped with sufficient postage.

Address all correspondence to: IHS Press

> Attn: Senior Editor
> 450 West Ohio Street
> Indianapolis, IN 46202-3269
> rboomhower@indianahistory.org

Author Guidelines for Connections

Connections is a family and social history journal of narrative articles telling engaging stories and histories about individuals, families and communities that also discuss how to research, document, and write memoirs, biographical sketches, and family and community histories.

The editors of *Connections* seek nonfiction articles based on solid primary and secondary research, with clear, compelling writing and vivid illustrations, including useful source material, and they encourage scholars, family historians, journalists and freelance writers to contribute to the journal.

The IHS Press will issue a standard contract on acceptance of an article and will pay a negotiated honorarium to the author. IHS Press will hold a royalty-free exclusive license to publish the article in *Connections*—which converts to a royalty-free nonexclusive license six months after publication. IHS Press owns the copyright in *Connections*, but the author owns the copyright in the article and is free to reprint the article after it is published in *Connections*. IHS Press is free to republish the article at a future time.

Manuscript Guidelines

Connections seeks articles and essays on topics such as—but not limited to—biography of individuals and/or families, personal narrative, immigration, cultural heritage, ethnic groups, women, folklore, geography, and military, medical, legal, archaeological, industrial, and agricultural history as these subjects provide historical context for family and social history research. In addition, we seek essays from family historians and other scholars discussing their personal experience in the fields of family and social history research and writing on Indiana topics.

In general, articles should be narrative in structure, have strong introductions and conclusions and weave research analysis into the larger framework. Essays should have genealogy and/or social history components and give historical context to the particular individuals, places, and time periods within the article, while also helping to explain research and writing methodologies for family and social historians. The editors give priority to submissions that meet standards of research and presentation and also display a direct Indiana connection. Prospective authors should be familiar with the journal before they submit articles or proposals.

Feature articles and essays should be 2,500 to 4,000 words in length. The editors primarily seek newly written material, although they will consider material that has been previously published. The editors will also respond to proposals submitted with writing samples and an indication of the means and costs of illustration.

Articles and essays should be written in clear and appealing prose that is free of jargon and undefined technical terms. Authors should avoid passive voice, lengthy quotations and one-sentence paragraphs. They should follow the guidelines of *The Elements of Style* by William Strunk Jr. and E. B. White and consult the latest editions of the *Chicago Manual of Style* and *Merriam Webster's Collegiate Dictionary*.

Authors should either submit a copy of each article—double-spaced throughout, with the author's name on the title page only—via e-mail or on standard 8½-by-11-inch paper. They should document their sources in endnotes. The editors will decide the form and extent of published documentation. A short biographical sketch of the author should also be included. The editors accept approved manuscripts via e-mail. Manuscripts will be returned to authors if they are accompanied by a self-addressed envelope stamped with sufficient postage.

Authors are responsible for providing illustrative material—in color or black-and-white—and captions that do not duplicate information in the text. IHS Press will provide staff assistance in locating—and will assume the cost of reproducing—photographs, maps, and documents in the IHS collections.

The editors initially review manuscripts submitted for publication and may send suitable ones to appropriate outside readers for evaluation. The editors make the final decision for or against publishing articles. Authors should allow 90 days or more for the evaluation process. Upon approval of an article, the editorial staff checks the sources of articles to ensure accuracy of facts and citations. The editors also reserve the right to copyedit accepted manuscripts to conform with the style and usage of *Connections.*

Authors of articles published in *Connections* may be nominated for the Willard C. Heiss Family History/Genealogy Award, given once each year by the Indiana Historical Society to "a family historian for his or her distinguished service and career in Indiana family history including presentations such as articles in *Connections.*"

Address all correspondence to: IHS Press

> Attn: Managing Editor
> 450 West Ohio Street
> Indianapolis, IN 46202-3269
> tbaer@indianahistory.org

Author Guidelines for Family History Resources

Within the Family History Resources section on the IHS website, the IHS Press publishes indexes to rare source material and other indexed material helpful to genealogical and historical researchers looking for ancestors and other historic individuals, including family genealogies.

The editors seek article and book-length manuscripts on topics such as—but not limited to—name and vital statistics lists or other pertinent data from unpublished source material, such as diaries, journals, ledgers, letter collections, and court, government, church, organizational, business and other records.

Prospective authors should be familiar with articles published within the Family History Resources section of the IHS website before they submit manuscripts or proposals. Manuscripts submitted for the "Regional Sources," "Genealogy Across Indiana" and "Family Records" departments of the Family History Resources section should include transcriptions and/or indexes of unpublished source material. These manuscripts should include introductions that describe the material, the historical background and repository of the source material and a guide describing the means of indexing and/or transcribing the material. Introductions should be no more than one to two pages in length and double-spaced.

Transcriptions from original documents should reflect an exact replication of the passages transcribed, including capitalization, spelling, punctuation and grammar that would be considered incorrect in today's usage.

IHS Press will issue a standard contract on acceptance of an article. IHS Press will hold a royalty-free exclusive license to publish the article in the Family History Resources section, which converts to a royalty-free non-exclusive license six months after publication. In the case of book-length publications, IHS Press will own the copyright in material that it finances and/or publishes. IHS Press owns the copyright in Family History Resources, but the author owns the copyright in the article and is free to publish the article after it is published in Family History Resources. IHS Press is free to publish the article elsewhere at a future time.

Submission of a manuscript by an author or receipt of a manuscript by IHS Press should not in any way be construed as an obligation by IHS Press to publish a manuscript.

MANUSCRIPT GUIDELINES

IHS Press editors seek newly written material. The editors will also respond to proposals submitted with writing samples. Articles and longer essays should be written in clear and appealing prose that is free of jargon and undefined technical terms. Authors should avoid passive voice, lengthy quotations and one-sentence paragraphs. They should follow the guidelines of *The Elements of Style* by William Strunk Jr. and E. B. White and consult the latest editions of the *Chicago Manual of Style* and *Merriam Webster's Collegiate Dictionary*.

Authors should either submit a copy of each article—double-spaced throughout, with the author's name on the title page only—via e-mail or on standard 8½-by-11 inch paper. They should document their sources in endnotes. The editors will decide the form and extent of published documentation. A short biographical sketch of the author should also be included. The editors accept approved manuscripts via e-mail. Manuscripts will be returned to authors if they are accompanied by a self-addressed envelope stamped with sufficient postage.

No illustrative material is required for articles and longer pieces in the Family History Sources section of the IHS website.

The editors initially review manuscripts submitted for publication and may send suitable ones to appropriate outside readers for evaluation. The editors make the final decision for or against publishing articles. Authors should allow 90 days or more for the evaluation process. The editorial staff checks the sources of articles to ensure accuracy of facts and citations. The editors also reserve the right to copyedit accepted manuscripts to conform with the style and usage of the Family History Resources section of the IHS website.

Address all correspondence to: IHS Press
Attn: Managing Editor
450 West Ohio Street
Indianapolis, IN 46202-3269
tbaer@indianahistory.org

Appendix 2

Sample Contract for an Article

Published with permission of the Indiana Historical Society Press

AGREEMENT

This AGREEMENT is entered into by and between _____ (hereinafter referred to as the AUTHOR), a citizen of _____, whose address is _____, and the Indiana Historical Society Press (hereinafter referred to as the PRESS), a division of the Indiana Historical Society whose address is 450 West Ohio Street, Indianapolis, Indiana 46202-3269, for the publication of an article "_____ _____" (hereinafter referred to as the ARTICLE) in *Traces of Indiana and Midwestern History* (hereinafter referred to as *TRACES*), a quarterly illustrated magazine.

In consideration of the mutual covenants and agreements set forth below and other valuable consideration, the sufficiency of which is hereby acknowledged, the parties hereto agree as follows:

1. *Author's Warranty:* The AUTHOR represents and warrants that he or she is the sole author of the ARTICLE; that he or she has full power and authority to make the AGREEMENT; that the ARTICLE does not infringe the copyright or other proprietary right of any other person; that it contains no libelous or other unlawful matter; that it makes no improper invasion of the privacy of any person; and that it has not been published previously in its present form.

2. *Author's Indemnification:* The AUTHOR agrees to defend the PRESS against any claim or action arising out of facts which constitute a breach of any of the representations and warranties set forth in paragraph 1 of this AGREEMENT and to indemnify and hold harmless the PRESS against any settlement or any final judgment for damages

arising out of such claim or action, provided that the PRESS gives the AUTHOR prompt notice of any claim or action against the PRESS alleging facts which, if proved, could constitute a breach of these warranties. In the defense of any such claim or action, the AUTHOR may use counsel of his or her choosing, at the AUTHOR's expense, and the PRESS may participate in the defense with counsel of the PRESS's choosing and at its expense. If any such claim or action is settled, or if there is a final judgment for damages arising out of any such claim or action, then the AUTHOR shall pay all reasonable costs and attorneys' fees incurred by the PRESS in defending such claim or action.

3. *Grants of License:* The AUTHOR grants to the PRESS a royalty-free exclusive license to reproduce and distribute (publish) copies of the ARTICLE in *TRACES* and on the PRESS's World Wide Web site (http://www.indianahistory.org), and the right to permit Indiana newspapers to reprint the ARTICLE in their newspapers. The PRESS shall own the copyright in *TRACES* and its Web site, but the AUTHOR retains ownership of the copyright in the ARTICLE. Six months after the ARTICLE is published in *TRACES*, the license granted herein to the PRESS shall automatically convert to a perpetual royalty-free nonexclusive license to publish copies of the ARTICLE as the PRESS chooses, in all print and electronic media, in a manner that may or may not include other portions of *TRACES*. Further, the AUTHOR shall thereafter be free to publish the ARTICLE elsewhere as he or she chooses. Once the license has become nonexclusive, the PRESS will refer to the AUTHOR requests from other publishers to reprint the ARTICLE, except AUTHOR agrees that all subsequent publication of the ARTICLE by the AUTHOR or by those to whom the AUTHOR has given permission must provide attribution to the PRESS and cite the volume and number of *TRACES* in which the ARTICLE was first published.

4. *Permission for Material:* If the ARTICLE incorporates any material (including, but not limited to, text, photographs, and illustrations) copied from a work by another, or any material copied from a previously published work by the AUTHOR, the AUTHOR shall acknowledge in the notes or captions of the WORK the source of such material and shall ascertain if permission is necessary to publish such material as part of the ARTICLE. If permission is necessary, the AUTHOR shall obtain such permission in writing from the owner of the copyright in such material. The PRESS shall pay fees for such permission, when required, subject to the approval of the PRESS's editor.

5. *Publishing Details:* The PRESS agrees to publish the ARTICLE in *TRACES* within one (1) year from the effective date of this AGREEMENT. If the PRESS has not published the ARTICLE within one year

from the effective date, then the licenses granted to the PRESS in paragraph 3 above shall automatically convert to royalty-free nonexclusive licenses, and the AUTHOR shall thereafter be free to publish the ARTICLE elsewhere as he or she chooses. The PRESS reserves the right to choose the issue of *TRACES* in which the AR-TICLE will appear and to copyedit the ARTICLE to conform to the style and usage of *TRACES*. The AUTHOR will be given an opportunity to read the edited manuscript, but if he or she fails to return it to the editor of *TRACES* by the date set by the editor, production and publication will proceed without delay.

6. *Copies for Author:* The PRESS agrees to furnish the AUTHOR five (5) free copies of the issue of *TRACES* in which the ARTICLE is published at the time of printing. The AUTHOR shall also have the right to purchase additional copies of such issue of *TRACES* from the PRESS at a discount of fifty percent (50%) off the retail (nonmembers') price.

7. *Payment to Author:* As consideration for this AGREEMENT, the PRESS will pay the AUTHOR _____ dollars ($____).

8. *Choice of Law:* This AGREEMENT has been entered into in the State of Indiana and the validity, interpretation, and legal effect of this AGREEMENT shall be governed by the laws of Indiana.

9. *Entire Agreement:* This AGREEMENT sets forth the entire agreement between the parties with respect to the subject matter hereof, and this AGREEMENT supersedes all proposals or prior agreements, oral or written, and all other communications between the parties relating to the subject matter hereof. No modification, amendment, waiver, termination, or discharge of this AGREEMENT or any provision hereof shall be binding upon the PRESS unless confirmed in writing by an officer of the PRESS.

10. *Effective Date:* The effective date of this AGREEMENT is the date of the signature of the last party to sign and date this AGREEMENT.

If the foregoing terms are satisfactory, please sign and date this AGREEMENT, return one copy to the PRESS, and retain the second copy for your own files.

For the PRESS: AUTHOR:

_____   _____

Date: _____   Date: _____

                                       Social Security Number: _____

Appendix 3
Sample Book Contract

PUBLISHER'S CONTRACT

THIS AGREEMENT is made between The Press, _____address_____
(hereinafter referred to as "the Publisher," "we," "us," or "our") and
_____author's name____, _____address_____ (hereinafter referred to
as "the Authors," "you" or "your") concerning "Working Title" (hereinafter referred to as "the Work").

Now, therefore, in consideration of their mutual promises and for other
valuable consideration, the parties hereby agree to the terms and conditions hereinafter set forth.

1. AUTHOR'S GRANT

You hereby grant and assign to us full and exclusive rights in the Work,
including the copyright and the rights (a) to reproduce, distribute, market, and sell the Work in whole and in part throughout the world in all
forms, languages, and media now or hereafter known or developed, including but not limited to electronic and digital media and (b) to license
others to do the same. This grant will endure for the full term of copyright
unless, in accordance with the U.S. Copyright Law, you notify us in writing that you wish to terminate it; this termination must occur within the
period specified by law. You authorize us to register the copyright in our
name in the United States and, if required, in other countries.

2. AUTHOR'S WARRANTY

You represent and warrant that you are the sole creators of the Work
and that you have full power to make this Agreement and grant; that
the Work is original; that the Work has not been published previously in
whole or in part; that the Work is not in the public domain; that the Work

119

does not infringe the copyright or other proprietary rights of any other person, institution, or corporation; that the Work contains no libelous or other unlawful matter and makes no improper invasion of the privacy of any other person; that any recipe, formula, or instruction contained in the Work is not injurious to the user; and that you have not previously assigned, pledged, or otherwise encumbered the Work or agreed to do so. You accordingly agree to indemnify, hold harmless, and defend us from and against any and all liability whatsoever for claims, demands, suits, penalties, damages, losses, and all manner of costs, fees and expenses arising out of and/or resulting from an alleged violation of any of these representations and warranties. You shall defend us through counsel you choose albeit subject to our advice and approval, such approval not to be unreasonably withheld. The provisions of this section shall survive any termination of this Agreement.

3. INFRINGEMENT

You agree to pay, equally with us, one-half of the expenses of any suit we may bring against any other party for infringement of copyright or violation of other related property rights and shall receive one-half of any damages or profits, less attorneys' fees and disbursements, that may be recovered in any such suit, or you may, at your option, decline to participate in the risks and proceeds of any such suit, leaving both open to us. You agree to notify us immediately of any claim made against you or us relating to the Work.

Initial

4. AGREEMENT TO PUBLISH

We shall publish the Work in book form, within a reasonable time, subject to market conditions and availability of funds, except as provided for elsewhere in the Agreement. The style and manner of publication, including but not limited to title, price, copyediting, format, production, print run, marketing, advertising, promotion, storage, and distribution, shall be under our exclusive control. This Agreement to publish is contingent upon our receipt of a manuscript that is professionally competent in style and content and that is endorsed by two peer reviewers and the Press's Faculty Advisory Board.

5. COMPETING WORKS

You agree that during the term of this Agreement you will not, without our prior written consent, given at our sole discretion, publish or allow your name to be used in connection with, any other edition of the Work in any language or any book, print or electronic, that may conflict or compete with the sale of the Work.

6. PHYSICAL SPECIFICATIONS

a. You agree to deliver to us the complete Work, including a preface, other front matter and back matter, together with camera-ready or digital copy for all illustrations, maps, charts, drawings, or other material (except index) to be included in the Work, **not later than (date)**. If you fail to deliver a complete manuscript we deem acceptable in form and content by this date, we may, then or at any subsequent time prior to your delivery of the manuscript, terminate this Agreement by giving you written notice. Under no circumstances, however, shall you be free to submit the Work elsewhere until it has been reoffered to us under the terms of this Agreement.

b. The final and completed manuscript shall consist of **no more than __ words** (including preliminary pages and reference matter) and no more than ___black & white illustrations and _maps. In any revision you undertake before the Work goes into production, you will not add to or subtract from the word count or the number of illustrations unless we agree in writing to such changes.

c. You agree to present the final manuscript to us in a digital file using a word-processing software approved by us, including extracts, notes, bibliography, and legend copy. All elements of the Work shall be prepared in accordance with a commonly recognized manual of style and in consultation with us. If you wish to use nonstandard spelling, punctuation, capitalization, or typographic style, you will discuss that matter with our editor before copyediting begins.

d. You agree to supply, at your own expense, all illustrations, including maps and drawings.

e. If you supply illustrations in electronic format, you will do so in a format acceptable to us.

f. You will give us the copyright owners' written authorization for us to use copyrighted materials (including, but not limited to, textual material, illustrations, contributions to collective works, and interviews) for publication in all forms and media, and you will pay any fees required for the use thereof. All necessary authorizations shall be delivered to us by the time the copyedited Work enters production. Otherwise, we reserve the right to postpone publication of the Work.

Initial

We will perform customary copyediting of the Work and will direct to you queries and suggestions regarding changes we believe are desirable. We will not make substantive changes in the manuscript without your prior written approval, which you will not unreasonably withhold. After your review and approval, you agree to treat the edited manuscript as final copy and to make no changes to it.

g. If you submit the manuscript to us in a form that requires editing beyond that normally expected of a publisher, retyping, or redrawing or other processing of illustrations, we shall do this work at your expense.

h. If in proofs or illustrations you should make any changes other than correcting typesetter's and printer's errors, you agree to pay the costs thereof. You agree to read, correct clearly and legibly, and return to the Publisher all proofs within fifteen (15) days after you receive them. You agree that if you unreasonably delay the return of proofs beyond the schedule agreed upon when the book is put into production, we may proceed with publication (including proofreading) without waiting for your return of proofs.

i. You agree that if we request an index, you will prepare it, or have it prepared by another person at your expense, promptly after you receive page proofs. If you fail to provide a suitable index within thirty (30) days after receipt of the page proofs, we will have an index professionally prepared and will charge the cost to you.

7. INSURANCE AND LIABILITY

Except for loss or damage attributable to our negligence, we shall not be responsible for loss or damage to any property submitted by you that is in our possession, in the possession of our independent contractors, or in the possession of anyone else to whom we make delivery in the normal course of our operations. If any unique or especially valuable material, such as a rare photograph, is in your manuscript, you must inform us and place on record with us a valuation of it. If special insurance is needed, you must arrange for it at your expense.

8. ROYALTIES AND OTHER PAYMENT

We prepare royalty statements annually as of June 30; any payment due will be paid within sixty days thereafter. If the accumulated royalty is less than $50, no payment will be made until the end of the accounting period in which the amount exceeds $50. We may establish a reasonable reserve for returns and reduce the amount payable accordingly. If we overpay on copies reported sold but subsequently returned, we may deduct the overpayment from any future payment owed.

The amount of royalty or other payment shall be calculated as follows:

Royalties

We will pay you a royalty, based on our net sales, of 8 percent on the first 1,000 copies, 10 percent thereafter for all print and electronic editions of the Work. Net sales shall be defined as gross regular sales less discounts and returns.

Subsidiary rights

For the licensing of any subsidiary right, including but not limited to foreign publication and translation; first or second serial publication; anthology, selection or excerpt; abridgment; condensation; digest; microform; duplication; photocopy; reprint by another publisher; book- club edition; and audio, motion-picture, television, radio, or stage production or transcription, we will pay you 40 percent of our actual net receipts from any such sale.

Royalty-free copies

On any copies lost or destroyed, on copies sold at or below the sum of the manufacturing unit cost plus 10 percent, on Braille transcription or other service edition published for the physically disabled, and on copies given away for the purpose of aiding the promotion and sale of the Work or given to you gratis, we will pay you no royalty.

9. PAYMENTS DUE AND OWING

Any payment due and owing from you to us, whether or not it arises from this Agreement, will be paid within thirty days of invoice unless prior written arrangements have been made between you and us. If payment is not received within thirty (30) days, we reserve the right to deduct the amount owed to us from your future royalty payments until the amount due has been paid in full.

10. COMPLIMENTARY COPIES

On initial publication of the Work, we will give each Author five (5) complimentary copies. You may purchase additional copies of the Work at list price less 40 percent discount, plus postage.

As our Authors you are entitled, as well, to purchase at a 40 percent discount, plus postage, any other OU Press book. Such orders should be addressed to our Order Department with a request for an author's 40 percent discount; otherwise they may be processed with the regular orders billed at list price.

11. REVISED EDITIONS

You agree to revise the Work when we determine that a revised edition is desirable. If you are unable to do so, or are deceased, we shall have the right to prepare and publish the said revision. In this event the author(s) we commission to revise the Work shall be compensated by a share of the royalty and other income, as determined by us, from the sale of the revised edition, or by a fee determined by us and charged against the royalty and other income accruing to you from the sale of such revised edition. We may display in the revised edition, and in advertising, the name of the said author(s). We may, at our discretion, use your name in connection with the publication, sale, or promotion of the revised Work.

Initial

12. TERMINATION

If we advise you (in a letter addressed to you at your last known address) that we intend to discontinue publication, or if we fail to keep the Work in print and neglect to reprint it or license an edition within nine (9) months after your written request that we reprint the Work, then you have the right to terminate this Agreement by written notice to us. We shall, within three (3) months of receipt of such request, (a) declare in writing our intention to reissue an edition of the Work, (b) enter a license providing for the publication in the United States of a new edition of the Work, or (c) return to you all rights granted to us herein except those rights granted to third parties prior to the receipt of your notice and in effect at the time of termination. If we declare our intention to reissue the Work and do not do so within nine (9) months from the date of our receipt of your request, the rights shall revert to you. The Work shall be deemed "in print" as long as copies in an English-language edition are offered for sale. We shall continue to receive our share of the proceeds from any license granted prior to the receipt of your notice and in effect at the time of termination.

13. SUCCESSORS AND ASSIGNS

This Agreement shall be binding upon, and inure to the benefit of, the heirs, executors, administrators, successors, and assigns of both parties. Either party shall give the other written notice of any assignments.

14. ENTIRE AGREEMENT; MODIFICATIONS; NOTIFICATION

This Agreement constitutes the entire agreement and understanding between the parties and supersedes all prior agreements and understandings, whether written or oral with respect to the subject matter of this Agreement. No modification or claimed waiver of any of the provisions hereof shall be valid unless in writing and signed by authorized representatives of both parties. Any notices required or permitted to be given shall be in writing and shall be sent to the respective addresses previously set forth, or at such addresses as the parties may from time to time designate by written notice.

15. CHANGE OF ADDRESS

The Author is responsible for notifying the Publisher of any permanent change of mailing address. The Publisher is not responsible for any failure to meet the terms of this Agreement resulting from the Author's failure to give notification of change of address.

16. SEVERABILITY

If any provision of this Agreement is judicially declared invalid, unenforceable, or void by a court of competent jurisdiction, such decision shall not have the effect of invalidating or voiding the remainder of this Agreement, and the part or parts of this Agreement so held to be invalid, unenforceable, or void shall be deemed deleted from this Agreement, and the remainder of this Agreement shall have the same force and effect as if such part or parts had never been included.

Initial

17. GOVERNING LAW

This Agreement shall be governed by the laws of the State of _____, without giving force and effect to its choice of law provisions. Any legal action in connection with this Agreement shall be filed in a court of competent jurisdiction in Oklahoma, to which jurisdiction and venue you expressly agree.

In the event of any suit arising from publication of such Work, the signatories and agents of the University of _____ and the State of _____ whose signatures are affixed hereto, and the members of the Board of Regents of the University of _____, in their individual capacities shall in no manner, individually or collectively, be liable for any damages to anyone, and any suit or claim hereunder shall be filed against the Board of Regents of the University of _____ in its corporate capacity, or against the State of _____, as duly provided by the laws of the State of _____.

18. EFFECTS OF HEADINGS

Descriptive words and statements used as headings in this Agreement to summarize the contents of succeeding paragraphs are not to be deemed a part of this Agreement or an interpretation or representation of the contents of such paragraphs.

_____   _____

Citizenship   Author's name

_____   _____

Author   Date of Birth

(The above information is used for registering the copyright.)

For the Press

In witness whereof, the parties have duly executed this Agreement this _____ day of _____, 202_, at _____city, state_____.

Appendix 4

Sample Contract with a Photographer

Published with permission of the Indiana Historical Society Press

AGREEMENT

This AGREEMENT is entered into by and between _____, (hereinafter referred to as the PHOTOGRAPHER), a citizen of _____, whose address is _____, and the Indiana Historical Society (hereinafter referred to as the SOCIETY), whose address is 315 West Ohio Street, Indianapolis, Indiana 46202-3299, for the publication of color photographs of _____ (hereinafter referred to as the PHOTOGRAPHS) in a publication tentatively titled "_____."

In consideration of the mutual covenants and agreements set forth below and other valuable consideration, the sufficiency of which is hereby acknowledged, the parties hereto agree as follows:

1. *Photographer's Warranty:* The PHOTOGRAPHER represents and warrants that he is the sole creator of the PHOTOGRAPHS; that he has full power and authority to make this Agreement; that the PHOTOGRAPHS do not infringe the copyright or other intellectual property rights of any other person; that they contain no libelous or other unlawful matter; that they make no improper invasion of the privacy of any person; and that they have not been published previously in their present form.

2. *Photographer's Indemnification:* The PHOTOGRAPHER agrees to defend the SOCIETY against any claim or action arising out of facts which constitute a breach of any of the representations and warranties set forth in paragraph 1 of this Agreement and to indemnify and hold harmless the SOCIETY against any settlement or any final judgment for damages arising out of such claim or action, provided

that the SOCIETY gives the PHOTOGRAPHER prompt notice of any claim or action against the SOCIETY alleging facts which, if proved, could constitute a breach of these warranties. In the defense of any such claim or action, the PHOTOGRAPHER may use counsel of his or her choosing, at the PHOTOGRAPHER's expense, and the SOCIETY may participate in the defense with counsel of the SOCIETY's choosing and at its expense. If any such claim or action is settled, or if there is a final judgment for damages arising out of any such claim or action, then the PHOTOGRAPHER shall pay all reasonable costs and attorneys' fees incurred by the SOCIETY in defending such claim or action.

3. *Grant of License:* The PHOTOGRAPHER grants to the SOCIETY a royalty-free exclusive license to reproduce and distribute (publish) copies of the PHOTOGRAPHS. The SOCIETY shall own the copyright in the publication in which the PHOTOGRAPHS are published, but the PHOTOGRAPHER retains ownership of copyright in the PHOTOGRAPHS. The SOCIETY will refer to the PHOTOGRAPHER requests from other publishers to reprint the PHOTOGRAPHS. One year after the PHOTOGRAPHS are published by the SOCIETY, the license granted herein to the SOCIETY shall automatically convert to royalty-free nonexclusive license. The PHOTOGRAPHER shall thereafter be free to publish the PHOTOGRAPHS elsewhere as he or she chooses.

4. *Publishing Details:* The PHOTOGRAPHER shall deliver to the SOCIETY the finished PHOTOGRAPHS no later than _____. The SOCIETY agrees to publish the PHOTOGRAPHS within two (2) years from the effective date of this Agreement. If the SOCIETY has not published the PHOTOGRAPHS within two (2) years from the effective date, then the license granted to the SOCIETY in paragraph 3 above shall automatically convert to a royalty-free nonexclusive license, and the PHOTOGRAPHER shall thereafter be free to publish the PHOTOGRAPHS elsewhere as he or she chooses.

5. *Copies for Photographer:* The SOCIETY agrees to furnish the PHOTOGRAPHER three (3) free copies of the publication in which the WORK is published at the time of first printing. The PHOTOGRAPHER shall have the right to purchase from the SOCIETY additional copies of the publication in which the WORK is published at the members' price.

6. *Payment to Photographer:* As consideration for this Agreement, within thirty (30) days after receipt of the PHOTOGRAPHS by the SOCIETY's editor and Publications Division, the SOCIETY will pay the PHOTOGRAPHER _____.

7. *Choice of Law:* This Agreement has been entered into in the State of Indiana and the validity, interpretation, and legal effect of this Agreement shall be governed by the laws of Indiana.
8. *Entire Agreement:* This Agreement sets forth the entire agreement between the parties with respect to the subject matter hereof, and this Agreement supersedes all proposals or prior agreements, oral or written, and all other communications between the parties relating to the subject matter hereof. No modification, amendment, waiver, termination, or discharge of this Agreement or any provision hereof shall by binding upon the SOCIETY unless confirmed in writing by an officer of SOCIETY.
9. *Effective Date:* The effective date of this Agreement is the date of the signature of the last party to sign and date this Agreement.

If the foregoing terms are satisfactory, please sign and date this Agreement, return one copy to the SOCIETY, and retain the second copy for your own files.

FOR THE SOCIETY: PHOTOGRAPHER:

For the PRESS: AUTHOR:

_____   _____

Date: _____   Date: _____

                  Social Security Number: _____

Appendix 5

Sample Request for Proposal for Typesetting and Printing a Journal

Courtesy of the authors

The original of this request for proposal (with details of date and recipient here removed) resulted in the typesetting and printing of *Documentary Editing*, the quarterly journal of the Association for Documentary Editing.

As we have discussed, I would like Typesetting Company, Inc., to provide me with an estimate of expenses for typesetting, printing, and mailing *Documentary Editing* during the calendar year ____. In general, you can use the previous issues that Typesetting Company produced in ____ [year] as a model. I have organized the categories of specifications (especially numbers 10–13) to coincide with the categories that you currently use in billing the Association for Documentary Editing (ADE). I will need the estimate no later than 23 October, which is the day before I leave for the ADE annual meeting, where I will present the estimates to the Council. I will FAX you this letter, with hard copy to follow by mail.

1. *Item: Documentary Editing*, the journal of the Association for Documentary Editing (ADE).
2. *Frequency:* Quarterly (March, June, September, and December).
3. *Schedule:* Typesetting Company to provide a production schedule for each issue during the calendar year ____.
4. *Trim size:* 8½ × 11 inches.
5. *Paper:* Typesetting Company or its subcontractor to supply 70-pound one-color acid-free coated (matte) text stock and 80-pound two-color acid-free coated (matte) cover stock.
6. *Ink:* Black and one PMS color.
7. *Binding:* Saddle-stitched on the 11-inch side.
8. *Billing:* ADE is the fiscal agent. Bills will be sent to me at the above address; I will approve payment and send the bills to the ADE treasurer for payment.

9. *Pages:* Text, 24 pages, black-and-white on both sides; plus cover black-and-white inside and two-color outside. With typesetting and printing quotes, please also indicate additional cost for 28 text pages and 32 text pages.

10. *Typesetting and Page Makeup:* ADE will supply diskettes containing all text, with typesetting codes input using the codes specified by Typesetting Company in ____ [year]. Typesetting Company supplies galley proofs, from which ADE will make up rough dummy pages. Typesetting Company will supply page proofs. Please quote base price for typesetting and page makeup, unit cost of alterations, and hourly cost of page makeup alterations.

11. *Illustrations:* ADE will supply illustrations. Please quote unit cost for halftones and screen tints.

12. *Printing:* Typesetting Company or its subcontractor will provide silverprints (blues). Quote printing cost for 550 copies base press run. Also quote per-copy price above 550. Please state policy on percent over or under press run.

13. *Mailing:* ADE to supply pressure-sensitive labels, sorted in ZIP code order. Typesetting Company or its subcontractor to supply 9 × 12-inch envelopes printed with return address and postal permit information, affix labels, insert the journal in the envelopes, deliver envelopes containing journals to the post office, and deliver overage to the editor of the journal in Indianapolis, Indiana. Please quote unit cost to stuff, label, sort, and mail the journal. Also quote cost of envelopes.

Appendix 6

Sample Request for Proposals for Writing a Book

Courtesy of the authors

This request for proposals resulted in the writing of E. Bruce Geelhoed, *The Rotary Club of Indianapolis: A Club, A Community, and a Century, 1913–1998* (Carmel: Guild Press of Indiana, 2000).

REQUEST FOR PROPOSALS FOR WRITING A NEW HISTORY OF THE ROTARY CLUB OF INDIANAPOLIS

The Rotary Club of Indianapolis seeks proposals to write a history of the club.

Purpose: The purpose of the history of the Rotary Club of Indianapolis will be:

- to orient new members to the background of our organization.
- to increase an understanding of the club among our existing membership and, to whatever extent possible, the wider reading public.

Several preliminary tasks must be undertaken as part of the background research, as follows:

- A questionnaire has been drafted to be circulated to all club members, asking them if they have recollections or records (papers, pamphlets, minutes, photographs, or other audiovisual materials) that would be useful for this project. A form of the questionnaire must be submitted to the 650 members.

- Oral history interviews need to be conducted with older members whose recollections will be important to the history. The interviews could be conducted by the author or by other persons, but all interviewers should receive some basic training in oral history interviewing techniques. Signed release forms need to be obtained from the interviewees. We should come up with a pattern for those interviews. History Committee members are willing to conduct oral history interviews. The History Committee can be expanded to include more people who will conduct those interviews.
- Club records dating back to 1913 are deposited in a storeroom on the sixth floor of the Indianapolis Athletic Club, down the corridor from the Rotary office. These records need to be processed and organized, and a basic guide or finding aid needs to be created. A History Committee member has made an initial inventory—which is printed on the reverse side of this request for proposals—of the records in the storeroom. Depending on the skills and experience of the author, we might contract separately with a person or organization to process and organize the collection. The History Committee has recommended that, after the history project is completed, the Board of Directors place the club records (including photographs) in a professionally staffed archive where they can be well cared for. If any records turn out to have no archival value, the person working on the collection could make recommendations to the Board of Directors concerning the disposition of such records.

Timeline:

1997: History Committee searches for author to write the book and a person to organize the records (who might or might not be the same person). We hope to make a selection in June.

1997–98: Records are organized. Author conducts research and writing. History to be complete prior to the international meeting in Indianapolis, 14–17 June 1998. The author will then attend and write an account of the international meeting, and make that the book's concluding event. The goal is to bring the book out in late 1998 or early 1999.

We seek an author with the following profile:

- a proven ability to organize a research project and carry it to a successful conclusion
- a writing style that will engage a wide audience
- knowledge of recent Indiana history and its documentation
- an established publication record is highly desirable

General Information:

Proposals should include a narrative specifying the project director's plan and how it will be implemented, a budget including all costs (including provision for transcription of approximately thirty oral history interviews), and résumés of persons who will be involved with the project. Persons making proposals may request an inspection copy of John McDowell's *From Flood to Fire: The History of Indianapolis Rotary Club, 1913–1969* (1969). Proposals received by 31 May are assured consideration, but the search will continue until a selection is made. Proposals should be sent to the chair of the History Committee: Thomas A. Mason, Indiana Historical Society, 315 West Ohio Street, Indianapolis, Indiana 46202–3299; phone: (317) 232-6546; fax: (317) 233-3109; e-mail: tmason@statelib.lib.in.us.

The History Committee will create teasers on the history project to appear in the club's newsletter. A short brochure on our club should be created as a spin-off from the book project.

From Flood to Fire contains approximately 80,000 words of text plus 72 illustrations in 251 pages, plus three appendixes. The appendixes cover current members, past members, and other Indiana Rotary Clubs and their charter dates. A full list of past members is not feasible today because of large numbers, but the new history will include appendixes on past officers and other Indiana Rotary Clubs and their charter dates. It will also include an index, a feature not in *From Flood to Fire*. The History Committee has recommended that a long-term plan be developed to produce ongoing supplements every decade.

The history will be a fully integrated, stand-alone study to replace *From Flood to Fire*, to be somewhat shorter and less detailed than that earlier book, stressing broad themes, and covering from the club's founding in 1913 through the Rotary International Convention here in Indianapolis in June 1998. For the years already covered by *From Flood to Fire*, the author of the new history will be charged to edit and condense material from the earlier book, the copyright of which the club owns. The contract will call for the author to deliver a typescript of 200–250 pages or approximately 64,000 words. At least one chapter will be devoted to the 1998 Rotary International Convention.

Appendix 7

Sample Request for Proposals for Publishing a Book

Courtesy of the authors

This request for proposals resulted in the publication of E. Bruce Geelhoed, *The Rotary Club of Indianapolis: A Club, A Community, and a Century, 1913–1998* (Carmel: Guild Press of Indiana, 2000).

REQUEST FOR PROPOSALS FOR PUBLICATION OF A NEW HISTORY OF THE ROTARY CLUB OF INDIANAPOLIS

The Rotary Club of Indianapolis seeks proposals for publication of a book on the history of the club. Responsibilities will include production—design, production coordination, prepress (typesetting and page makeup), printing, binding, and marketing/publishing/distribution. The club also seeks proposals to produce a color brochure for marketing the book. The goal is to bring the book out in late 1998 or early 1999.

Written by E. Bruce Geelhoed, professor of history at Ball State University and director of the Center for Middletown Studies, the book is tentatively titled "A Club, A Community, and A Century: The Rotary Club of Indianapolis, 1913–1998." It will have the following elements and chapters: Introduction; 1. The Formative Years, 1913–1919; 2. The Emergence of a Community Identity, 1920–1929; 3. The Rotary Club Amidst the Depression, 1930–1939; 4. The War Years and Postwar Resurgence, 1940–1949; 5. Strengthening the Roots in the Community, 1950–1959; 6. A New Surge of Activism, 1960–1969; 7. The Rotary Club as a Mature Organization, 1970–1979; 8. The Rotary Club Faces the Challenges of Growth, 1980–1989; 9. A Fixture in the Community, 1990–1998; 10. The 1998 Rotary International Convention in Indianapolis; Conclusion.

The vendor(s) will provide:

- Design and printing a color brochure for marketing the book, incorporating an order form for the book, 2,000 copies, to be produced by 5 June.
- A finished book with the following specifications:

  Rotary will provide, by 1 September 1998, a typescript and computer disk with Macintosh-generated text of the book (including index), and glossy photographs for illustrations. The text delivered by Rotary will have been edited by a member of Rotary who is an experienced copy editor. For purposes of cost estimates, assume: a typescript of 200 pages or 64,000 words, 100 halftone illustrations, 6 × 9-inch cover size, and a press run of 1,500 copies printed on acid-free paper. Binding: Please quote three ways: (1) a 2-color paper cover; (2) 4-color paper cover; (3) split press run of 500 clothbound copies with 4-color jacket, and 1,000 copies with 4-color paper cover.

- Marketing/advertising/distribution for the book.

These services will not necessarily all be provided by the same vendor. Proposals should state the estimated cost for the service to be provided. Proposals received by 19 May are assured consideration, but the search will continue until a selection is made. Proposals should be sent to the chair of the Rotary History Committee.

Appendix 8

Permission Request (Image)

Date

Dear,

I am writing to request permission to reprint the following material from you or your publication:

This material is to appear in the following work to be published by Rowman & Littlefield Publishers, an academic press based in Maryland.

Author/Editor:

Title of Work:

Date of Publication:

This book is scheduled to be published in _____ in both print and electronic editions. We are seeking

- nonexclusive rights to publish above listed _____ in the print and electronic editions of _____.

Unless you indicate otherwise, the following credit line will appear in the book: _____.

Thank you for your attention to this matter. I look forward to a timely response.

Sincerely,

I agree to the uses of the material as described above.

Signature: _____

Date: _____

Appendix 9

Permission Request (Text)

Courtesy of Rowman & Littlefield Publishers

Date

Dear,

I am writing to request permission to reprint the following material from you or your publication:

This material is to appear in the following work to be published by Rowman & Littlefield Publishers, an academic press based in Maryland.

Author/Editor:

Title of Work:

Date of Publication:

This book is scheduled to be published in _____ in both print and electronic editions. We are seeking

- nonexclusive rights to publish above listed _____ in the print and electronic editions of _____.

Unless you indicate otherwise, the following credit line will appear in the book: _____.

Thank you for your attention to this matter. I look forward to a timely response.

Sincerely,

I agree to the uses of the material as described above.

Signature: _____

Date: _____

Appendix 10

Interview Release Form

Courtesy of Rowman & Littlefield Publishers

Requestor Name:

The role of the requestor(s) in the publication is as (check more than one, if necessary)

☐ Interviewer   ☐ Author   ☐ Editor

The working title of the publication in which response in writing or as the result of interview(s) will appear in part or in whole is:

The work is expected to appear in:

Publisher of the publication is:

Date(s) of interview(s) or contribution(s) in writing:

Interview / Respondent:

Name:

Address:

Telephone:

Email:

Date of birth:

By signing the form below, you give your permission for any audio recordings, written responses, or photographs made in reply to and specifically for this project to be used for the above listed publication in print, audio and electronic form in all languages by the publisher and potential licensees of the publication.

By giving your permission, you do not give up any copyright or performance rights that you may hold.

I agree to the uses of these materials described above, except for any restrictions, noted below.

Name (please print): _____

Signature: _____

Date: _____

Requestor's signature: _____

Date: _____

Appendix 11

Contributor Agreement

Courtesy of Rowman & Littlefield Publishers

CONSENT TO PUBLISH AGREEMENT

FOR CONTRIBUTOR TO AN EDITED VOLUME

Dated xx/xx/xxxx

I, _____ (print name here), understand that my contribution(s), "_____" (contribution title here), will be published in the book entitled _____ (book title here) to be published by Rowman & Littlefield Publishers. I understand that I will receive one (1) gratis copy of the book from the publisher and may order additional copies at a fifty percent (50%) discount from the list price. If more than one individual is designated as the Contributor, then all obligations and indemnifications are joint and several.

The Contributor hereby agrees with the Publisher to the following terms and conditions in connection with its publication of the Contribution:

1. **Rights granted**
   a. The Contributor grants to the Publisher during the term of copyright, and during any renewals or extensions thereof, the exclusive right to publish and sell, including the right to permit others to publish and sell, the Contribution in whole or in part in any and all editions whether print, electronic, or audio, in all languages throughout the world.
   b. The Publisher grants the Contributor the right to place a copy of their contribution in their university's institutional repository at any point after 12 months post-publication of the work.

2. Delivery and Acceptance

a. The Contributor shall deliver to the Volume Editor no later than _____ (Delivery Date) one electronic copy of the final Work, including bibliography or bibliographical essay; all necessary permissions, licenses, releases, and consents; and art. All accompanying figures (photographs, illustrations, maps, and charts) shall be in camera-ready form. All accompanying tables shall be provided as electronic files. The Author shall keep a copy of all materials sent to the Publisher. Tables and figures shall not exceed ___ in number. The Work shall be approximately _____ words (including notes and bibliography), plus art.

b. In order to be considered satisfactory, the Contribution must be factually accurate and original and must acknowledge all intellectual debts. The Publisher may choose to engage scholars, consultants, or other experts in the topic covered by the Contribution to help determine its accuracy and originality. Any permissions necessary in order to reprint already published and/or copyrighted material quoted in the Contribution shall be obtained and paid for by the Contributor.

3. Publication

The Publisher shall publish the Work at its expense in a manner and style and at a price that it determines. All decisions and details as to the editing and publication of the Work, including style, edition or format, illustrations, time and manner of production, advertisement, and the number of free copies distributed will be left to the Publisher's sole discretion.

4. Copyright

a. The Publisher undertakes to print the copyright line on the imprint page of the Work as follows:

Selection and editorial matter © _____ [followed by the year of publication]

Copyright in individual chapters is held by the respective chapter authors.

5. Warranties

Please select A or B:

☐ **A.** I certify that my article has never been previously published or copyrighted. I hereby assign the right to publish the article as part of the above-named volume to Rowman & Littlefield Publishers, Inc. I retain copyright to the article.

Signature: _____

☐ **B.** My article(s) have been previously published in _____

_____

Permission has been obtained to reprint this article(s) in the book described above. A copy of that permission is attached.

Signature: _____

6. **Assignment**

   All rights and licenses granted or assigned by the Publisher, pursuant to this Agreement, to any division, affiliate, subsidiary, or parent company or successor of _____ Publishers, Inc., shall be construed as though the Work was still in the Publisher's hands; and all parts of this Agreement would still be in full force and effect.

7. **Signature of Agreement**

   a. This Agreement constitutes the whole agreement between the Contributor and the Publisher and supersedes all preexisting agreements or arrangements, written or oral, between the parties relating to the subject matter of this Agreement.

   b. This contract offer is valid if signed within ninety days of the issue date on page one.

Accepted and Agreed to: _____ Date: _____

_____ **Author Name**

Preferred Mailing Address, E-mail Address, and Phone Number (please **print** *legibly*):

Street Address: _____

City, State/Province, Postal Code: _____

Country: _____

Phone number (including country and area code): _____

E-mail address: _____

Please return this signed form to the editor of your book.

Appendix 12

Marketing Questionnaire

Courtesy of Rowman & Littlefield Publishers

This packet is your opportunity to provide information that will assist us in marketing and promoting your book. It is shared by various departments and personnel within Rowman & Littlefield and is consulted when plans for your book are being developed. Please, take some time to fill out each section as thoroughly as you can and submit it electronically with your final manuscript. Thank you!

Title:

Author(s):

Mailing address:

Phone:

Email:

1. Book Pitch/Short Description: Please summarize your book in one or two sentences and list, in order of importance, the main sales features of your book.
2. Long Description: Please provide a 250–300 word summary of your book. We'll revise and review this with you before we use it on the book's cover. Make sure to point out what is new and unique about your book.
3. Author Bio(s): Please provide a 50–100 word bio of yourself for use on the book cover. You may include a longer bio as an About the Author page in the book.
4. Keywords: Supply at least ten keywords/phrases that you think would allow readers to most easily find your book in an online search. Please limit key phrases to no more than three words.

5. New to this Edition: If the book is a new edition, please detail the changes from the previous edition.
6. Endorser Suggestions: Please provide, in order of priority and/or likelihood, the names and email addresses of recognized authorities on the book's subject matter whom you believe would be interested in providing prepublication comment for promotional purposes. If you will be reaching out to anyone directly, please also list those people so we do not overlap.

This is your opportunity to let us know how you plan to promote your book and how we might support those efforts. These suggestions will help our publicity team create a dynamic promotional plan for your book. But it's also a reminder that as the sole author of your book, you are in a great position to help promote it through mostly free and easy avenues. Social media is a great place to start, and we encourage every author to take advantage of these opportunities. Please don't rearrange or delete info below; if you don't have a response to a particular area, just leave it blank.

PUBLICITY TIP SHEET

1. Selling Points (what are the selling points for your book—include at least three, starting with an active verb; e.g., Offers insight into . . .):
2. Will you be hiring a PR firm? If so, please provide their contact information:
3. Your Website (if applicable):
4. Your Blog (if applicable):
5. Your Social Media Handles:

   - Facebook:
   - Twitter:
   - LinkedIn:
   - Instagram:
   - Goodreads:
   - Amazon Author Page:
   - YouTube Channel:
   - Are you active on any other social media sites? (Explain)

6. Planned Author Promotional Activities (book signings, appearances, talks, conferences, radio, assistance from your school/place of work, etc.):
7. Columnists/journalists/popular bloggers who may have an interest in your book (names, websites, and contact information if possible):

8. Podcasts related to your book topic:
9. Radio/TV (list any programs that might have an interest in your book—be specific about program names, and indicate if you've appeared on any of these before):
10. Organizations (alumni, professional, national, etc., that might be interested in helping to publicize your book):
11. Bookstores (list of names and addresses of any bookstores where you are known personally or that specialize in the book's subject area):
12. Special sales (list any people, companies, or organizations that might be willing to purchase your work in bulk quantities of more than 100). For interested parties, we can offer various special discounts for bulk purchases. Please include a contact name, his/her role in the organization, and a contact email or phone number.

MARKETING TIP SHEET

1. Meetings and Conferences: Please list the annual professional meetings at which your book would be suitable for display.
2. Review Copy Requests: Supply a list of 10–20 media outlets (journals, newspapers, magazines, and blogs) that you believe might be interested in reviewing or featuring your book, including your alumni magazine and any outlets in which you have published previously. Indicate any that you know personally or have reviewed or featured your previous works. Please provide contact names and mailing addresses whenever possible.
3. Academic Cross-over: Is your book suitable for use in any college courses? If so, please provide details on the course, including normal student enrollment and schools or professors noted for teaching the course.
4. Book Prizes: Provide, in order of priority and/or likelihood, prizes for which your book would be a strong contender, including contact information.
5. Product Mentions: List the names and addresses of any companies or individuals whose products or services are mentioned in your book.
6. Previous Publications: List your other books, including title, publisher, year of publication, and type of book. Specify quantity sold, book-club adoptions, paperback reprints, foreign editions, serializations, movies, etc.
7. Résumé: Attach or insert your current résumé or curriculum vitae.

8. Q&A: Please list of up to ten questions and answers relating to your book that could be posed to you in an interview to spark lively, interesting, revealing, or controversial conversation.
9. Published Reviews: If your book is a reprint or new edition, please attach copies of reviews or articles in which it was featured. Please do not include Amazon.com user reviews.

SUBSIDIARY RIGHTS TIP SHEET

1. **Rights:** Have all permissions for art or text in the book been secured for all languages, formats, and territories? If not, please specify restrictions below.
2. **Foreign Publishers:** Do you have connections with any foreign publishers who might be interested in co-publishing or translation rights? Please supply specific contact names.
3. **Book Clubs:** Do you know of any book clubs that might be interested in considering your book as a selection.
4. **Serial Rights:** Outlets that might be interested in first serial rights.
5. **Additional comments and suggestions**

Glossary

Acquisitions editor (AE)—Key decision-maker in the publishing process, responsible for finding and acquiring new content that will contribute to the success and reputation of the publishing company.

Advance contract or contract on proposal—Presses will often offer a contract to an author for a book based on the quality of the proposal. Some presses will send the proposal out for peer review before offering the contract; others will offer a contract without peer review of the proposal. In both cases the final submitted manuscript will be sent to outside readers for peer review.

Advance on royalties—Contracted payment to author in advance of book publication that must be repaid by earnings received from future sales.

Agent—An intermediary between an author and a publisher who signs promising authors and works and negotiates with prospective publishers on their behalf.

AI (artificial intelligence)—A branch of computer science concerned with the simulation of human intelligence processes by machines.

Antiquarianism—The compilation of minute data with little or no analysis, explanation, or narrative.

Backlist—Books on a publisher's list that have been on sale for more than a year. Books that make it to the backlist and sell over several years without being actively promoted are highly sought after by publishers.

Bound book date (BBD)—Date when printed and bound book is scheduled to be received in the warehouse.

ChatGPT—One of a growing number of artificial intelligence-based software products that simulate human speech and conversation. It can respond to questions and compose various written content, including articles, social media posts, essays, songs, scripts, code, and emails. Launched by OpenAI on November 30, 2022, it received a great deal of media attention and criticism and a $10 billion investment from Microsoft.

Contributed volume—A book containing articles by several authors that are all related to an overarching theme or idea. The articles are commissioned, edited, and organized by a volume editor or editors, who are responsible for the quality and consistency of the contributions.

Copy editor—Once a manuscript has been contracted, reviewed, revised, and submitted, the copy editor reviews the work for errors, consistency, clarity, and quality. Copy editors are often freelancers assigned by an in-house manuscript editor to work directly with the author and are paid for by the press as part of the fixed costs of a project.

Developmental editing—Also known a substantive editing, this type of editing goes beyond grammar and correctness to focus on structure, content, and coherence of a written work. Development editors can be recommended to authors by an acquisitions editor to help an author bring out a manuscript's full potential, but the author is generally responsible for paying for these services.

Discounts—Books are discounted for sale by bookstores and online booksellers at different rates, depending on the channel to market. Bookstores and other retail outlets generally require a trade discount in the range of 50 percent, while academic books sold to libraries and online are generally discounted at a short discount or in the 20 percent range.

Dots per inch (or pixels per inch)—Dots per inch (DPI) and pixels per inch (PPI) are measures reflecting the quality of digital images. DPI is mainly relevant to printed materials and refers to the number of printed dots per inch, while PPI is relevant to digital displays and refers to the number of pixels per inch in a digital image. Press production departments usually require images to be a minimum of 300 DPI (or PPI) at the size the image will appear in the book—e.g., 4×5 @ 300 PPI.

Editorial, Design, and Production (EDP)—The EDP department works with Acquisitions, Editorial, and Marketing to determine the specifications for each book project, including trim size, page design, cover design, print run, and schedule.

Fixed costs—Fixed costs in publishing are expenses that do not change regardless of the number of copies of a book that are produced or sold. Examples of fixed costs include editorial costs, design, composition, and author advances.

Frontlist—Books on a publisher's list that have been available for a year or less and are being actively promoted and featured in the press's catalog.

Gray scale—Grayscale printing is often used for black-and-white photographs, illustrations, and text documents. Images submitted to production departments, such as color photographs or maps, may not appear clearly in a book printed only with black ink.

Gross margin—Gross margin is a financial metric that measures the profitability of a book project. It is calculated by subtracting the cost of goods sold (COGS) from the revenue earned from sales. Gross margin is expressed as a percentage and represents the percentage of revenue that remains after deducting the COGS. The formula for gross margin is Gross Margin = (Revenue–Cost of Goods Sold) / Revenue × 100%.

ISBN (International Standard Book Number)—a unique identifier used to distinguish and catalog books, eBooks, and other published works. Each ISBN is tied to a particular edition, format, and publisher of a book.

JPEG (Joint Photographic Experts Group)—A commonly used method of image file compression to represent content, especially photographs.

Letter of inquiry—A letter sent to an editor by a prospective author to gauge interest in receiving a full proposal.

List—The collection of a publisher's work that is currently in print and available for sale.

Manuscript editors / project editors—Editors who work with authors and assign copy editors after a manuscript has been transmitted from Acquisitions are often located in the EDP department.

Marketing questionnaire (MQ)—A questionnaire sent to an author by a publisher's marketing department once a book project has been contracted and transmitted for design and production. The questionnaire will provide marketing with a foundation for a marketing plan, including catalog copy, review copies, awards, press connections, and more. It should be filled out thoroughly and returned quickly, with the understanding that the marketing department will be working on many projects simultaneously.

Monograph—A detailed and comprehensive written work that focuses on a single subject, topic, or theme.

Net revenue—The amount earned from book sales after deducting costs for returns and discounts. Author royalties are commonly based on a percentage of the net revenue of sales received.

PDF (Portable Document Format)—A widely used file format developed by Adobe that allows documents to be shared and viewed reliably across different platforms and devices while preserving their formatting.

Peer review—A process by which manuscripts, research papers, and articles are evaluated by experts in the relevant field before they are published in a journal or a book. The goal of peer review is to ensure the quality, accuracy, and validity of the content being published.

PPB—A variable cost that includes paper, print, and binding.

Print on demand (POD)—A publishing and printing process in which books, documents, and other printed materials are produced individually or in small quantities as needed. POD allows for the printing of copies on an as-needed basis in response to customer orders.

Proposal—A book proposal is a comprehensive document that provides an in-depth overview of a book project. It is typically submitted by authors to publishers, literary agents, or editors as a way to persuade them to consider publishing the book. A book proposal includes various elements and details about the book, the author, the target audience, and the market.

Prospectus—A shorter document than a proposal that provides a brief overview of a book project. It is often used to initially pique the interest of publishers or agents and may serve as a preliminary step before submitting a more detailed book proposal.

Publication date—The official date on which a book is made available to the public for purchase and distribution.

Returns—A convention of trade publishing in which books ordered by retailers and distributors can be returned for a full refund.

Royalty—Payment made to author by a publisher based on the sales of a book. Royalties are generally based on net revenue received.

Sliding scale—Royalty payments that increase as certain sales benchmarks are met.

Slush pile—Unsolicited manuscripts received "over the transom."

Subsidiary rights—Rights negotiated in a book contract for additional rights that can be granted to third parties beyond the primary publication of the book. These include but are not limited to audio, visual, dramatic, electronic, serial, periodical, and book club rights.

Subvention—A financial contribution or subsidy provided by an author, institution, or entity to support the publication of a book or other written work. A logical funding prospect for a local history project is your local community development foundation.

TIFF (Tag Image File Format)—A widely used image format for storing high-quality graphics, photographs, and other images. TIFF files are known for their ability to maintain a high level of detail and color accuracy, making them desirable and often required for book publication.

Trade book—Any book published for general bookstore or public library sales.

Variable cost—Variable costs in publishing are expenses that change based on the number of copies of the book that are produced or sold. Examples include printing costs such as ink, paper, and binding, as well as shipping, distribution and storage costs, and royalties to the author.

Bibliography

Ambrosius, Lloyd E., ed. *Writing Biography: Historians and Their Craft*. Lincoln: University of Nebraska Press, 2004.

Association of American University Presses and Joyce Kachergis, eds. *One Book / Five Ways: The Publishing Procedures of Five University Presses*. Chicago: University of Chicago Press, 1994.

Bailey, Herbert S., Jr. *The Art and Science of Book Publishing*. 1970; 3d ed., Athens: Ohio University Press, 1990.

Barlow, Jeffrey G. "Historical Research and Electronic Evidence: Problems and Promises." In *Writing, Teaching, and Researching History in the Electronic Age: Historians and Computers*. Dennis A. Trinkle, ed. 194–225. Armonk, NY: M. E. Sharpe, 1998.

Barzun, Jacques, and Henry F. Graf. *The Modern Researcher*. 1957; 6th ed., Belmont, CA: Thomson/Wadsworth Publishing, 2004.

Beasley, David R. *Beasley's Guide to Library Research*. Toronto: University of Toronto Press, 2000.

Beckett, John. *Writing Local History*. Manchester, UK: Manchester University Press, 2007.

Benedict, Michael Les. *A Historian's Guide to Copyright*. Washington, DC: American Historical Association, 2012.

Bielstein, Susan M. *Permissions: A Survival Guide*. Chicago: University of Chicago Press, 2006.

Britton, Gregory M. "Thinking Like a Scholarly Editor: The How and Why of Academic Publishing." In Peter Ginna, ed., *What Editors Do: The Art, Craft, and Business of Book Editing*. Chicago: University of Chicago Press, 2017.

Buenger, Walter L., and Arnoldo De León, eds. *Beyond Texas through Time: Breaking Away from Past Interpretations*, new ed., twentieth anniversary ed. College Station: Texas A&M University Press, 2011.

Caro, Robert A. *Working: Researching, Interviewing, Writing*, Kindle edition. New York: Alfred A. Knopf, 2019.

Cohen, Daniel, and Roy Rosenzweig. *Digital History: A Guide to Gathering, Preserving, and Presenting the Past on the Web*. Philadelphia: University of Pennsylvania Press, 2005.

Collins, M. H. [Marilyn H. Collins]. *Write History Right: How to Research, Organize, and Document the Past for Your Hometown, Region, Family, Sports Team, School, Events, Organization, Church: A Step-by-Step Guide.* Rogers, AR: CHS Publishing, 2009.

Cook, Tony. "Self-Publishing Comes in from the Cold with Sale." In *Indianapolis Star*, July 20, 2012, A-5.

Felt, Thomas E. *Researching, Writing, and Publishing Local History.* 1976; 2d ed., Nashville, TN: American Association for State and Local History, 1981.

Fiering, Norman. *A Guide to Book Publication for Historians.* Washington, DC: American Historical Association, 1979.

Fischer, David Hackett. *Historians' Fallacies: Toward a Logic of Historical Thought.* New York: Harper & Row, 1970.

Germano, William. *Getting It Published: A Guide for Scholars, and Anyone Else Serious about Serious Books.* 2001; 3rd ed. Chicago: University of Chicago Press, 2016.

Greco, Albert M., Clara E. Rodriguez, and Robert M. Wharton. *The Culture and Commerce of Publishing in the 21st Century.* Stanford, CA: Stanford Business Books, 2006.

———, Jim Milliot, and Robert M. Wharton, *The Book Publishing Industry*, 3rd ed. New York: Routledge, 2014.

Harman, Eleanor, Ian Montagnes, Siobhan McMenemy, and Chris Bucci, eds. *The Thesis and the Book: A Guide for First-time Academic Authors.* 1976; 2d ed., Toronto: University of Toronto Press, 2003.

Harstad, Peter T. "Indiana Historical Society." In Bodenhamer, David J., and Robert G. Barrows, eds. *The Encyclopedia of Indianapolis.* Bloomington: Indiana University Press, 1994.

Kammen, Carol. *On Doing Local History.* 1986; 3rd ed., Lanham, MD: Rowman & Littlefield, 2014.

——— and Amy H. Wilson, eds., *Encyclopedia of Local History.* 2000; 2nd ed., Lanham, MD: AltaMira Press, 2013.

Kirsch, Jonathan. *Kirsch's Guide to the Book Contract: For Authors, Publishers, Editors, and Agents.* Los Angeles: Acrobat Books, 1999.

———. *Kirsch's Handbook of Publishing Law: For Authors, Publishers, Editors, and Agents.* 1995, Los Angeles: Silman-James Press, 2005.

Krug, Steve. *Don't Make Me Think, Revisited: A Common Sense Approach to Web Usability.* 2000; 3rd ed., San Francisco: New Riders, 2014.

Kyvig, David E., and Myron A. Marty. *Nearby History: Exploring the Past around You.* 1982; 4th ed., Lanham, MD: Rowman & Littlefield, 2019.

Lee, Marshall. *Bookmaking: Editing, Design, Production.* 1965; 3rd ed., New York: Norton, 2004.

Luey, Beth E. *Handbook for Academic Authors.* 1987; 6th ed., New York: Cambridge University Press, 2022.

———, ed. *Revising Your Dissertation: Advice from Leading Editors.* 2004; 4th ed., Berkeley: University of California Press, 2011.

Lynch, Patrick J., and Sarah Horton. *Web Style Guide: Basic Design Principles for Creating Web Sites.* 1999; 4th ed., New Haven, CT: Yale University Press, 2016.

Mann, Thomas. *The Oxford Guide to Library Research.* 1987; 4th ed., New York: Oxford University Press, 2015.

Marius, Richard, and Melvin E. Page. *A Short Guide to Writing about History*. 1989; 8th ed., Boston: Pearson, 2012.

Mason, Thomas A. "Partnerships in Publications." In *History News* 47, no. 4 (1992): 12–14, 32.

McCullough, David. *John Adams*. New York: Simon & Schuster, 2001.

———. *The Pioneers: The Heroic Story of the Settlers Who Brought the American Ideal West*. New York: Simon & Schuster, 2019.

McLean, Gavin. *How to Do Local History: Research, Write, Publish: A Guide for Historians and Clients*. Dunedin, New Zealand: Otago University Press, 2007.

Milligan, Ian, *The Transformation of Historical Research in the Digital Age*. Cambridge, UK: Cambridge University Press, 2022.

Morville, Peter, and Louis Rosenfeld. *Information Architecture for the World Wide Web: Designing Large-Scale Web Sites*. 1998; 3rd ed., Sebastopol, CA: O'Reilly Media, 2007.

Park, Karin R., and Beth E. Luey. *Publication Grants for Authors and Publishers: How to Find Them, Win Them, and Manage Them*. Phoenix, AZ: Oryx Press, 1991.

Parker, Donald Dean. *Local History: How to Gather It, Write It, and Publish It*. Revised and edited by Bertha E. Josephson for the Committee on Guide for Study of Local History of the Social Science Research Council. New York: SSRC, 1944.

Phillips, Lori Byrd, and Dominic McDevitt-Parks. "Historians in Wikipedia: Building an Open, Collaborative History." In *Perspectives in History: The Newsmagazine of the American Historical Association*, vol. 50, no 9 (December 2012): 55–56.

Portwood-Stacer, Laura. *The Book Proposal Book: A Guide for Scholarly Authors*. Princeton, NJ: Princeton University Press, 2021.

Posner, Richard A. *The Little Book of Plagiarism*. New York: Pantheon, 2007.

Presnell, Jenny L. *The Information-Literate Historian: A Guide to Research for History Students*. 2007; 3rd ed., New York: Oxford University Press, 2019.

Redman, Samuel J. *Historical Research in Archives: A Practical Guide*. Washington, DC: American Historical Association, 2013.

Samuels, Edward. *The Illustrated Story of Copyright*. New York: Thomas Dunne Books, 2000.

Schrag, Zachary M., *The Princeton Guide to Historical Research*. Princeton: Princeton University Press, 2021.

Storey, William Kelleher. *Writing History: A Guide for Students*. 1999; 6th ed., New York, Oxford University Press, 2021.

Thompson, John B. *Book Wars: The Digital Revolution in Publishing*. Cambridge, UK; Medford, MA: Polity Press, 2022.

———. *Books in the Digital Age: The Transformation of Academic and Higher Education Publishing in Britain and the United States*. Cambridge, UK; Malden, MA: Polity Press, 2005.

Trinkle, Dennis A., and Scott A. Merriman, eds. *The American History Highway: A Guide to Internet Resources on U.S., Canadian, and Latin American History*. Armonk, NY: M. E. Sharpe, 2007.

Trubshaw, Bob. *How to Write and Publish Local and Family History Successfully: Books, Booklets, Magazines, CD-ROMs, and Web Sites*. Loughborough, UK: Heart of Albion Press, 2005.

[Williams, Roger Lloyd]. *Self-Publishing: Planning for a Better Book*. 1983. Nappanee, IN: Evangel Press, 1992.

Wilson, Amy H., ed. *Encyclopedia of Local History*, 3rd ed. Lanham, MD: Rowman & Littlefield, 2017.

Zinsser, William. *On Writing Well: The Classic Guide to Writing Nonfiction*. 1976; 7th ed., New York: HaperCollins, 2006.

AASLH Technical Leaflets are available from the AASLH website (www.aaslh .org/leaflets.htm) in downloadable copy or hard copy. These are dated on the technology of printing, but the fundamental principles of publishing books on state and local history remain unchanged:

007   Warner, Sam Bass, Jr. *Writing Local History: The Use of Social Statistics*. 1970.

034   Walklet, John J., Jr. *Publishing in the Historical Society*. 1966.

039   Derby, Charlotte S. *Reaching Your Public: The Historical Society Newsletter*. 1967.

051   Alderson, William T. *Marking and Correcting Copy for Your Printer*. 1969.

053   Gore, Gary. *Spotting Mechanical Errors in Proof: A Guide for Linecasting Machine Proofreaders*. 1969.

103   ———. *Phototypesetting: Getting the Most for Your Money*. 1978.

142   Purcell, L. Edward. *Writing Printing Specifications: A Systematic Approach to Publications Management*. 1981.

145   Enstam, Elizabeth Y. *Using Memoirs to Write Local History*. 1982.

210   Sommer, Barbara W., and Mary Kay Quinlan. *A Guide to Oral History Interviews*. 2000.

277   Lupton, John A. *How to Find and Use Legal Records*. 2017.

Index

About the Authors

Thomas A. Mason is adjunct senior lecturer at Indiana University–Indianapolis. He previously served as director of publications at the Indiana Historical Society.

J. Kent Calder is retired as editorial director of the University of Oklahoma Press and served as executive director of the Texas State Historical Association from 2008 to 2014.